The ANGEL

of Dartmouth

Elly Wentworth was a finalist in *MasterChef: The Professionals*, Winner of the South West Chef of the Year, representative of the South West on the *Great British Menu* and is now Executive Chef at the award-winning Angel restaurant.

Each of the recipes in this collection has featured on the menu at the iconic riverside Angel restaurant, with stunning flavours and exquisite presentation at their heart. Following in the footsteps of Joyce Molyneux, celebrated previous owner of the Angel and one of the first women ever to receive a Michelin star, Elly's dishes pay tribute to some of the finest seasonal ingredients the coast of Dartmouth has to offer.

'Elly is one of the country's finest young chefs.'
Hywel Jones

Elly Wentworth at

The ANGEL

of Dartmouth

In Loving Memory of Craig Akehurst

When I joined the Angel in 2018, Craig was already working in the kitchen as head of pastry. We very quickly struck up a friendship and the perfect working relationship. I have enjoyed working with pastry since my time in this section of the kitchen with Chris and James Tanner. Craig was one of the very best and most level-headed pastry chefs I have ever come across. He was such a calm and collected person, who went about his daily tasks with enthusiasm and a smile on his face.

After working together for three years, creating recipes and seeing our diners enjoy them, Craig was sadly diagnosed with mesothelioma, a particularly virulent form of cancer, in March 2021. He passed away on 26 July 2021 at the far too young age of 34. The team and I lost a lovely, talented and highly intelligent colleague. For those three years together, he was not only my partner in crime, but also my best friend. Each day, the feeling of not seeing him in the kitchen still makes me sad. However, we have promised we will make the Angel the best we can with Craig in our memories. Rest in peace, dear friend.

Foreword

From a young age, I enjoyed cooking for my family. By my early teens, my ambition was to become a chef. The journey I have been on since those days has been both enjoyable and full of challenges. I relished dealing with each one as it came along. The experiences they gave me have greatly contributed to the person and chef I am today.

My journey has taken me to the kitchens of some of the South West's best chefs. I owe a great deal of the skills and techniques I have today to the chefs I worked alongside. Their continued friendship and encouragement are very much appreciated.

When the opportunity arose to become head chef at the iconic Angel restaurant in Dartmouth, I knew the time was right for me to strike out on my own. I am passionate and 100 per cent committed to delivering great food, using locally sourced ingredients that are sustainable and in season. My food is a reflection of both me and the wonderful location of the Angel restaurant. The majority of my life has been lived in the South West, close to the sea and surrounded by countryside growing fabulous produce.

I knew when taking on the head chef role at the Angel that I was following in the footsteps of some highly acclaimed chefs. Therefore, my food needed to be of the highest quality and deliver a fine dining experience. Since joining the Angel in 2018, I have built up a collection of recipes that showcase the great food and ingredients of the South West. So, when the opportunity came along to write this book, I could not let it pass me by.

When choosing recipes for the book, I wanted to make sure that all four seasons were covered. I also wanted to include a mix of everything, from appetisers through to fish and meat dishes, as well as desserts. These are recipes that any competent home cook can work through to provide memorable meals for special occasions.

To ensure optimal results, always source the best and freshest ingredients you can find. For those more specialised ingredients, I have included names of the suppliers I use. They all have websites where the ingredients can be purchased online. All my suppliers have become like family to me and understand my requirements, so you can buy from them with confidence.

Each recipe has been broken down into individual elements, many of which can be prepared in advance. I have tried to write them in such a way that they feel as if I am in the kitchen working alongside you. I hope you enjoy working from these recipes and that those you are cooking for leave the dinner table with great memories.

Page 8 The Angel

SPRING
Page 34 March – May

SUMMER
Page 100 June – August

AUTUMN
Page 164 September – November

WINTER
Page 216 December – February

Page 270 A little extra

Page 282 Index

Page 287 Acknowledgements

The ANGEL
A Very Special Restaurant

Lying on the west bank of the River Dart, on the picturesque south coast of Devon, is the town of Dartmouth, with its sloping streets and grey stone castle. Set into the hills above the town is the imposing red-brick Britannia Royal Naval college. The Royal Navy has been training its officers in Dartmouth since 1863, but before the college was built in 1905, students lived in wooden hulks moored on the River Dart.

When Isambard Kingdom Brunel was building the rail network across the South West of England, he saw Dartmouth as a key destination. Despite the challenges posed by the steep terrain, he was so confident that he would be able to run the line through to the town that he had a terminus built on the banks of the Dart. However, the task proved impossible and Brunel had to settle for building a line from Paignton through to the village of Kingswear, which is located directly opposite, on the other side of the river. The line opened in 1864 and today it is served by a heritage steam train during the summer season. There are regular ferries crossing the river between Kingswear and Dartmouth. The station building, perched between the river and the inner harbour, is now home to the Embankment Bistro.

Shipbuilding was once a major industry in the town, but this gradually declined as the Royal Navy and commercial shipping companies needed larger vessels, and it was difficult to create the infrastructure to build these in the shallow waters of the Dart, with the steep hills on both sides.

In 1944 Dartmouth's naval college became home to American troops as they planned and practised for the D-Day landings in France. Much of the local area, including the nearby town of Slapton, was transformed by the presence of American soldiers in the months leading up to the operation. On 4th June 1944, a flotilla of 480 ships, carrying close to half a million men, left the area very early in the morning and headed to Utah Beach in Normandy. Life then started to return to some sort of normality for the locals.

The Naval College was also the setting for a world-famous love story. It was here, in July 1934, that a 13-year-old Princess Elizabeth first became smitten with dashing 18-year-old Philip Mountbatten. They married on 20th November 1947 in an extravagant ceremony at Westminster Abbey in London.

Since the early twentieth century, as a consequence of the railway, Dartmouth has been a highly popular tourist resort. Visitors now travel from all over the UK and abroad to enjoy the many attractions that the South West of England has to offer – from the annual regatta to the sandy beaches. Consequently, hospitality has become a major industry for the town, including a wide range of restaurants for visitors to choose from.

2 South Embankment

Number 2 South Embankment is a mock-Tudor building, its façade adorned with intricate carved patterns and white-railed balconies. It is perfectly situated just a stone's throw from the jetty, offering a splendid view across the Dart to the village of Kingswear, with its array of pastel-coloured cottages set into the steep hill and the steam train puffing along, its whistle carrying across the water.

There has been a restaurant at this address since as far back as the 1950s, when Britain was still in the grip of post-war rationing and austerity. At the time, it was rare to find restaurants serving truly high-quality food outside of major cities. Even in London, very few restaurants were recognised as delivering an excellent dining experience, and most of those that did were based in luxury hotels, far beyond the reach of most diners.

Charles Glenie and his wife Margaret were the first proprietors, opening their eponymous restaurant in the late 1950s. Glenie's specialised in seafood, with Margaret heading up the kitchen and Charles running operations front of house. Charles also ran a taxi business from the restaurant and was a well-known character, often seen by locals and visitors to Dartmouth sitting in the window watching the world pass by.

The Glenies built up a reputation for exceptional food and excellent service, earning glowing reviews published in early editions of *The Good Food Guide* throughout the 1960s. In the early 1970s, when they decided to retire to Spain, a young local couple took on the restaurant, still using the Glenie name. They chose to run it as a standard fish and chip shop, but it was not the success they had hoped for, and by 1973 the property was placed for sale with a local estate agent. It was then that Joyce Molyneux entered the scene.

Joyce Molyneux: A Life Dedicated to Cooking

The early years

Joyce was born on 17th April 1931 in Handsworth, Birmingham. It was on a French exchange, staying with a family in St Dié des Vosges, that she had her first taste of classic French cooking. When she left school at the age of 16, she was eager to learn the skills required to become a professional cook. The first step in her journey was to attend the Birmingham College of Domestic Science.

Joyce affectionately referred to her tutors there as the 'Scottish Mafia'. The college's syllabus followed the Edinburgh School of Cookery approach, which meant learning recipes from 1907, alongside a selection of high-class dishes. Although this was far from the style of cookery she longed to pursue, it did provide her with core knowledge and skills.

Her first cookery job after graduating was working in the staff canteen of Birmingham-based W. Canning & Co., who manufactured electroplating equipment. Then, in 1951, a good friend told her that there was a position going at the Mulberry Tree in Stratford-upon-Avon. She applied and was promptly offered the job as assistant to chef Douglas Sutherland.

Douglas was a classically trained chef who was well regarded by his peers. His style was very much based on traditional French cooking. Until appointing Joyce as his assistant, he had previously worked solo in his kitchen. The restaurant had just thirty covers and the kitchen used a coal-fired stove. Over the next eight years, under Sutherland's tutelage, Joyce herself became a classically trained chef.

Joyce and Stephen Markwick in the kitchen, 1974.

The Hole in the Wall

In 1959, Joyce moved from the Mulberry Tree to work alongside owner and head chef George Perry-Smith at The Hole in the Wall in Bath. George was a self-taught chef who relied on his own instincts and adapted recipes from great cookery book writers. Working together, a now classically trained Joyce was able to pass on her skills to George as well as learning from his freestyle approach.

Along with other pioneering restaurants in the 1960s, such as Sharrow Bay (under Francis Coulson and Brian Sack) in the Lake District, Walnut Tree (under Franco Taruschio) in Abergavenny, and Box Tree (under Malcolm Reid and Colin Long) in Ilkley, The Hole in the Wall was part of a wave of new and exciting food, the beginning of what we now know as British-style cooking. These chefs used the best and freshest locally sourced seasonal produce, which was prepared and cooked using classic French culinary techniques. Their food was also affordable for a much wider range of diners.

George insisted that his kitchen staff spent a little time working front of house and that the waiting staff experienced some time in the kitchen. He believed this would enable each staff member to fully understand the workings of a restaurant and customers' expectations. He also operated an open kitchen, which was unheard of at the time. As well as allowing his diners to observe the workings of the kitchen, it also created a calmer working environment. Later, when Joyce opened the Carved Angel, she also embraced this approach.

After selling The Hole in the Wall, in 1973 George opened the Riverside restaurant in Helford, Cornwall, with Joyce, his wife Heather Crosbie and his stepson Tom Jaine. They also looked for a second location to open another restaurant and, after visiting a number of locations around Devon and Cornwall, they decided that Dartmouth was the perfect place.

Hand-illustrated card of Joyce and Tom in the kitchen, 1974.

The Carved Angel, 1974 to 1999

It was decided that Joyce and Tom would run the new restaurant. After months of major refurbishments, they opened in June 1974, having settled on the name the Carved Angel. It is not a large restaurant. The ground floor can accommodate 40 covers, the first floor a further 16. The additional capacity was particularly useful during the holiday seasons when demand was at its height. The first floor was also used for private dining events. However, the lack of a dumbwaiter meant everything needed to be carried up and down a flight of stairs.

Joyce required a calm and professional attitude from all staff members. She brought a touch of theatre to the restaurant by carving duck, chicken and other meats at the table, inviting diners to choose how much they would like.

All ingredients were locally sourced where possible. Menus frequently changed to reflect the best produce that was available and in season. Joyce enjoyed foraging, both in the countryside and around the seashore, and she would later have her own small vegetable garden on the edge of town. She firmly believed that the items on a plate should each individually stand out and the overall dining experience should be enhanced by sauces or other ingredients, allowing the natural food flavours to shine through rather than masking them.

Under Tom's expert eye, a superb wine list was assembled, featuring many great French wines sold at reasonable prices. With Joyce cooking in an open kitchen and Tom out front, they started to build a national reputation for excellent food and a memorable dining experience. Fish and seafood featured on the menus, alongside meat and locally grown vegetables. Offal was a regular item, as it was popular in the 1970s through to the early 1990s. It was not uncommon to see sweetbread and kidney dishes, stuffed pigs' trotters and hearts on the menu. Joyce drew on many European influences and the great cookery book writers of the day, such as Elizabeth David and Jane Grigson.

The carved angel statue, 1974.

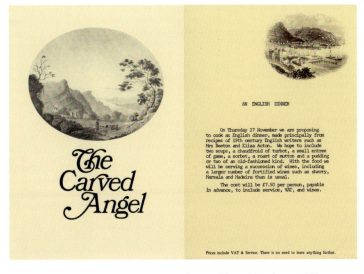

Illustrated Carved Angel menu, 1979.

13 The Angel

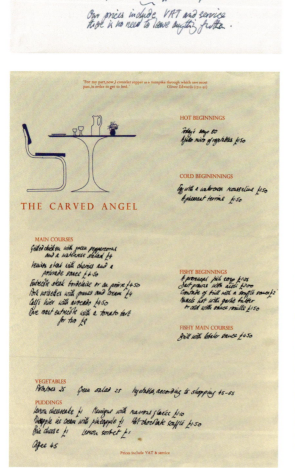
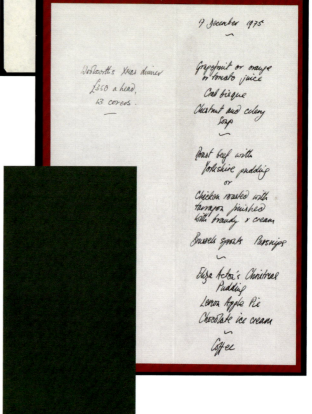

Tom Jaine's handwritten menus, 1974 and 1975. Letter of thanks for the Woolworth's Christmas lunch, 1975.

Joyce's reputation was such that top London chefs and celebrities would make the long journey down to Dartmouth. In 1978, Joyce was awarded a Michelin Star, which she held for a number of years. She was only the second UK-based female chef to achieve a star (the first was awarded in 1976 to Sonia Stevenson, chef and co-owner with her husband Peter of the Horn of Plenty, just a few miles away in Gulworthy, Tavistock). The restaurant was also regularly reviewed in *The Good Food Guide*. By 1984, the Carved Angel had made such an impact with diners that the Guide crowned it 'The Best Real Food Restaurant' for that year.

Joyce's first cookery book, *The Carved Angel Cookery Book*, written with Sophie Grigson (daughter of Jane, an established cookery book writer and TV personality in her own right) was published in 1990. First edition copies, particularly those personally signed by Joyce, are much prized by collectors. The various editions have now sold over 50,000 copies, and although it is over 30 years old, many top chefs still refer to this cookbook today.

In 1993, the Egon Ronay Cellnet Guide made the Carved Angel their Restaurant of the Year. A plaque-style plate, provided by the guide to commemorate this achievement, can still been seen in the restaurant today. Egon Ronay himself was a regular visitor over the years.

As Dartmouth was mainly a holiday destination, busy with tourists over the summer, Joyce and Tom looked for other projects to occupy them in the quiet winter months. Joyce developed a range of jams, preserves and chutneys to sell around the country. The most notable success, though, was the Carved Angel Christmas Pudding, which can still be bought today, although it is now made using an updated recipe.

The Egon Ronay Restaurant of the Year Award, 1993.

Joyce with a carved angel.

The AA Rosette Award, 1975.

New arrivals

In 1986, Tom Jaine left the Carved Angel to pursue other projects, although he remained a very close friend and confidant of Joyce's right up until her passing. For the remaining years that Joyce ran the Carved Angel, her long-time close friend Meriel Matthews (née Boydon) was her business partner. Together, they kept the restaurant as one of the most sought-after places to dine during the 1990s.

In the late 1980s, Joyce bought a second property in Dartmouth and opened the Carved Angel Café, which served daily breakfast and afternoon tea. The café enabled Joyce to sell more of her own products and allowed diners to enjoy her food in a more relaxed setting.

As Joyce's profile grew, she appeared as a judge in two episodes of *MasterChef* and in the programme *Take Six Cooks*, which featured top-class chefs such as Nico Ladenis, Pierre Koffmann, Albert Roux and a very young Raymond Blanc.

Helping hands

To deliver the style of food Joyce firmly believed in, she needed other chefs to work alongside her. She was very good at identifying young chefs who had natural talent and understood her ethos. During the years Joyce was in the kitchen, she engaged a number of chefs to work with her who then went on to have great careers of their own.

The first chef Tom and Joyce recruited was Stephen Markwick. He was already an experienced chef working in a hotel restaurant in the north east of England when Joyce and Tom persuaded him to make the move down to the South West. With a young family in tow, it was a brave decision for him to make. However, it turned out to be a very good one. After a number of years at the Carved Angel, Stephen moved on to set up his own restaurant in Bristol. This became one of the top restaurants in the city, with people coming from miles around to enjoy his food. After running Markwick's for 35 years, Stephen retired in 2012. His eponymous restaurant is still greatly missed.

Another accomplished chef who worked with Joyce in the early stages of her career was Jane Baxter. After college, Jane made the decision to become a full-time chef and pursued her dream wholeheartedly, going through a copy of the 1985 *Good Food Guide* and writing to many of the most notable restaurants of the day. From the replies she got back, one stood out. It was from George Perry-Smith at the Riverside restaurant. He said that he did not currently have a position for her, but would get back in touch if one arose. A few weeks later he sent Jane a postcard inviting her down to Helford for an interview. Jane made the long journey down by train. It was a worthwhile trip as George offered her a junior chef role with immediate effect.

Joyce Molyneux and Tom Jaine in the kitchen at the Carved Angel, November 1977.

Jane worked with George through 1986, which was to be his last full year running the restaurant. In 1987, when her parents came to visit her, they made a trip up to Devon to have lunch at the Carved Angel. Jane introduced herself to Joyce, an interview followed and she moved up to Dartmouth to work with Joyce from February 1987. With Joyce's full support, Jane later moved to a more senior role working under Richard Cranfield at Bistro 13, and then at his next Dartmouth-based restaurant, Mansion House. She then went on to work with Rick Stein at his restaurant in Padstow, with chef, journalist and author Rosie Sykes (who also worked at the Carved Angel) and at London's River Café alongside Rose Gray and Ruth Rogers, before establishing The Riverford Organic Field Kitchen. Today, Jane and her business partner Samantha Miller run Wild Artichoke, a catering and events business in Kingsbridge, Devon. Jane has written a number of cookery books, is a regular chef on the BBC series *Saturday Kitchen Live* and featured in Matt Tebbutt's 2022 series *Go Veggie And Vegan*.

Working for Joyce at the Carved Angel led to some lifelong friendships being forged, and even a marriage. Tim Withers had previously worked at The Hole in the Wall and The Riverside, before moving over to the Carved Angel. It was during his time there that he met his future wife Helen, a Dartmouth girl who had been waiting tables for Joyce since she was at college. In 1986 Tim moved on to work with Colin White at his award-winning restaurant White's in Cricklade, Wiltshire, then in 1989, he and Helen took over a Wadworth pub, The George & Dragon, in Rowde, near Devizes in Wiltshire. The pub gained AA rosettes along with regular positive reviews in *The Good Food Guide*. After running the pub from 1989 to 2004, they sold up and bought a house called the Old Vicarage in the small town of Dulfer, Wales, which they have been running as a guesthouse since 2006.

One day during the early 1980s, a young lad named Nick Coiley, fresh from the local catering college, went along to see if he could get a job in the kitchen of the Carved Angel. Initially, Tom and Joyce thought he was a salesman and tried to turn him away. However, his enthusiasm and endeavour persuaded them to offer him a position working alongside Joyce. Over the years, he rose through the ranks of the kitchen brigade, becoming a very accomplished chef. When he became her head chef, Nick fondly recalls sitting down with Joyce each Sunday evening to put together the coming week's menu, based on what ingredients were in season and readily available from local suppliers.

The Carved Angel suppliers, 1975

17 The Angel

Joyce always kept up to date with other restaurants and chefs around the UK, travelling long distances to sample their food. Nick remembered one particular trip vividly. They travelled up to London for lunch at Bibendum, where Simon Hopkinson was receiving rave reviews. When they walked into the dining room, there was a table of very well-known chefs who were clearly having a good time and enjoying the food. Once they saw Joyce enter the room, every chef rose from his seat, bowed his head and then sat back down to continue lunch. The chefs around this table included Michel and Albert Roux, Pierre Koffmann and Nico Ladenis.

Nick Coiley worked with Joyce for over 16 years and remained a lifelong friend. After the Carved Angel, he went on to run his own highly regarded restaurant, Agaric, a few miles away in Ashburton. Nick has now retired to a new life in Normandy, where he runs a cookery school. He continues to enjoy foraging, both in the fields and along the seashore.

Life after the Carved Angel

In 1999, Joyce made the decision to retire and sell both the Carved Angel and the Carved Angel Café. Although she gave up running her own restaurant and being a chef, Joyce did not disappear from the world of food. In October 2011 her second cookbook *Born To Cook: Angel Food* was published, with proceeds going to Save The Children. It was written with Gerard Baker, a protégé from the Carved Angel kitchen.

In October 2017, the *Observer* honoured Joyce with a Lifetime Achievement Award, which was presented over a special lunch at chef Mitch Tonks's Seahorse Restaurant, just two doors down from the Carved Angel.

All those who worked alongside Joyce remember her calmness and willingness to help, although she also demanded high standards of professionalism. They appreciated Joyce's unbridled passion to pass on her knowledge and skills to those working with her.

Dartmouth never forgot Joyce. She was often invited back to the town, attending the festivals and annual regatta as an honoured guest. When she was invited to the 2018 Dartmouth Food Festival, Joyce met Elly for the first time, and she returned again to have lunch at the Angel with her niece in 2019. This visit holds very special memories for Elly and her team.

Joyce's passing in 2022, at the age of 91, was greeted with an outpouring of emotion and tributes from across the cookery world, along with the media and diners who all loved her food and the wonderful person she was.

Joyce Molyneux at 80, 2011

New owners and a new name: 2000 to 2016

When Joyce retired, Michelin-starred chef Peter Gorton and his business partner Paul Roston jumped at the chance to acquire both the Carved Angel and the Angel Café. They took over in February 2000, having already appointed David Jones as head chef, which meant that David had the chance to spend a few weeks working with Joyce before the restaurant formerly changed ownership.

David already had an impressive CV, including head chef at the Box Tree in Ilkley and Ynyshir. He was awarded 3 AA rosettes by the time he was 26 and a Michelin Star at 28. He spent two years at the Carved Angel, leaving in January 2002, but he still visits Dartmouth regularly and is fondly remembered by the locals.

In 2004, Peter Gorton and Paul Roston decided to sell the Carved Angel. Over a few drinks in a local hostelry, they agreed a deal with renowned chef John Burton-Race, who had recently returned to the UK from France, a period of his life that was documented in the TV series *French Leave*. He had been looking for a restaurant that was close to his Devon home and The Carved Angel was perfect.

Peter Gorton

After some refurbishment work, the restaurant was opened in 2004 as the New Angel. Already a well-known chef, John had gained Michelin stars at previous establishments such as L'Ortolan, near Reading, and London's Landmark Hotel. His food immediately gained the attention of critics and diners alike. In 2005, Michelin awarded him a star, which he would retain until he left in 2010.

Although the restaurant closed for some time in 2007 due to family issues, John got it back up and running with the help of his former business partner Clive Jacobs, owner of *Caterer* magazine, reopening it in early 2008. When John left in 2010, Clive enticed chef Nathan Thomas to leave the Ledbury and take up the head chef role to keep the restaurant open. He then approached Michelin-starred chef Alan Murchison, who had worked with John at L'Ortolan, to see if he was interested in taking on the restaurant. At this time, Alan was running his company 10 in 8 Fine Dining and was building up a range of fine dining restaurants around the country, each with a top chef in the kitchen. The New Angel was an ideal addition to this project. A deal was agreed for Alan to run a restaurant from the premises, but Clive retained ownership of the building.

Alan Murchison

Alan wanted to have a fresh start, so he decided to rename the restaurant. After canvassing the locals for suggestions that would be in keeping with the past, he settled on Angélique. The restaurant briefly closed for refurbishment, then opened under this name in January 2011. Unfortunately, this new era was not to last very long. By November 2013, Alan and his company had gone into liquidation. The restaurant closed and the empty shell of the grand mock-Tudor building was a sad sight by the river for the next few years.

A NEW BEGINNING...

Elly Wentworth

In 2016, the family-owned Holland Group, who operate a number of restaurants, holiday apartments and retail businesses across Dartmouth, bought the building from Clive Jacobs. They developed the first and second floors into high-quality holiday apartments and started work to bring the ground floor back as a functioning restaurant, under the name the Angel.

Knowing the venue's tradition of fine dining and wishing to recapture the status it had enjoyed in Joyce's time, the Group looked for a female chef who had the ability to elevate the restaurant and its reputation.

In the early months of 2018, 26-year-old chef Elly Wentworth was working with Michelin-starred chef Hywel Jones at Lucknam Park Hotel & Spa, and was already considering a number of attractive offers to move her career forward. It was a friend who first alerted Elly to the opportunity at the Angel. Following his recommendation, she visited the restaurant a number of times before finally deciding to take up the role of head chef. The unique challenges presented by the Angel, along with its illustrious history, were too good to turn down.

Like Joyce, Elly is very much a champion of using fresh, seasonal and sustainable produce in her dishes. She works closely with local suppliers who all fully understand her requirements. Her modern British cooking, drawing on influences from around the world, is enjoyed by diners and food critics alike. Like Joyce and her chefs before them, Elly and the team work within an open kitchen, so diners can observe them in action.

With Elly at the helm, the Angel has gone from strength to strength, regularly winning awards and gaining attention around the country. Those who enjoyed dining at the Carved Angel during Joyce's time have started to return. They frequently comment about how happy they are to see another female chef in the kitchen delivering great food.

Elly Wentworth was born in Wimborne Minster, Dorset, on 23rd December 1991. She grew up in Plymouth and has been a passionate cook since she was young, often preparing family meals at home.

Her unbridled enthusiasm and desire to learn the culinary arts led Elly to become a kitchen porter at The Mussel Inn in the small Devon village of Down Thomas, where she bombarded the chef with questions every day about how the dishes were being prepared.

When Elly was 14, the family moved to Cornwall, where they ran a farm that included pigs, horses and 4,000 chickens. She used to get up at 5am each morning to collect eggs before going to school. Living on the farm gave her an appreciation for the importance of locally grown food, which she still uses in her cooking to this day.

At the age of 16, Elly enrolled at Plymouth College on a two-year professional catering course. Using the knowledge and skills she was gaining at college, she would go home each evening to create meals for the family. She did not follow recipes verbatim but constructed her own interpretations of traditional dishes, drawing on her natural understanding of the mechanics of cooking to produce balanced and tasty meals for the family. After just 18 months, Elly had successfully completed the course and left with an NVQ Level 2 qualification.

Following the course, Elly took up an apprenticeship as a commis chef at the St Mellion Golf Club in Cornwall. When the opportunity arose to move to the luxury Lake Country Hotel & Spa in Llangammarch Wells, Powys, Wales, she made the step up to work in a fine dining kitchen. After 14 months in the kitchen at the Lake, Elly was offered a position with brothers Chris and James Tanner – first in their Barbican restaurant, then at their flagship Tanners restaurant in Plymouth. She started in the pastry section and quickly rose to demi chef.

When she was offered the chance to work at a Michelin-starred restaurant, Elly seized the opportunity with both hands. With the support of both Tanner brothers, she joined Simon Hulstone at his Torquay-based restaurant The Elephant, as demi chef. At The Elephant, Elly expanded her knowledge and started to learn about using flowers in dishes, visiting Simon's nearby allotment in the afternoons between service to gather both flowers and vegetables for the evening.

After 18 months working with Simon, in 2012 an opportunity arose to join Michelin-starred chef Richard Davies, who is particularly renowned for his fish and seafood dishes, at his then restaurant The Manor House, located in Castle Combe, Wiltshire. Elly was engaged as a chef de partie, in charge of a specific section in the kitchen during service. While working with Richard, she learnt a wide range of skills specific to the preparation and cooking of fish as well as seafood. When a position in the kitchen at the Michelin-starred Lucknam Park was advertised in 2015, Richard saw that this was a natural next step for Elly and encouraged her to submit an application.

On arriving for her interview at Lucknam Park, Elly was greeted by one of the sous chefs, the second most important role in the commercial kitchen. He asked her to fillet a selection

of fish as a skills test. At the time, head chef Hywel Jones was running a cookery school within the building. After a few minutes, the sous chef was so impressed with Elly's skills that he phoned Hywel and asked him to come over to the kitchen and see Elly in action. It did not take Hywel very long to see the potential in front of him and offer Elly the position of chef de partie. Within just three months of joining, she was promoted to junior sous chef.

By 2016 Hywel had seen such progress and potential with Elly's work in the kitchen, across all sections, that he persuaded her to apply for a place on that year's BBC series *MasterChef: The Professionals*. She was a very late, in fact a last-minute entrant, to this widely watched annual competition, which aims to showcase the talents of aspiring chefs. From the very first episode she appeared in, Elly's skills and ability to think on her feet greatly impressed the judges. Throughout the series, her inventive food gained praise from all who were fortunate enough to sample her work. Elly made the final three, narrowly missing out on the ultimate prize.

In 2016, another event took place that would, a couple of years later, become a big part of Elly's life. The Holland Group – a family-owned company who run a number of businesses throughout Dartmouth, including retail outlets, holiday apartments, secure parking and hospitality venues – bought 2 South Embankment. The Holland Group already owned the wine bar and eatery Platform 1, which sits just a few metres away on Dartmouth's jetty, so taking on the former Carved Angel premises and opening a dedicated restaurant was a natural next step.

The Group converted the building's first and second floors into high-quality holiday apartments. The ground floor, where once great restaurants had thrived, was only being used for storage, so they began work to restore it to its former glory. Initially, it was opened as a standard restaurant catering to summer tourists. However, knowing the restaurant's illustrious history and wishing to recapture the magic of the Carved Angel when Joyce Molyneux was at the helm, in 2018 The Holland Group decided to shift the focus to fine dining. To elevate the dining experience and re-establish the restaurant's reputation amongst diners around the UK, they looked for a female chef who could take it to the next level.

Following her *MasterChef* experience, and with the extra skills she had acquired from working with Hywel and the team, in 2018 Elly was looking for her next career move. She

Joyce Molyneux and Elly Wentworth at the Dartmouth Food Festival, 2019.

was already considering a number of attractive offers when a friend told her about the opportunity in Dartmouth. Despite her initial reservations, Hywel persuaded Elly that it was the right career move and, given the restaurant's history, a very unique opportunity. She visited the restaurant a number of times before finally deciding to take up the role of head chef at what was soon to be named the Angel: Taste of Devon.

She made a promising start. The restaurant's reputation was building and Elly's cooking was evolving now she had complete control of a commercial kitchen for the first time. Awards and accolades started to pour in.

What no one could have foreseen at the close of 2019 was the Covid pandemic and the impact it would have on everyone. As it was for all those working in hospitality, 2020 was a challenging year, marked by lockdowns. Like other restaurants, the Angel had to operate with reduced table numbers once indoor dining was allowed again. Throughout this difficult period, Elly managed to maintain a viable restaurant, and it was even included in the 2020 Michelin Guide. Once again, a restaurant and its chef operating at 2 The Embankment, Dartmouth, had come to the attention of one of the world's most recognised authorities on the best dining establishments.

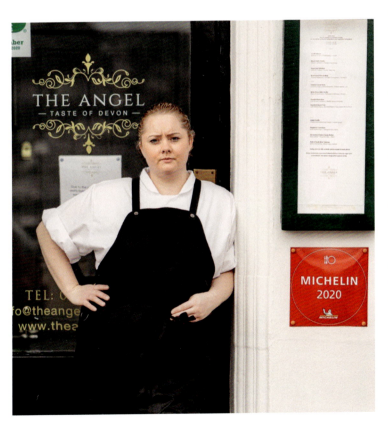

Elly outside the Angel, 2021

During one of the lockdowns, Elly was contacted to see if she would like to participate for the South West in the 2021 BBC series the *Great British Menu*. Although she did not make it through to the final, her dishes received excellent scores and comments from the judges. One dish in particular, her dessert Black Penny, received a maximum score of ten and can still be enjoyed today at the Angel.

For Elly and the team, 2021 was also a challenging year. There were the ongoing issues of the Covid epidemic and staff shortages across all parts of the hospitality sector. As if this wasn't enough to contend with, Elly and the team lost talented pastry chef and dear friend Craig Akehurst to cancer. Elly had known Craig for a number of years and he was a great asset to have at her side while she was building her career as head chef. He is greatly missed.

The *Great British Menu* came calling once more, asking Elly to be part of their 2022 series. She made it to the final two during her heat week, getting high scores for her dishes and receiving admiring comments from judge and renowned chef Tom Kerridge.

With her reputation growing, the restaurant industry trade magazine *The Caterer* featured Elly on its front cover with a five-page article inside. She also appeared in the five-part Channel 4 series *Best of Britain by the Sea*. Presenters Grace Dent and Ainsley Harriott enjoyed a three-course lunch in the restaurant in March 2022, and the episode aired two months later.

Throughout 2022, Elly and the restaurant continued to gain awards and national recognition. In September, James Pike was appointed General Manager of The Holland Group, and he saw the potential for Elly to extend her head chef role beyond the Angel, by opening a French-style bistro across the road at the company's other dining establishment, Platform 1. Elly was appointed to the role of Group Executive Chef and would oversee operations for both establishments, whilst still being very much hands on day to day with the Angel. The early months of 2023 saw a major refurbishment program and rebranding for Platform 1, while the Angel was also upgraded and redecorated. On 31st March, the Embankment Bistro was launched, with a very enthusiastic audience enjoying samples of the new menu.

Elly was in demand as a champion of women building successful careers in catering. Along with four other female chefs, she was invited to provide a course for the dinner held on 6th March at Deer Park Country House as part of Hospitality Action's International Women's Day celebrations. Elly provided the dessert. She was one of four women celebrated in the 'Inspiring Women' feature that appeared in the Spring issue of *Quality Matters*, and the Angel gained a 'New Restaurant' entry in *The Good Food Guide*. In the same week, the restaurant had confirmation that it had retained its entry in the 2023 edition of *The Great Britain and Ireland Michelin Guide*.

Elly Wentworth and Angela Hartnett during filming for the Great British Menu, 2022 series.

Brandon Head, Elly and Jordan Wiltshire, 2023.

Elly's awards before the Angel

Winner of South West Young Professional Chef of the Year 2012 and 2014
Winner of South West Chef of the Year (overall) 2014
Finalist Craft Guild of Chefs Young National Chef of the Year competition 2015
Winner of Royal Academy of Culinary Arts Awards of Excellence 2015

Awards with the Angel

Entry in Michelin Guide since 2018
2 rosettes from the AA since 2019
Best Fine Dining Restaurant by Food & Drink Devon 2020/21
Gold Standard Dining by Food & Drink Devon 2020/21
Good Food Guide 2023

My Journey to The Angel

Chris Tanner
RESTAURANTS: THE BARBICAN KITCHEN, PLYMOUTH; THE KENTISH HARE, BIDBOROUGH, ROYAL TUNBRIDGE WELLS.

A chef or restaurateur is only as good as the people they surround themselves with. When we opened the doors to our very first restaurant, Tanners, in July 1999, we could never have envisaged the talent that would come through our kitchen.

After being established for ten years and having some phenomenal people in the kitchen, we were receiving CVs constantly. In 2009 a young cook's CV landed on the office desk. It was from an 18-year-old named Elly Wentworth. She arrived well-presented and on time (for once!) for her interview. From the start we could see she was serious and hungry to succeed. We started her on the pastry section, where she soon threw herself into the professional environment. Our job was to focus and guide her in the kitchen. She quickly demonstrated her passion to learn and soon found her rhythm. The pastry section is probably one of the most technical areas of cookery, where the recipes must be methodically followed. Elly soon mastered this, with nobody getting near her recipe book or even daring to try!

Tanners was a busy restaurant that opened Tuesday to Saturday for lunch and dinner. It was demanding work and by Saturday we were all looking forward to our couple of days off. The break in the afternoon was particularly welcome; some went to the gym, others would go into the town and some went home for a cheeky siesta. Elly was quite partial to the latter. One particular Saturday evening, we and the kitchen team were gearing up for a busy service at 5.30pm, front of house had been briefed and we were all set for a full house, but Elly was nowhere to be seen. 6pm came and went. By this time we were getting concerned as she was normally all over it. 6.30pm came, with the first couple of orders starting to come into the kitchen. By 7pm we were starting to rock and still there was no sign of Elly. At 7.15pm the kitchen's back door nearly came off its hinges as – you guessed it – a rather red-faced Elly Wentworth hurtled into the kitchen, receiving a standing ovation from the entire crew. She had not set an alarm and her cheeky little siesta had overrun... She did, however, survive the night and lived to see another service!

Throughout the three years she was with us, Elly progressed on to all the kitchen sections and demonstrated a great love for her chosen craft. Her bubbly personality is infectious, her work ethic second to none, and for both James and me, it has been a joy to watch her progression over the years. It is great to see her now leading her own team. This is just the start and we are yet to see the best of Elly Wentworth.

The world is absolutely her oyster!

Simon Hulstone
THE ELEPHANT, TORQUAY. 1 MICHELIN STAR

I have many fond memories of Elly's time at The Elephant. She arrived at a time when I was particularly busy with international competitions and ambassador roles, and of course running a Michelin-starred establishment, so I relied on my high-quality and consistent team, and Elly was integral to that. The team also played their part in the competitions, making for great days out and trips all around the country, and we continued to add to our awards. Elly was fun and really lit up the team with her humour and strong West Country accent, which was a constant source of banter. It's great to see how far she has come since leaving the team here and now for her to be in such an iconic building as the Angel. It's a pleasure to watch her grow and take the reins as a head chef. This is only the start of her journey and we will see and hear (you always hear her first) a lot more of Elly in the next few years as she champions the best of British cuisine and hospitality.

Richard Davies
CALCOT MANOR, TETBURY.

I have known Elly for almost 15 years. She came to me at The Manor House, Castle Combe, as a young demi chef de partie. She was dedicated, hard-working and strong willed. I knew immediately that we would get on and that she would go on to do wonderful things and inspire the younger generation around her.

I have watched her grow in confidence as a young woman and an exceptional chef, and I know that she will continue to succeed within the industry.

Elly likes to have fun at work. She always had a funny story and her laugh alone would be enough to make me laugh out loud – you could hear her laughing a mile away! We spend more time with friends at work than with our loved ones, so I think it is important to surround yourself with good people, and to build a tight team, a team that would do anything to help each other create the very best food possible. Elly was the perfect team player, and you would want her on your team without question.

Hywel Jones
LUCKNAM PARK, CHIPPENHAM. 1 MICHELIN STAR

Every once in a while a new chef joins the kitchen team who just stands out from the rest. Elly Wentworth was that chef the day she came for a trial at Lucknam Park.

I asked one of the junior sous chefs to test Elly and to see what she could do. Within an hour I was being told that I had to offer her a job. She was that good.

No single thing set Elly apart. It was pretty much everything. She was an incredibly talented cook, had infectious enthusiasm for her craft, was highly motivated to develop herself and, even as a junior chef, displayed the leadership qualities required to become a head chef.

Her bubbly personality and cheeky sense of humour made her a popular member of the team and I was delighted when her appearance on *MasterChef* helped introduce Elly to a far greater group of fans than just her workmates.

Elly was a model professional but never took herself too seriously. She enjoyed the kitchen banter and gave as good as she got. She certainly had her share of comical moments, none more so than when she ordered ten whole halibut instead of ten kilos of halibut – something she still denies to this day!

Elly's move to the Angel has been the making of her. She's developed and evolved her cooking, become a great leader and is an example to all aspiring young chefs.

Elly is one of the country's finest young chefs. I'm fortunate that she decided to dedicate some of her career to my kitchen and I could not be any prouder of her.

SPRING

March – May

Bread

Milk Bread Rolls

Amuse Bouche

Carrot Cream | Miso | Black Garlic

Starters

Cured Brill | Exmoor Caviar | Granny Smith Dressing

White Asparagus Tortellini | Potato | Truffle Tea

Free Dived Scallops | Cucumber Butter | Pickled Mustard Seed

Mains

Roasted Brill | Turnip | Smoked Sea Lettuce Sauce

Red Mullet | Baby Artichokes | Langoustine Bisque

Lamb Loin | Apricots | Hispi Cabbage | Smoked Almond

Pre-desserts

Apricot Sorbet | Toasted Honey | Chamomile | Bee Pollen

Desserts

Gin And Tonic 'Angel Style'

Coconut | Lychee | Yuzu 'All White'

Devonshire Clotted Cream Parfait | Golden Raisin | Sesame And Apple

Malt Mousse | Blackout Coffee Sponge | Hazelnut Ice Cream

'Chocolate Bar' Poached Cherries | Salted Almond

Milk Bread Rolls

Makes 15 – 18 rolls

First, make the **starter**. Combine the flour and water in a small saucepan. Whisk the mixture until there are no lumps and the flour has totally combined with the water. Then place the saucepan over a low heat, whisking constantly for 4–5 minutes. Make sure during this process that the liquid does not boil. Remove the saucepan from the heat and allow to cool for at least 10 minutes.

Now make the **dough**. Put the butter into a medium saucepan and place on a low heat to melt. Once melted, take off the heat. In another saucepan, pour in the milk and warm until tepid, not boiling. When it is warm, take this saucepan off the heat as well.

In a stand mixer, pour in the cooled starter. Then add the flour, yeast and sugar. Gently whisk until the ingredients have combined. Now add the salt and whisk for a few more seconds. With the dough hook attached, start the mixer on the low speed setting.

With the mixer working at low speed, slowly add the milk, followed by the melted butter. Allow the ingredients time to fully combine. Then add one of the beaten eggs. Once the egg has combined with the mix, increase the speed to medium and continue mixing until a smooth, elastic dough has formed. You will know it has reached the correct consistency when you can take a small piece of the dough and stretch it between your fingers and the light shines through it.

Lightly grease a bowl and a sheet of cling film with trennwax spray. Then remove the dough from the mixer, shape it into a ball and place into the bowl. Cover the bowl with the cling film, ensuring the greased side is face down on top of the dough. Put the bowl aside to enable the dough to prove and roughly double in size. The proving process should take about 1 hour.

Once the dough has proven, carefully remove the cling film and put it aside with the greased side facing upwards. On a lightly floured surface, gently knead the dough into a ball. During this process, you will see it deflate. Do not overwork the dough. It should only take a minute to form into a ball. Now put the dough back into the bowl, place the cling film back on top of the bowl and put it into the fridge to rest for at least 2 hours. It will happily stay in perfect condition for up to 24 hours. So, you can make it in advance.

If you have ring moulds, lightly grease a flat-bottomed oven tray and the inside of the moulds. Take the bowl of dough from the fridge and remove the cling film. On a work surface that has been dusted with flour, place the dough ball. Divide the dough into 12g pieces and form each into a ball. With the moulds on the baking tray, press five balls into each one. You should be able to make 15-18 rolls from the dough mix. Once all the dough has been placed into the moulds, brush the tops with the remaining beaten egg. Cover them all with a sheet of lightly greased cling film (greased side down) and set aside to rest for 40-50 minutes.

If you do not have ring moulds, lightly grease each muffin hole. Take the bowl of dough from the fridge and remove the cling film. On a work surface that has been dusted with flour, place the dough ball. Divide the dough into 60g pieces and form each into a ball. Place each one into a muffin hole. You should be able to make 15–18 rolls from the dough mix. Once all the dough has been placed into the muffin holes, brush the tops with the remaining beaten egg. Cover them all with a sheet of lightly greased cling film (greased side down) and set aside to rest for 40–50 minutes.

Preheat the oven to 160°C (140°C fan/Gas Mark 3). If you have an oven with humidity control, set it to 60%. If not, put some water into a tray and place it on the bottom of the oven. Remove the cling film from your baking tray and then place the tray in the oven. It should take about 22 minutes for the rolls to reach a golden brown colour. Once they are golden brown, remove the baking tray from the oven and allow to cool. When they have had sufficient time to completely cool, remove the rolls from the moulds or muffin tins and gently sift a light dusting of flour over the top.

At the Angel I serve these rolls with smoked whipped buttermilk butter and sea salt flakes.

> "A memorable meal is not just about the main dish. It is the little things served alongside the main which help to make the overall dining experience unforgettable. These milk bread rolls are a light and tasty way to start your meal."

For the starter

28g white bread flour
   (I use Wessex Mill)
90ml tap water

For the dough

30g unsalted butter
120ml full-fat milk
300g white bread flour,
   plus extra for dusting
7g fresh yeast or 2.3g dried yeast
38g caster sugar
1 tsp table salt
2 large free-range eggs, beaten
   separately
Trennwax spray, for greasing

Equipment

Stand mixer with a whisk and a dough
   hook
15–18 x 35 x 70mm ring moulds (for
   best results, although not completely
   necessary) or muffin trays

Carrot Cream | Miso | Black Garlic

Serves 8

For the **carrot velouté**, start by washing the carrots. Peel the carrots and thinly slice them all. Place a large pan on the heat, add the butter and gently melt. Add the sliced carrots and cook for 5 minutes, stirring. Add 2 good pinches of salt to the carrots. Add the water to the carrots, cover, then simmer for 10 minutes. When the carrots are cooked, start to blend the mixture. You want to make sure it has a good consistency and is not too thick. If it is too thick, add some more water. Season the velouté. Pass the velouté through a fine sieve and allow to cool.

For the **carrot cream**, measure out 700ml of the carrot velouté. In a mixing bowl, add water and ice. Add the gelatine leaves and allow to bloom. Bring the carrot velouté to the boil, add the bloomed gelatine and whisk well. Once all whisked in, pour into a measuring jug. Pour the carrot cream liquid into 8 small dishes; I usually weigh this to 70g per portion. Place the dishes into the fridge to set. Cool the remaining carrot cream. You can reheat this the following day. This will keep in the fridge for 2 days maximum.

Next, I move on to the **Granny Smith purée**. Gently wash the apples under cold water. Peel and core the apples, then slice them into very thin pieces. Put the slices into a large pan and add the caster sugar. Now add the water and bring to the boil, stirring continuously. Simmer the apples for 5–10 minutes or until soft. You want no colour on the apples, as they should remain as white as possible. Using a blender, blend the apples to a thick purée. Pass through a fine sieve and put into a piping bag straight away. Allow the purée to cool in the fridge. It can be kept in the fridge for up to 2 days.

For the **puffed potato**, pour the rapeseed oil into a medium pan and place on the heat. The oil needs to remain at 180°C, so use a thermometer to maintain the heat. If it gets too hot, take the pan off the heat and allow to cool to the correct temperature. When the oil is ready, place the air bag patata into the oil and gently fry for 30 seconds using a slotted spoon to stir the air bag in the oil. Spoon out onto a J cloth and season with salt and the cumin. This can be kept for up to 3 days, if left in a cool, dry place and kept in an airtight container.

Now for **miso and black garlic purée**: in a mixing bowl, weigh out 75g Granny Smith purée. Add the black garlic paste and white miso paste. Mix all three ingredients together and put into a piping bag. Leave this purée in the fridge until needed.

Assembly and Plating Up

Take the carrot cream out of the fridge and allow to come up to room temperature for 5–10 minutes. Place 12–14 dots of the black garlic purée on top of each portion of carrot cream. Place 8–10 dots of the coriander oil on top of each portion, as well. Add the puffed potato air bag on top; you want to make sure you cover the oil and purée, so add a good couple of spoons of this.

> "This amuse-bouche starts your meal off perfectly. The Angel uses the best black garlic available in the south-west, from the South West Garlic Farm. The flavours are deep, almost caramelised, with a wonderful sweet-sour balance. There is a strong umami kick and hints of aged balsamic, black cardamom, leather, smoke, tamarind and liquorice. Black garlic is a unique, truly artisan ingredient and very special in its own unique way. For me, this is one of the best amuse-bouche we have made at the Angel. It did take us a few weeks of tweaking to perfect this recipe, so I hope you enjoy it as much as I do!"

For the carrot velouté
400g carrots
120g unsalted butter
450ml tap water
Salt and black pepper, to taste

For the carrot cream
700ml carrot velouté (see above)
4½ bronze gelatine leaves

For the Granny Smith purée
8 Granny Smith apples
1 tsp caster sugar
100ml tap water

For the puffed potato
Rapeseed oil (enough to cover the patata)
20g Sosa air bag patata (potato – I get mine from Ritter's)
2g ground cumin (toasted before use)
A pinch of salt

For the miso and black garlic purée
75g Granny Smith purée (see above)
100g black garlic paste (I use South West Garlic Farm paste)
15g white miso paste

To garnish
Coriander oil (see page 278)

Equipment
Blender
Fine sieve
Piping bags
Temperature probe
Squeezy bottle

Serves 6

Cured Brill | Exmoor Caviar | Granny Smith Dressing

Start by **curing the brill**. Add the sugar and salt to a mixing bowl. Next, add in the lime, lemon and orange zest and juice. Use a spatula to mix all the ingredients together, making sure the salt and sugar are both thoroughly mixed with the juices. Pour half the mixture into a deep oven tray. Put the brill fillets in the tray. Now gently pour the remaining mixture over the fillets. I usually cure the brill on the day I serve the dish, so they are as fresh as possible. Place cling film over the top of the tray and put into the fridge. Depending on the size of the brill, it will take 20–40 minutes for them to be cured. Halfway through the process, peel back the cling film, turn the brill fillets, re-cover and give them about another 20 minutes to finish curing. Have a mixing bowl ready, filled with cold water. Once cured, take the brill out and gently wash each fillet in the water to remove all the cure. Pat dry with kitchen paper or J cloth and place them on a small tray. Cover the small tray with cling film and put into the fridge so the fish can firm up.

You can prepare the **pre hy** up to a week in advance. Pour half the water into a blender. On high speed, slowly add the xanthan gum, and then gradually add the rest of the water. This is an effective thickening agent and emulsifier. Continue to blend for a further minute so the mixture comes together and thickens. Once blended, put into a container, cover with cling film and keep in the fridge until needed.

The last element to prepare is the **Granny Smith dressing**. Make sure you have all the ingredients weighed and ready to use before starting. Add the verjus, citric acid, table salt and sugar into mixing bowl. Set up the juicer. Cut the apples (with core and peel) into quarters. Feed the apples into the juicer, one by one. You will need to be as quick as you can juicing the apples, so they keep their vibrant green colour for as long as possible. Once all the apples have been juiced, pour 300ml juice into a measuring jug. Skim off any pieces that have come to the surface. Now add the juice to the mixing bowl. Whisk together and add the pre hy. Strain the mixture through a chinois into a medium bowl, pressing down on the solids with a spatula to extract all the juice. Pour the strained mixture straight into a squeezy bottle and keep the fridge.

Assembly and Plating Up

Using a Parisienne scoop, scoop out five small balls of apple per serving and set aside. Slice the cured brill fillets into 1.5cm-wide pieces. I use five pieces per portion – three are placed in the centre of a small bowl-style plate, with the other two on top to create height. Place five Parisienne apple balls on top of the brill with three small quenelles of caviar. Add the purslane and fennel over the brill between the apple balls and caviar. Pour 50ml Granny Smith dressing into the bowl, so it is just below the height of the brill. Add a couple of drops of dill oil and olive oil into the apple dressing, giving additional flavour and colour to the dish. Now serve straight away.

> " This cured brill recipe works perfectly with the refreshing flavour of the Granny Smith apple. It showcases seasonality at its best. To add that extra special touch, I have paired it with the best caviar we have in the South West. This fish comes into season in British waters during May and is caught until December. It is at its best between June and August. As with all fresh fish, check for a clean smell of the sea, bright red gills and clear eyes as signs of both quality and freshness. For the restaurant, I usually buy our brill from Flying Fish in Cornwall. They send the fish filleted and include the bones, which I use to make a fish stock. Any good fishmonger will happily prepare the fillets for you. Be sure to ask them for the bones as well. "

For the cured brill

150g caster sugar

150g table salt

Zest and juice of 1 unwaxed lime

Zest and juice of 1 unwaxed lemon

Zest and juice of 1 unwaxed orange

2 fillets from a 2–3kg brill

For the pre hy

125ml tap water

6.5g xanthan gum (I use MSK)

For the Granny Smith dressing

12ml Minus8 verjus

1.5ml citric acid

3g table salt

10g caster sugar

8 Granny Smith apples

6g pre hy (see above)

To garnish

1 Granny Smith apple

Exmoor caviar (I buy the 50g tins)

4 leaves of sea purslane

4 leaves of sea fennel

Dill oil (see page 278)

Olive oil

Equipment

Blender

Juicer

Chinois

Squeezy bottle

Parisienne scoop

Serves 6 – 8

White Asparagus Tortellini | Potato | Truffle Tea

Make the **pasta dough** first. Place the eggs, egg yolks and olive oil in a mixing bowl. Whisk all the ingredients together and add the salt. Pour this mixture into a measuring jug and leave to one side. Set up a food processor; I usually use a robot-coupe in the restaurant, but a food processor or a stick blender with all attachments will work. Put the flour into the food processor with a quarter of your egg mixture. Blitz the dough to large crumbs; they should come together to form a dough when squeezed. If it feels too dry, gradually add more egg mixture until it comes together. Empty the dough onto a floured surface and begin to knead the dough together for 2-3 minutes until nice and smooth. Wrap the dough in cling film and put in the fridge to rest for at least 45 minutes. Bring the pasta dough out of the fridge and cut in half. Set up the pasta machine and feed the dough through the widest setting. Repeat this process with the dough, narrowing the rollers one notch at a time until you have a smooth sheet of pasta. On the lowest setting, feed the sheet through twice until it's semi-transparent. Using a 5cm ring cutter, cut out the pasta sheets and place them on a tray. Keep covered until needed.

To prepare the **lemon oil**, add all the ingredients to a mixing bowl and whisk together. Season with table salt and sugar. You may need to add more sugar if it tastes too sharp.

Now move on to the **glazed white asparagus**. It has a thick outer skin, so needs to be peeled before cooking, as it can be very stringy to eat. Run a peeler across the skin, rotating constantly to avoid creating flat edges. Bring the water, butter, lemon juice, sugar and salt to the boil. Add the peeled white asparagus and bring back to the boil. Once boiling, set aside and allow to cool. It is best to let the asparagus cool in this liquid to retain flavour and moisture. Leave for 1-2 hours to cool completely.

Next, prepare the **white asparagus salsa**. Once the white asparagus has cooled, cut the bottom of the stem away. You do not want this part as it tends to be very woody to eat. Remove the tips and keep for the plate. You just need the stems for the salsa. Dice them into 5mm pieces, finely chop the chives and mix with the lemon oil. Season to taste and keep in the fridge until required.

To make the **pre hy**, pour the water into a blender. On high speed, slowly add the xanthan gum and blend for a further minute until fully combined. Place into a container and leave in the fridge. It will last for up to a week.

Begin preparing the **truffle vinaigrette** by adding the water, verjus, sugar and pre hy to a mixing bowl. Slowly whisk while adding the olive oil, followed by the black truffle. Once all the ingredients have been fully incorporated, add salt to taste, then set aside.

For the **mushroom essence**, put the mushrooms in a food processor. and blend until you have a fine duxelles. Remove and place in a pan, cover with the water and bring to the boil. Add the garlic, rosemary and thyme. Reduce heat to a light simmer and cook for a further 30 minutes. Allow to cool, then store overnight in the fridge. The next day, bring the mushroom essence back up to the boil and then pass through a fine sieve with a double layer of muslin cloth to remove all impurities. Once strained, set aside until required.

Next, prepare the **truffle tea**. Place a pan on a medium heat. Add in the rapeseed oil, leek, carrot, celery and shallot. Sweat down until transparent, making sure they do not colour. Add the mushroom essence and bring to the boil. Then add the dried mushrooms and vinegar. Grate black truffle into the stock and add the bay leaves. Finish with the sugar and salt. Bring the tea to a light simmer for 1 hour and then sit for 30 minutes. Pass through a fine sieve with a double layer of muslin. Now set aside for use later.

Finally, make the **potato tortellini filling**. Preheat the oven to 180°C (160°C fan/Gas Mark4). Make a bed of sea salt on an oven tray. Place the potatoes on top and cook in the oven for up to 1 hour until the potatoes soften in the middle. The larger the potatoes, the longer the cooking time. Once soft, remove the potatoes, scoop out the insides and discard the skins. Put the potatoes into a pan on a medium heat, then add the double cream and milk. Whisk until combined, then fold in the crème fraîche, black truffle and salt. Cook for a further 5 minutes. Add the vegetarian Parmesan and glazed white asparagus. Set aside to cool.

Assembly and Plating Up

Place a circle of pasta on a floured surface, then add 25g of the potato filling to the centre. Brush a little egg wash around the circumference of the pasta. Fold the circle in half, keeping the filling in the centre, then seal the outside of the pasta together so the mixture is enclosed with no air gaps. Brush a little egg wash on the bottom of the corners and fold around your index finger until the corners meet and pinch together to seal. You want two tortellini per portion. The tortellini can be kept on a floured tray in the fridge for an hour or so before serving.

In a frying pan, fry the morels in rapeseed oil and salt. Get good colour on them, then add the butter and melt until it begins to foam. Add a small amount of water to the pan to create a glaze and stop the butter from burning. Remove from the heat and set aside for plating.

Half-fill a medium pan with tap water, place on a high heat and bring to the boil. Then add the olive oil and salt. Now put in the tortellini and cook for 2–4 minutes. Meanwhile, in another pan, glaze the remaining white asparagus in their own liquor. Warm up the truffle tea in another pan and keep hot. Remove the tortellini and glaze with the truffle vinaigrette.

To plate up, cut the white asparagus tips in half lengthways and place at the righthand side of each bowl, moving vertically from 5 o'clock to 1 o'clock. Garnish with two wild garlic shoots and three morels. Put 2 tablespoons of white asparagus salsa, in a round circle, at the centre of the plate. Place two cooked tortellini on top of the salsa. Now Microplane the black truffle and place on top. Pour on the truffle tea and serve immediately.

> "This classic spring vegetarian dish showcases asparagus at its seasonal best. The combination of flavours work very well together and the Wiltshire truffle just enhances the dish when used alongside the rich umami flavour from the mushroom essence."

For the pasta dough

2 large eggs

3 large egg yolks

5ml olive oil

Pinch of table salt

275g extra fine 00 flour, plus extra for dusting

1 egg, for egg wash

For the lemon oil

25ml fresh lemon juice

75ml olive oil

25g caster sugar

Salt, to taste

For the glazed white asparagus

16 spears of white asparagus

200ml tap water

100g unsalted butter

10ml fresh lemon juice

8g caster sugar

8g table salt

For the white asparagus salsa

2 spears of glazed white asparagus (see above)

20ml lemon oil (see above)

20g chives, finely chopped

Salt, to taste

For the pre hy

125ml tap water

6.5g xanthan gum (I use MSK)

For the truffle vinaigrette

100ml tap water

10g verjus

10g caster sugar

2g pre hy (see above)

10ml olive oil

15g Wiltshire black truffle, grated

Salt, to taste

For the mushroom essence

1.5kg button mushrooms

750ml tap water

1 garlic clove

2 sprigs of rosemary

2 sprigs of thyme

For the truffle tea

1 tbsp rapeseed oil

1 leek, diced

1 carrot, peeled and diced

2 celery sticks, diced

2 shallots, finely sliced

Mushroom essence (see above)

25g dried mushrooms (I use dried ceps)

20ml sherry vinegar

45g Wiltshire black truffle

2 bay leaves

10g caster sugar

A pinch of sea salt

For the potato tortellini filling

2 medium potatoes (you need 125g cooked potato)

30ml double cream

25ml full-fat milk

25ml crème fraîche

12g Wiltshire black truffle, finely grated

15g vegetarian Parmesan, finely grated

6 spears glazed white asparagus, diced (see above)

Sea salt

To garnish

24 morel mushrooms

Rapeseed oil, for frying

100g unsalted butter

25ml olive oil

Sea salt

16 small wild garlic shoots

Wiltshire black truffle

Equipment

Food processor or stick blender

Pasta machine

5cm ring cutter

Blender

Fine sieve

Muslin cloth

Microplane

Free Dived Scallops | Cucumber Butter | Pickled Mustard Seed

Serves 4

To prep the **scallops**, use a boning knife to pop the hinge of the scallop to open it up, allowing the knife to fillet flat across the head of the scallop to separate the top shell, then discard the shell. Next, remove the bottom shell from the scallop. Find the white firm muscle to the top side underneath the scallop which attaches it into place. Using a knife, you need to carefully cut away the muscle, allowing the scallop to be easily dispatched from the shell. Discard the shell. Carefully remove the scallop's membrane, muscle and roe using a knife or just your hands. If you look at a scallop from its head, the muscle beside will be exposed. Therefore, you can place your thumb in between the muscle and protein and start to separate them, while slowly going around the protein of the scallop with your thumb to dispatch the rest, leaving the pure protein. Repeat this process for all the scallops, then keep the scallops in the fridge for later.

For the **reduction**, julienne the shallots. Now add all the ingredients to a pan and bring to the boil. Remove from the heat, cover with cling film and leave it to infuse. Once cooled, place in the fridge. This reduction can last for up to a week in the fridge. I weigh out the reduction each day for all the sauces.

Now on to the **cucumber beurre blanc**. Add the reduction and fish stock to a medium pan, bring to the boil and reduce the liquid by half. Once reduced, remove from the heat and stir in the cream. Put back on a low heat and bring to a simmer. Reduce further until you have just a quarter of the original amount of liquid. Take off the heat and emulsify the butters into the mixture using a stick blender for best consistency. Once fully emulsified, peel the cucumber to the core and blitz the skins into the sauce, pass through a fine sieve and use the lime juice and salt to taste. Set aside until the dish is ready to serve.

For the **pickled mustard seed dressing**, bring a pan of water to the boil, then add the mustard seeds. Boil for a further minute, then remove from the heat and allow to cool. Refresh the mustard seeds again by filling the pan with water and bringing the seeds to the boil. You want to repeat this process three times, then set the pan aside. To make the pickle liquor, add the vinegar, water and sugar to a pan. Place on a low heat and bring to a simmer until the sugar is dissolved. Add the mustard seeds to the pickle and set aside to infuse.

To make the **cucumber relish**, Microplane the cucumber skin only, place into a muslin cloth and squeeze out all the moisture until it's dry. Add salt to the cucumber and set aside for 15 minutes. Then squeeze the cucumber through a muslin cloth again. Add the pickled mustard seed dressing, the banana shallot and dill. Mix all the ingredients and keep in the fridge until needed. This will only last one day.

For the **crispy sea beet**, in a small mixing bowl, add the flour, soda water and salt. Whisk the ingredients together until they form a light batter. You are looking for one with a consistency that is not too runny or thick. A good example of the perfect consistency is tempura batter. Coat the sea beet in the batter. Once your fryer is at 170°C, place the coated sea beet in the oil and cook until golden brown. Make sure you keep turning them so they get an even colour. Drain the sea beet on a J cloth and season with salt. This needs to be done on the day you are serving, as you want the sea beet to be nice and crispy.

Assembly and Plating Up

Pour the cucumber butter into a small saucepan and gently bring to a simmer. While it's coming to the heat, cook the scallops. Place a medium frying pan on the heat and allow to heat up slowly. You don't want a hot pan, as this will burn the scallops. Add the rapeseed oil to the pan, pat dry the scallops with a J cloth and season the scallops with table salt. Add the scallops to the pan, flat-side down, and cook until golden brown. You want to see a good caramelisation on each scallop with a slightly translucent centre. As a general rule, cook scallops for 2 minutes on one side and anything from 10 seconds–1 minute on the other side. Once cooked, serve immediately. On the bottom of each bowl, add three cucumber slices, which have been gently warmed with olive oil. Add a scallop on top the cucumber and seven dressed cucumber balls. Place a good teaspoon of cucumber relish on top of the scallop. Place the crispy sea beet on top with a few dots of pickled mustard seed dressing. Finish the dish with the cucumber butter and fennel and purslane flowers.

For the scallops

12 fresh scallops

1 tsp rapeseed oil

Table salt

For the reduction

3 shallots

400ml dry white wine

200ml white wine vinegar

225ml tap water

50g tarragon

50g flat-leaf parsley

50g dill

For the cucumber beurre blanc

200ml reduction (see above)

200g fish stock (see page 273)

200ml double cream

100g smoked butter, cubed

100g unsalted butter, cubed

2 large cucumbers

Juice of 1 lime

Salt, to taste

For the pickled mustard seed dressing

25g mustard seeds, soaked overnight

100ml white wine vinegar

100ml tap water

100g caster sugar

For the cucumber relish

1 large cucumber

3g table salt

1 banana shallot, brunoised or finely diced

8g dill

For the crispy sea beet

62g gluten-free flour

20ml soda water (you might need to add a little more if needed)

3g Maldon sea salt

80g sea beet (I buy mine from local forager Flying Fish)

Oil, for frying (quantity depending on appliance)

To garnish

1 cucumber, cut into 2mm slices

Olive oil

28 cucumber balls

12 sea fennel leaves

16 sea purslane flowers

Equipment

Boning knife

Stick blender

Fine sieve

Microplane

Muslin cloth

Deep-fat fryer

> " At the Angel we are very particular about our scallops and have a fantastic local supplier (Jamie, Greenstraight Scallops) who dives to catch every scallop with a single breath. No tanks or equipment is used, meaning the ethos is environmentally friendly and as natural as it can be. He delivers the scallops directly from his boat to the restaurant. When we get them delivered, they have only been out of the water for a maximum of 10 minutes. They are therefore as fresh as you will ever get and I am very lucky to be using them in the restaurant. They are a regular feature on our signature tasting menu. "

Roasted Brill | Turnip | Smoked Sea Lettuce Sauce

Serves 6

To brine the **brill**, put the salt and sugar into a saucepan, then add the water. On a high heat, boil the mixture, then allow 20 minutes for it to cool. Once cooled, put the brill into a dish and pour over the liquid. Cover the dish with cling film and place in the fridge for about 20 minutes. Once the brill has had time to brine, remove it from the fridge and pat dry with kitchen paper.

To make the **preserved lemon gel**, in a medium saucepan, add the sugar, lemons and water. Bring the mixture to the boil, then pour it into a blender and blitz on a high speed until you have a smooth gel. With a spatula, transfer the contents from the blender back into a saucepan on a medium heat. While constantly whisking, add the agar-agar. Then, still gently whisking, cook for 4 minutes. Pour the mixture into a dish, cover with cling film and place in the fridge to set. Once it has set, use a spatula to put it into the blender. Blitz on high speed and add the saffron. After a couple of minutes blitzing, pass the mixture through a chinois or sieve. Once sieved, pour it into a squeezy bottle or piping bag. You can prepare the gel up to a day in advance of serving, but it must be kept in the fridge.

To make the **turnip fondants**, peel the turnips, then slice into 1.5cm-thick pieces. Using the ring cutter, cut into circles. Put the fondants into a vacuum pack bag, add the kombu, smoked butter and salt, then vacuum seal. If you have a water bath, get it to 85°C and then put in the bag to cook for 25–30 minutes. If you do not have a water bath, use a saucepan of water, ensuring the water gets to 85°C and remains at that temperature during the whole cooking time. Once cooked, remove the turnip fondants from the water and allow to cool in the bag.

Preparing the **smoked sea lettuce sauce** begins by putting the water, vinegar, wine, shallots, chervil and dill into a saucepan. Place on a medium heat and bring to the boil. Remove from the heat and allow to cool and infuse for 20 minutes. Pass the cooled mixture through a chinois or sieve into another saucepan. Place it on a medium heat, then add the fish stock and cream. Bring to a simmer, stirring occasionally, and reduce by half. Once reduced, remove from the heat. Using a stick blender, add in the unsalted and smoked butter. Next, blend in the sea lettuce, then season with the sugar and lime juice. Pass through a chinois or sieve and set aside. Keep on the side until needed; this will be warmed up when you're ready to plate.

For the **baby turnips**, add ice cubes to a mixing bowl and fill with cold water. Using a turning knife, trim the green leaves off the top and place the turnips into a pan of salted water. Gently simmer the turnips for 3–4 minutes, then place straight into the iced water.

Gently take the skin off the turnips and place a medium pan on the heat. Add the rapeseed oil to the pan. Halve the turnips and place, flat-side down, in the pan. Season with sea salt and thyme and cook until a nice golden colour. Add the butter and keep warm for plating up.

To prepare the **crispy sea lettuce**, put the green split peas into a blender and blitz on high speed until you have a powder. In a food processor, add the flour, salt and 15g of the green split pea powder, followed by the beer. Mix on medium speed until you have a light, smooth batter. The ideal consistency is that of tempura batter. Dip the sea lettuce into the batter and deep-fry at 180°C for 2 minutes until golden brown. Drain on a J cloth or kitchen paper.

Start preparation for the **pickled turnips** by half-filling a bowl with ice cubes and then fill with cold water until the ice cubes are covered. Put a medium saucepan of water on a medium heat and bring it to a simmer. Now add the turnips and simmer for 15–20 minutes. They need to become soft in the middle but not fully cooked. Once soft, place them into the iced water to quickly cool and stop the cooking process. In a medium saucepan, pour the apple juice, white port and vinegar. Place on a high heat and bring to the boil. Once boiling, reduce the heat to medium and reduce the liquid by half. While the liquid is reducing, slice the turnips thinly on a mandoline. Stamp out discs with a 1.6cm pastry cutter. Place all the discs into a container. When the liquid has reduced by half, stir the olive oil and sugar into the liquid with a spatula. Pour the mixture over the turnip discs and leave to cool.

We are now at the final stage. Place a frying pan on a medium-high heat and add a splash of oil. Once the oil has become hot, put in the brill and fry for a minute or two until it gets a nice golden colour. Now add the butter and cook until the butter is foaming. Then turn the fish over and let the butter start to noisette (become brown and nutty but not burnt). Add a splash of water to the pan to create an emulsion and glaze the fish. Cook for a further minute. Remove from the heat and let the fish continue to cook in the pan off the heat.

"A wonderful fish dish to enjoy and spoil your family and friends. Many of the elements can be prepared up to a day in advance of serving."

Assembly and Plating Up

Place a turnip fondant on the lefthand side of each bowl. Next add six pickled turnip discs around the fondant and add the sea aster on top of the fondant. Add four baby turnips around the pickles and three dots of the preserved lemon gel. Place the brill on top of the fondant, sea purslane and bronze fennel on the fish. Warm the smoked sea lettuce sauce and pour into sauce jugs. To finish this dish, add the crispy sea lettuce and the dill oil.

For the brill

25g table salt

40g sugar

500ml tap water

2 fillets from a 3–4kg brill (I buy mine from Flying Fish)

100ml rapeseed oil

150g unsalted butter

For the preserved lemon gel

125g caster sugar

125g preserved lemons

400ml tap water

9g agar-agar

1g saffron

For the turnip fondants

6 medium turnips

5–6g kombu flakes

100g smoked butter

Maldon sea salt

For the smoked sea lettuce sauce

180ml tap water

180ml white wine vinegar

375ml dry white wine

1½ shallots

2 sprigs of chervil

2 sprigs of dill

150g fish stock (see page 273)

150ml double cream

150g unsalted butter

150g salted smoked butter

100g foraged sea lettuce

40g caster sugar

50ml fresh lime juice

For the baby turnips

3 bunches of baby turnips

1 tsp rapeseed oil

100g unsalted butter

25g thyme

Maldon sea salt, to taste

For the crispy sea lettuce

50g green split peas

125g gluten-free flour

3g table salt

300ml bottled beer (an IPA-style ale works best)

25g sea lettuce

Oil, for frying

For the pickled turnips

2 large turnips

150ml apple juice

150ml white port

125ml apple cider vinegar

50ml olive oil

35g caster sugar

To garnish

36 leaves of sea purslane

12 fronds of bronze fennel

Dill oil (see page 278)

Equipment

Blender

Chinois or fine sieve

Squeezy bottle or piping bag

2cm ring cutter

Vacuum pack bag

Water bath or temperature probe (optional)

Deep-fat fryer (optional)

Mandoline

1.6cm pastry cutter

Red Mullet | Baby Artichokes | Langoustine Bisque

Serves 4

For the **langoustine bisque**, preheat the oven to 180°C (160°C fan/Gas Mark 4). On a large gastro tray, roast the langoustine heads and claws for 15–20 minutes. While the heads are cooking, in a large pan cook the mirepoix: in a large pan, add the rapeseed oil, then the diced celery, fennel, onions and carrots. Sweat down, then add the fresh chopped tomatoes. Cook out until a jammy consistency. Add the tomato purée and the bay leaf and roast down. You want to see a good colour on the purée before adding the brandy. Add the brandy and burn off the alcohol. Add the white wine and reduce this by half, then add the roasted langoustine heads and claws and fill up with water to just cover the shells. Bring to the boil and then add the tarragon. Simmer the stock for 45 minutes. Leave to rest for 10 minutes, then pass the stock through a chinois and then a double layer of muslin. Return to the pan and reduce by three-quarters. Add butter and cream, if needed, to create a good, foamy consistency.

For the **baby violet artichokes**, fill a large pan with water and ice cubes, then squeeze the lemons in. Once all the juice has been squeezed from the lemons, add the skins to the water. Pull off the green outer leaves of the artichokes to expose the pale yellow ones inside. Using a knife, trim an inch off the top of the baby artichokes. Peel the outer layers away with a peeler. Now trim each artichoke into a circular shape. Ideally you want to take off the tough layer of the stem and the underside from the heart. Once you have a nice, round artichoke heart, put it in the water. Prepare all the baby artichokes this way. Then, using a serrated knife, trim off the tops of the artichokes and place back into the water. You are now ready to cook the baby artichokes. In a pan on medium heat, sweat off the mirepoix and coriander seeds. Add the tap water and wine and then the baby artichokes along with the salt and pepper. Bring to a simmer, then place a sheet of baking paper over the top and gently cook on a low heat for 10–15 minutes.

Fillet the **red mullet**, making sure you remove the pin bones. Place each piece into a medium vacuum pack bag with a pinch of Maldon sea salt, 3g fennel pollen and two pinches of dukkah. Cook in a water bath at 52°C for 30 minutes. Remove from the bath and leave in the bag to keep warm until ready to plate.

To cook the **quinoa**, put both quinoas in a pan with the water and cook slowly for 15 minutes until water has evaporated. You know when this is cooked as there is no bite left to the grain. Add two pinches of Maldon sea salt. Allow the quinoa to cool in the fridge.

Now, to make the **honey dressing**, mix the vinegar and Dijon mustard together, then add the rapeseed oil and soaked yellow mustard seeds, and season to taste with the honey. Place into a squeezy bottle for later and chill in the fridge.

For the **artichoke salad**, scoop out the hearts of four of the cooked artichokes, then finely chop the artichokes and place into a small mixing bowl. Add the honey dressing, chopped parsley and chopped chervil. Season with sea salt. Leave in the fridge until needed.

To **garnish**, heat a fryer to 180°C and fry the flat-leaf parsley until crisp. Place on a J cloth and add a sprinkle of salt. Repeat this process for the capers. Before adding the capers to the fryer make sure you squeeze off the excess brine as they can spit with the hot oil. You can place a lid on the top for 30 seconds while the initial cooking part is done. Place the capers on a J cloth.

Assembly and Plating Up

Begin by scooping out the hearts from the remaining eight baby artichokes. Place a frying pan on the heat and add the 2 teaspoons of rapeseed oil. Now remove the stems from the artichokes, so you are left with a circular choke and a hollow centre. Cook the artichokes in the oil. You are looking for a good caramelisation on the top of each artichoke (on the presentation side). Add the butter and herbs and then foam the butter over the artichokes. Keep the artichokes warm while cooking the rest of ingredients.

Gently heat through the cooked quinoa, adding 1 teaspoon of the honey dressing. Take four artichoke shells and add a spoonful of cooked quinoa to each.

Now for the red mullet. Take the fish from the vacuum pack bags and place onto a metal tray for blowtorching. In the kitchen, I use a commercial blowtorch. You want to slowly blowtorch the skin, making sure you do not burn it. Once you have an even colour over the red mullet, assemble the fish back together on the plate. It should look as if it is still on the bone. Take the four remaining artichokes and fill the centres with the salad.

Gently heat the shellfish bisque while plating up the dish. Place the red mullet on the plate on the right-hand side and the two artichokes, one filled with the salad and one with the quinoa. On the top of each of the artichokes filled with artichoke salad, add an optional leaf of sea purslane, three sprigs of crispy parsley and some capers. Foam the bisque with a stick blender and pour into saucers. Enjoy!

For the langoustine bisque

3kg langoustine heads and claws
Rapeseed oil, for frying
1 bulb fennel, roughly chopped
2 large brown onions, roughly chopped
3 carrots, roughly chopped
2 celery sticks, roughly chopped
5 tomatoes, chopped
2 x 400g tins of tomato purée
1 bay leaf
50ml brandy
250ml white wine
2 litres tap water
35g tarragon leaves
100g unsalted butter (optional)
100ml double cream (optional)

For the baby violet artichokes

Juice of 3 unwaxed lemons
12 baby violet artichokes (300–350g each)
125ml extra virgin olive oil
1 carrot, roughly chopped
1 celery stick, roughly chopped
1 tsp coriander seeds
500ml tap water
250ml dry white wine
1 tsp Maldon Sea salt
A pinch of black pepper
2 tsp rapeseed oil
150g unsalted butter
4 sprigs of thyme
4 sprigs of rosemary

For the red mullet

4 x 350g red mullet, scaled and gutted (I buy mine from Flying Fish)
Maldon sea salt
12g fennel pollen
Dukkah (homemade or shop-bought from a supplier such as Wellocks)

For the quinoa

100g black quinoa (I buy this from Wellocks)
100g white quinoa
400ml tap water

For the honey dressing

50ml white wine vinegar
20g Dijon mustard
200ml rapeseed oil
25g yellow mustard seeds, soaked overnight
50g blossom clear honey

For the artichoke salad

4 cooked baby artichokes (see above)
Honey dressing, to taste
10g flat-leaf parsley, finely chopped
10g chervil, finely chopped
Sea salt, to taste

To garnish

2 tsp rapeseed oil, for frying
12 sprigs of flat-leaf parsley
75g small Lilliput capers
4 leaves of sea purslane (optional)

Equipment

Chinois
Muslin cloth
4 medium vacuum pack bags
Water bath
Squeezy bottle
Deep-fat fryer
Blowtorch
Stick blender

> "Red mullet is one of my favourite fishes to both cook and eat. It was during my time working with Hywel Jones that I learned how to prepare and cook this simple but great-tasting fish. Hywel's attention to detail always shines through, along with the ability to pass on his skills to chefs working with him, like me.
>
> For this dish I'm using small baby violet artichokes and cooking them à la barigoule, which is a cooking process that originates from the south of France and is perfect paired with the freshest red mullet. The recipe consists of small purple artichokes cooked with carrot, white wine and olive oil, which are then mixed with fresh herbs."

Lamb Loin | Apricots | Hispi Cabbage | Smoked Almond

Serves 4

To make the **brine**, fill a saucepan with the water. Place on a high heat, then add the salt and sugar. Stir, using a whisk, then add the bay leaves, lemon thyme and rosemary. Stir them in and bring to the boil. Once boiling, remove from the heat and allow to cool for 1 hour.

When the brine has cooled, prepare the **braised lamb necks**. Place the necks into the brine, ensuring they are fully immersed in the liquid. Cover and refrigerate for 12 hours. Once brined, wash them under cold running water and pat dry. Pour both stocks into a large saucepan. Place on a high heat, bring to the boil, then remove from the heat. In another large saucepan on high heat, add the lamb necks and sear them. Follow by adding the carrots, celery, herbs, garlic, coriander seeds, star anise and pink peppercorns. Now pour in the stock mixture and bring to the boil. Turn down the heat to low and simmer for 4–5 hours. The liquid should reduce by half during this time. Once reduced, add the dried apricots and stir them through the mixture. Reduce further until the liquid coats the back of a spoon and is rich and glossy. This can take anywhere from 30 minutes to 1 hour.

You can make the **apricot and lemon thyme jam** up to a day before it is needed. Add all the ingredients to a large saucepan. Place on a high heat and bring to the boil. Once boiling, reduce the heat to low and simmer until reduced to a thick and sticky mix. Transfer to a food processor and blitz on high for 2 minutes until smooth. Pass through a chinois or fine sieve and refrigerate in a tight container until needed. If it is too thick to blend, add a splash of water. Transfer to a piping bag or squeezy bottle when ready.

Another element you can prepare in advance is the **spring onion pommes purée**. Preheat the oven to 180°C (160°C fan/Gas Mark 4). Make a bed of sea salt on a baking tray and put the potatoes on top. Bake in the oven for 45 minutes–1 hour. Once the potatoes are soft, remove from the oven and allow to cool for 10 minutes. Cut them in half and scoop out the insides. Pass through a moulin (or ricer). Place the potato in a pan, then add the butter. Fold together and stir in the milk. Add the spring onions, then season with salt and pepper. Stir to ensure the ingredients are evenly mixed, then put the mixture into a piping bag and set aside. I would recommend making this only 1–2 hours before you are going to serve your meal. Wrap the piping bag in a tea towel then keep in a warm place (if your oven has a grill above it that is not being used, put the bag there, as this is an ideal place for it to benefit from rising heat). Alternatively, you can opt to keep the pommes purée in a container in the fridge until required. You will then need to reheat it and probably add a knob of butter plus a little more milk, stirring them in with a spatula to restore the consistency of the purée to when it was first made. Place in a piping bag ready to use when plating up.

For the **lamb sauce**, pour the lamb sauce into a large saucepan, place on a medium heat and simmer until reduced by half. In another saucepan, pour in the apricot liqueur, then reduce on a medium heat by half. Combine the two into one saucepan that is not on the heat and whisk in the butter. Now stir through the cream. Decant into a container and put on the lid (or cover with cling film). This will keep in the fridge for 2 days.

Prepare the **lemon thyme crumble** by preheating the oven to 160°C (140°C fan/Gas Mark 3). Add the oats, butter and sugar to a food processor and slowly mix for 3 minutes. Now add the lemon thyme, rosemary and salt and mix for a further 2 minutes. Transfer the mixture to a baking tray, then cook for 15–20 minutes. Once the oats are golden brown, remove from the oven and set aside to cool. The crumble will keep in a cupboard for 3 days, in an airtight container.

Another element you can make in advance is the **apricot and Sauternes jelly**. Pour the water into a large saucepan, then add the dried apricots, mandarins, Sauternes and tea leaves. Place on a high heat and bring to the boil. Leave to cool completely and infuse for 2–3 hours. Once infused, pass through a chinois. Pour 200ml of the strained liquid into a saucepan. Add the apricot purée and kappa. Place the pan on a high heat and bring to the boil. Remove from the heat and pour into the silicone moulds. Put aside to chill and set. This can be prepared 2–3 days before serving and stored in the fridge. If you do make this element in advance, first cover the moulds with cling film or remove the moulds and put into a container with a lid, using baking paper to prevent sticking.

Take the **lamb loin** and score the fat on the top, then vacuum pack with the rosemary, thyme and dried apricots. Cook in a water bath at 58°C for 35 minutes. Once cooked, remove the lamb from the bag and season all over with salt and pepper. Place face down onto a roasting tray and sear the lamb on all sides, then add the butter and all the remaining herbs from the bag. Let the butter foam and then begin to baste the lamb with the butter. Sprinkle all over with Maldon sea salt, then allow to rest for 15–20 minutes.

To make the **smoked almond salsa and hispi cabbage**, preheat the oven to 190°C (170°C fan/Gas Mark 5). Place the almonds on a baking tray and roast in the oven for 8–10 minutes until a lovely golden colour. Remove from the oven and leave to cool for 10 minutes. Once cool enough to handle, chop them into halves. In a medium saucepan on high heat, add the shallot and garlic, then sweat for a couple of minutes. In another saucepan on a high heat, add the cabbage and butter, then sweat down for 2–3 minutes, stirring frequently so they do not burn. Add a splash of water and continue to cook for another 2 minutes. Now combine with the sweated shallots and garlic from the other pan. Add the parsley, mustard and almonds. Mix well and season with salt and pepper to taste, then remove from the heat.

Assembly and Plating Up

First, make sure the lamb loin, lamb neck, lamb sauce, almond cabbage and the pommes purée are hot and ready. If you need to, preheat the oven to 180°C (160°C fan/Gas Mark 4) and warm up the lamb loin in it. The almond cabbage, while still in the pan, can be kept in the oven with the door open while you plate up to ensure it remains hot. Just be careful not put it in too early or it will overcook and ruin the dish.

On the main plate, we want the lamb loin carved and placed centrally, very slightly off centre to the left. Place the apricot and Sauternes jelly offset right to the lamb loin and pipe a large circle of apricot and lemon thyme jam above the jelly. You could add the lamb sauce now, but I recommend saucing at the table.

Use three side dishes per serving. Use one for the pommes purée, piped in a nice motion up and down to create a ruffled dome with a peak. Put the cabbage on another and lastly the glazed lamb neck and crumble on the main plate.

> "Lamb is one of my favourite meats to cook. At the Angel, we pride ourselves on using the best local Devonshire lamb. This dish is renowned for its simplicity along with the accompanying side dishes for their bold flavours."

For the brine

1 litre tap water

100g table salt

100g caster sugar

2 bay leaves

3 sprigs of lemon thyme

3 sprigs of rosemary

For the braised lamb necks

5 lamb necks, boned

1 litre veal stock (see page 275)

500ml chicken stock (see page 274)

2 large carrots, sliced

1 celery stick, sliced

50g thyme

50g rosemary

4 garlic cloves, crushed

5g coriander seeds

2 star anise

Pinch of pink peppercorns

100g dried apricots, finely diced

For the apricot and lemon thyme jam

250g dried apricots

1 shallot, sliced

100g demerara sugar

125g apricot purée

100ml apple cider vinegar

3 lemon thyme leaves

2 Granny Smith apples, peeled, cored and chopped

Pinch of saffron

350ml bottled freshly squeezed orange juice

For the spring onion pommes purée

4 large Maris Piper potatoes

250g unsalted butter, plus (optional) a knob for reheating

250ml full-fat milk, plus (optional) extra for reheating

½ bunch of spring onions, thinly sliced

Sea salt

Table salt and black pepper, to taste

For the lamb sauce

500ml lamb sauce (see page 277)

100ml apricot liqueur

100g unsalted butter, cubed

50ml double cream

For the lemon thyme crumble

150g rolled oats

120g unsalted butter

25g light brown sugar

10g lemon thyme leaves

4g rosemary, finely chopped

Pinch of table salt

For the apricot and Sauternes jelly

250ml tap water

150g dried apricots

2 mandarins

125ml Sauternes

10g apricot and peach tea leaves

200g apricot purée

2g kappa carrageenan or tapioca

For the lamb loin

1 x 4–5kg short Devon lamb saddle

100g rosemary sprigs

100g thyme sprigs

50g dried apricots

150g unsalted butter

Maldon sea salt

For the smoked almond and sweetheart cabbage salsa

75g smoked almonds

1 shallot, brunoised or finely diced

1 garlic clove, crushed

2 hispi cabbages, chopped

250g unsalted butter

Handful of flat-leaf parsley

1 tsp wholegrain mustard

Maldon sea salt and black pepper

Equipment

Food processor

Chinois or fine sieve

Piping bags

Squeezy bottle (optional)

Moulin or ricer

4 silicone quenelle moulds

Vacuum pack bag

Water bath

Apricot Sorbet | Toasted Honey | Chamomile | Bee Pollen

Serves 8

Start by making the **apricot sorbet**, which can be prepared a few days in advance. Add the water and apricot purée to a medium saucepan. In a mixing bowl, add the sugar and sorbet stabiliser. Mix together with a spoon, ensuring they are thoroughly mixed, otherwise you will end up with lumps in your sorbet. Pour into the saucepan and bring to the boil, whisking continuously, then add the apricot liqueur. Stir and remove from the heat. Allow to cool. Once cooled, transfer the liquid to a measuring jug and gently pour it into the silicone moulds, filling the moulds to the top. Place a piece of baking paper over the top and put straight into the freezer. Make sure they are laid on a flat surface.

Now for the **toasted honey crémeux**. Whisk the egg yolks and sugar together until light and fluffy. Soak the gelatine in ice-cold water and allow to bloom. Half-fill a bowl with ice cubes and cover them with tap water. Put the honey into a saucepan and place it on a medium heat. Watch over the pan, as you do not want the mixture to burn. Once it is a dark caramel colour, remove from the heat and gradually stir in the double cream. When both have thoroughly combined, slowly pour the mixture into the bowl with the egg yolks, sugar and salt, whisking constantly to bring the different ingredients evenly together. Once they have combined, transfer the mixture to a saucepan and place on a medium heat. Keep whisking and, using a probe, bring up to 82°C. Once it has reached 82°C, add the gelatine. Stir in and then remove the pan from the heat. Transfer the mixture to a bowl and place it over the bowl of iced water to cool. Once it has cooled completely, put the mixture into a piping bag and keep in the fridge until needed. You can keep this in the fridge for at least a week.

To make the **apricot gel**, place a medium pan on a low heat. Add the apricot purée, chamomile liquid and sugar. Turn up the heat and bring to the boil. Then add the agar-agar and bring to the boil again, whisking continuously. Keep whisking at boiling point for a further 2 minutes. Remove the pan from the heat and pour the mixture into a container. Allow to cool, then cover the container and put in the fridge to set. Once set, blend the gel in the blender and pass through a chinois. Spoon straight into a piping bag. Keep in the fridge until needed.

With all the other elements prepared, you can now make the **white chocolate dip**. Put the white chocolate and cocoa butter into a mixing bowl. Place a medium pan of water on the heat and put the mixing bowl over the pan. The chocolate will now gently melt. Make sure the water does not boil and the mixing bowl does not come into contact with the water. This is method of cooking is often referred to as bain-marie. Once the mixture has melted, add the Power Flowers or the white food colouring. Using a stick blender, blend the chocolate and white food colouring until completely combined. Once mixed, set the bowl aside until required. You can make the dip in advance and keep it in a covered container in the fridge for a couple of days. However, it is best when made and used on the day of serving. If made in advance, warm it through first before using.

Assembly and Plating Up

Remove the sorbet from the freezer and allow to stand at room temperature for 2–3 minutes so it can soften a little. Pop a portion out of the mould and put a cocktail stick through one end, through the flat side, and gently dip into the white chocolate, making sure it covers the sorbet. Once coated all over, place onto baking paper to set. It will set quickly. Repeat with the remaining sorbet. Pipe the apricot gel onto the plate first, then place the sorbet onto the gel. Add a dot of apricot gel on top of the coated sorbet and a nice peak of the toasted honey crémeux alongside. To finish, add a good pinch of bee pollen over the top. This can be left out for a good 10–15 minutes before serving to allow the sorbet to soften.

> "This little pre-dessert delivers a palate-refreshing burst full of flavour. The toasted honey and chamomile work very well with the apricot liqueur."

For the apricot sorbet

55ml tap water

250ml apricot purée

55g caster sugar

12g sorbet stabiliser

10ml apricot liqueur

For the toasted honey crémeux

3 egg yolks

30g caster sugar

4g table salt

3.5g bronze gelatine leaves

50g blossom honey

250ml double cream

For the apricot gel

350ml apricot purée

Two pinches dried chamomile

50g caster sugar

12g agar-agar

For the white chocolate dip

65g white chocolate pieces (I use Callebaut)

40g cocoa butter (I use Callebaut)

2 White Power Flowers or 20g white food colouring

To garnish

Bee pollen

Equipment

8 silicone pomponette moulds (I use a 24-cup Pavoni Formaflex Pomponette Mould)

Temperature probe

Piping bag

Blender

Chinois

Stick blender

Cocktail sticks

Serves 8

Gin and Tonic 'Angel Style'

For the **elderflower tonic granita**, add the water and sugar to a medium pan, then bring to a simmer. Allow to cool completely. Once cool, add the elderflower tonic, along with both the lime and lemon zest and juice. Place the mixture into a container, cover and freeze until completely frozen.

Now on to the **roasted orange curd**. Pour the orange juice into a saucepan. Place on a medium heat and reduce by half. Let the liquid slightly caramelise. You want to end up with 120ml reduced orange juice. Once reduced, add the butter and sugar. Bring to the boil and remove from the heat. Put the egg yolks into a ThermoMixer and temper them. Add the tempered yolks to the saucepan and cook until the mixture reaches 83°C. Pour over the white chocolate pieces, making sure to stir so you get an even mix, and then allow to set. Once set, transfer to a piping bag. This can be kept in the fridge for at least a week.

To make the **orange gin syrup**, pour the orange juice into a saucepan, place on a medium heat and reduce by half. Remove from the heat and let it cool completely. Once cool, add the gin and mix well.

Assembly and Plating Up

Put the orange segments onto a metal tray. Now, with a blowtorch, pass the flame over them until slightly burnt. When all the oranges have been torched, cut each segment into three pieces. We usually serve this pre-dessert in frozen martini glasses. However, you can use a small dish or a glass. First, add a large dot of the roasted orange curd. Then add four pieces of the burnt orange along with 2 teaspoons of the orange gin syrup. Take the elderflower tonic granita from the freezer and, using a fork, scrape it down. It will look icy and white in colour. Place 3 full dessertspoons of the granita on top of the curd. It is now ready to be served.

For the elderflower tonic granita

100ml tap water

100g caster sugar

500ml elderflower tonic (I use Fever-Tree)

Zest and juice of 4 unwaxed limes

Zest and juice of 2 unwaxed lemons

For the roasted orange curd

240ml smooth orange juice

75g unsalted butter

50g caster sugar

45g egg yolk

75g white chocolate (I use Callebaut), broken into pieces

For the orange gin syrup

500ml smooth orange juice

35ml orange gin (I use Conkers Orange Angel Gin)

To garnish

1 orange, peeled, pips removed and divided into segments

Equipment

ThermoMixer

Temperature probe

Piping bag

Blowtorch

Squeezy bottle

"Gin and tonic is an iconic drink which everyone loves. So this is my take on a refreshing pre-dessert, which I serve at the Angel, made with my very own orange gin."

Coconut | Lychee | Yuzu "All White"

Serves 8

Begin making the **lychee gel** by adding water, sugar and lychee purée to a saucepan. Bring to the boil, then add the agar-agar. Continue boiling for another 2 minutes, then pour into a container. Cover and allow to set. Once firmly set, transfer it to a blender and blend until smooth. Pass the gel through a chinois and then into a piping bag. Keep the bag in the fridge until required. You can make this in advance and it lasts up to 3 days.

For the **coconut and lychee centre**, add the coconut purée and lychee gel to a pan with 32g caster sugar and the lime juice, then bring to the boil. In a separate mixing bowl, add the 6g caster sugar and pectin and mix together well so there are no lumps in the mixture. Add to the pan and whisk the mixture for a further 2–3 minutes, making sure it comes to the boil again. Pour the liquid into a measuring jug and then into 16 of the individual circle moulds. Allow to cool, then put in the fridge until required later.

To prepare the **coconut dacquoise**, preheat the oven to 170°C (150°C fan/Gas Mark 3½). Sift the almond flour and icing sugar together. Beat the egg white on medium speed in a stand mixer with the whisk attachment. When the egg white is foamy and white, gradually add the sugar. Continue beating until you get stiff peaks. Fold the almond flour mixture into the meringue and evenly mix, being careful not to overwork the mixture and deflate it. Evenly spread the coconut mixture onto a greased silicone mat or sheet of baking paper. Try to make sure the mixture is all the same height and there is room around the edges, so it does not burn too quickly. Bake in the oven for 12–14 minutes until golden brown. Do keep an eye on it while baking, as the cooking time can vary depending on your oven. Remove from the oven and allow to cool completely at room temperature. Once cooled, use the ring cutter to divide the dacquoise into small pieces for the coconut mousses.

Next, move on to the **lychee compote**. Drain the lychees and make sure you keep the juice. Soak the gelatine in iced water until it's bloomed. Dice the lychees into a small pieces. Put the juice into a medium pan and add the sugar. Place on a medium heat and bring to the boil. Now add the bloomed gelatine, then the diced lychees. Stir and then remove the pan from the heat and allow to cool. Once cool, pour into 16 more of the circle moulds.

For the **coconut and white chocolate mousse**, place a medium pan on the heat and fill the pan three-quarters of the way up with water. Place a mixing bowl on the top and add the white chocolate. Gently melt the white chocolate; you don't want it to burn. Once melted, remove from the heat. Soak the gelatine in iced water until it's bloomed. In another pan, add the coconut purée and lychee gel and bring to the boil. Then add the bloomed gelatine and whisk together. In a large mixing bowl, add the double cream and whisk to semi-peaks.

Now add the coconut purée to the melted chocolate and, using a stick blender, blitz the purée and chocolate together. Gently fold in the whipped cream and transfer the mixture to a piping bag. I use two different types of moulds for the coconut mousses, to give the plate a different look. Half-fill 8 quenelle moulds with the coconut mousse and place a coconut and lychee centre in the middle, topped by a lychee compote. Fill up the quenelles with the remaining coconut mousse and smooth off with a palette knife. Add a coconut dacquoise disc to the top of each mould and smooth off again. Repeat the same process using the half sphere moulds. Place a piece of baking paper on the top and put in the freezer to set.

To make the **coconut crémeux**, put the chocolate in a small bowl over a pan of water over a low heat. Then put the gelatine into a small bowl of iced water and allow to bloom. Next, place a pan on a medium heat, then add the coconut purée and gently bring to the boil. Now add the bloomed gelatine and whisk. Then add in the double cream and coconut rum. Add the melted white chocolate and blend with a stick blender. Place in the fridge to set. Once set, put the mixture put into a piping bag. Put back in the fridge until needed. Do not whisk this as it will become too loose and you won't be able to use it.

To prepare the **yuzu sorbet**, first add the water, glucose and yuzu juice to a medium saucepan. Add the sugar and sorbet stabiliser to a mixing bowl. Mix together thoroughly with a spoon, otherwise you will end up with lumps in your sorbet. Pour into the saucepan and bring to the boil, whisking continuously, then add the lemon juice. Stir and remove from the heat. Allow to cool. Once cooled, transfer the liquid to a measuring jug and then pour it into 8 of the silicone quenelle moulds. Fill the moulds to the top. Place a piece of baking paper on top and put straight into the freezer. Make sure they are placed onto a flat surface.

With all the other elements prepared, now make the **white chocolate cocoa spray**. Put the white chocolate and cocoa butter into a mixing bowl. Fill a medium pan three-quarters full with water and put it on a medium heat. Now place the mixing bowl on top, making sure it does not touch with the water. The chocolate should now gently melt. Keep an eye on it, making sure the water does not boil. Once the mixture has melted, add the Flower Power tablets or the white food colouring. Using a stick blender, blend the chocolate and cocoa butter until completely mixed. Once mixed, set the bowl aside until required.

Assembly and Plating Up

Put the melted white chocolate cocoa spray into the chocolate sprayer, making sure the correct attachment is on the sprayer. Turn out all the mousses onto a silicone mat, making sure there is space between them all. Spray the mousses evenly, taking care there is an even covering. Once sprayed, place them back in the freezer to firm up and freeze again. Ideally this needs to be done in the morning or a few hours before serving.

Once the mousses have set, take out the circular and quenelle mousses and allow to defrost, I usually pull out all our mousses on the morning of the day I want to serve them. Remove the lychee compote and coconut crémeux from the fridge. Bring out the yuzu sorbet from the moulds, drizzle a little melted white chocolate over the top of each, and allow them to come up to room temperature.

Place a circular mousse on the right-hand side of each plate and the quenelle to the left. And three dots of coconut crémeux to the circular mousse and pipe the lychee compote in between. Add four white flowers on top of the crémeux. Add a small amount of coconut dacquoise on the plate to hold the yuzu sorbet.

" This white dessert, which is based on three flavours – coconut, lychee and yuzu – is all about simplicity and elegance. It features regularly on our signature tasting menu. "

For the lychee gel

150ml tap water

50g caster sugar

350ml lychee purée

6g agar-agar

For the coconut and lychee centre

125ml coconut purée

90ml lychee gel (see above)

32g plus 6g caster sugar

6g pectin NH

32ml fresh lime juice

32g caster sugar

15g glucose syrup

For the coconut dacquoise

35g almond flour

100g icing sugar

100g egg white

35g caster sugar

60g desiccated coconut

For the lychee compote

120g tinned lychees, diced (I use 2 tins)

2g bronze gelatine leaves

45ml lychee juice from the tins

20g caster sugar

For the coconut and white chocolate mousse

137g white chocolate

2g bronze gelatine leaves

50g coconut purée

20g lychee gel (see above)

190ml double cream

For the coconut crémeux

135g white chocolate

2.5g gelatine leaves

70g coconut purée

150ml double cream

10ml coconut rum

For the yuzu sorbet

250ml tap water

12ml glucose syrup

55ml yuzu juice

150g caster sugar

4g sorbet stabiliser

Juice of ½ lemon

For the white chocolate cocoa spray

250g white chocolate

125g cocoa butter (I use Callebaut)

6 Flower Powers (I buy mine from Ritter Courivaud)

To garnish

Melted white chocolate, for drizzling

32 white flowers

Equipment

32 1cm silicone circle moulds

16 quenelle moulds (I use the Silikomart Quenelle 10)

Stand mixer with whisk attachment

Silicone mats

5cm ring cutter

8 half sphere silicone moulds

Stick blender

Piping bags and small round piping nozzle

Blender

Chinois

Chocolate sprayer

Serves 8

Devonshire Clotted Cream Parfait | Golden Raisin | Sesame and Apple

For the **clotted cream parfait**, set up a stand mixer with the whisk attachment. Weigh out the sugar and water into a medium saucepan. Fill a separate mixing bowl halfway with ice-cold water and add the gelatine. Allow the gelatine to bloom. Place the sugar and water mixture onto the heat and cook to 118°C. This is the soft-ball stage (i.e. when a bit is dropped into cold water it will hold its shape). Always use a thermometer to keep checking the temperature. When the gelatine has bloomed, squeeze out the excess water and put on a small tray ready for the sugar. While the sugar is cooking, begin to whisk the egg yolk and vanilla in the mixer. This will double in volume and look like a thick sabayon. When the sugar reaches 118°C, pour the sugar mixture onto the yolk and continue to whisk until the mixture is room temperature. Lightly whip the double cream and clotted cream until at a soft peak stage. Fold into the sabayon mixture and pour into piping bags. Pipe the parfait into the half-sphere moulds and place a piece of baking paper on the top. Place in the freezer. This can be made a few days in advance and will need time to freeze.

Now move on to the **apple sorbet**. Add the water and apple purée to a medium saucepan. In a mixing bowl, add the sugar and sorbet stabiliser, then mix together with a spoon. Make sure they are completely mixed, otherwise you will get lumps in your sorbet. Once mixed, pour into the saucepan with the apple purée. Bring to the boil, whisking continuously. Pour into a Pacojet and allow to freeze. Once frozen, blitz in the Pacojet and put into a container. Place in a freezer until ready to plate. This can also be made in a household ice-cream churner.

For the **pickled golden raisins**, add the vinegars, sugar and water to a saucepan. Bring to the boil. Add the golden raisins and bring back to the boil. Pour into a small container and cover the raisins with cling film. Allow a little time to cool, then put into the fridge. These raisins can be made in advance and last in the fridge for up to 2 weeks.

For the **sesame seed tuile**, preheat the oven to 180°C (160°C fan/Gas Mark 4). Line an oven tray with a silicone mat or baking paper. In a medium pan, add the liquid glucose, orange juice and butter. Place on a medium heat and bring to a simmer. Add in the icing sugar and flour, then cook out for 2–3 minutes. Now add all the sesame seeds and mix well. Remove from the heat and spread evenly over the silicone mat or baking paper. Put the tray into the oven and cook for about 8 minutes. Remove from the oven and leave to cool for about 5 minutes. Once cooled, use the round cutter to cut out 16 tuiles. Ideally you want the same size ring as the parfait, so it fits perfectly on the top. Keep your tuiles in an airtight container at room temperature until needed.

For the **raisin purée**, first make a pickling liquor by boiling the verjus and sugar until the sugar is completely dissolved. Soak the raisins in the pickle for at least 2 hours, then add the water and vanilla extract. Blend to a purée and pass through a fine sieve. Put the raisin purée into a piping bag and keep in the fridge. This can be made well in advance and will keep for a week.

To make the **apple balls**, use a Parisienne scoop. Scoop out five small balls of apple per serving and place into a small vacuum pack bag with the cloudy apple juice. I tend to vacuum pack the apple balls to compress them in their own juices and they tend to go clear.

Assembly and Plating Up

Remove the sorbet from the freezer so it can soften a little as you prepare each plate. First, build the tuile. Use one tuile per person and place five apple balls on top for each plate. Evenly place the balls around the tuile. In between the apple balls, pipe five dots of the raisin purée. Place five pickled golden raisins on each drop of purée. Using a rocher spoon, place a scoop of sorbet on the left of the top of the tuile and line the three apple balls and raisins in a semicircle around it. Finish the sorbet by placing three pieces of lemon balm on the apple and pickled raisins. Add a big dot of raisin purée on the plate. Now remove the clotted cream parfait from the freezer and place onto a plain tuile on a dot of raisin purée. Gently place a prepared tuile on top. You are now ready to be serve.

For the clotted cream parfait

236g caster sugar
75ml tap water
1 gelatine leaf
160g egg yolk
1 vanilla pod (I use Zazou Emporium)
300ml double cream
175ml Devonshire clotted cream

For the apple sorbet

110ml tap water
500g green apple purée
110g caster sugar
25g sorbet stabiliser

For the pickled golden raisins

50ml maple white verjus (I use Minus8)
50ml white wine vinegar
100g caster sugar
100ml tap water
100g golden raisins

For the sesame seed tuille

25ml liquid glucose
1 tsp orange juice
50g unsalted butter
75g icing sugar, sifted
25g plain flour
25g white sesame seeds
25g black sesame seeds

For the raisin purée

50ml maple white verjus
50g caster sugar
150g seedless raisins
150g golden raisins
75ml tap water
1 tsp vanilla extract (I use Zazou Emporium)

For the apple balls

40 apple balls, from two Granny Smith apples
50ml cloudy apple juice

To garnish

Micro lemon balm

Equipment

Stand mixer with whisk attachment
Temperature probe
Piping bags
8 80ml silicone half-sphere moulds
Pacojet or ice-cream churner
Silicone mat
3cm round cutter
Blender
Fine sieve
Parisienne scoop
Vacuum pack bag

"This recipe is one I learned in the kitchen with Richard Davies when were both at The Manor House in Castle Combe. It is the best parfait recipe and so easy to make. To top it off, I use the top Devonshire clotted cream. The apple sorbet works perfectly alongside the pickled golden raisins, giving a unique twist to the dish."

Malt Mousse | Blackout Coffee Sponge | Hazelnut Ice Cream

Serves 8

Start with the **blackout coffee sponge**. Preheat the oven to 160°C (140°C fan/Gas Mark 3). Beat the butter and the sugar together in a stand mixer with the whisk attachment. Once fluffy, add in the whole egg and continue mixing. When combined, take the bowl from the mixer and using a silicone spatula, gently fold in the flour, cocoa powder, bicarb and baking soda. Place the bowl back in the mixer and add the coffee, milk and crème fraîche – make sure the coffee is cold – and mix well. Take a large shallow baking tray, line with a silicone mat or sheet of baking paper and evenly spread over the cake mixture. Bake in the oven for 9 minutes, or until cooked. Once cooked, place another silicone mat or sheet of baking paper over the top of the cake. Now place a heavy tray on top (or another heavy, flat-surfaced item) to cold-press the cake, then put into the fridge for at least 1 hour. Once pressed, remove the cake from the fridge. Now place the mousse ring in the centre of the tray and push down to cut out a square. Do not remove the mousse ring as you will build the dessert on this ring.

Next, prepare the **chocolate marquise**. Take a medium pan and half-fill with water. Place it on a medium heat. In a metal mixing bowl, add the chocolate and butter. Cover with cling film and place on top of the pan of water to melt. Make sure the bowl does not meet the water. In a stand mixer, whisk the egg yolk and sugar together until pale and creamy. In another mixing bowl, whisk the cream to soft peak stage, taking care not to overwork it or it will not combine properly with the other ingredients. Mix the egg yolk and sugar with the cocoa powder, melted chocolate and butter until fully combined. Then fold in the soft cream using a spatula until just combined, taking care not to beat the air out or overwork the cream. Transfer to a piping bag and pipe into the square mousse ring, on top of the cold-pressed cake. We are looking for about 3.5cm depth of marquise in the mousse ring. Smooth out with a palette knife and keep in the fridge until required.

For the **coffee curd**, boil the espresso, butter and sugar in a small saucepan. Put the chocolate in another bowl. In another mixing bowl, add the egg yolk and whisk them, then pour the hot espresso mixture over the eggs to temper them. Pour the whole mixture back into the saucepan and cook until it thickens, making sure to stir continuously as it cooks. You will know it's cooked when the mixture coats the back of a spoon. Pour this mixture over the chocolate and mix well until everything has combined. Add the chocolate curd to a piping bag and place into the fridge. This curd will last for up to 3 days. Before serving, remove from the fridge to bring back up to room temperature before serving.

To prepare the **malt mousse**, half-fill a pan with water. Place the white chocolate in a bowl. Place the bowl on top of the pan and then put the pan on a low heat. Melt the chocolate, making sure it isn't getting any hotter than 52°C. You should monitor this with a temperature probe. In a mixing bowl, filled with ice-cold water, add the bronze gelatine and allow the gelatine to bloom. When it's bloomed, squeeze out as much water as possible and place on a tray. In a separate medium pan, add the first batch of double cream, malt extract syrup and malt powder and bring to the boil. Once the mixture has boiled, add this liquid to the egg yolk. Whisk well and pour back into the saucepan to cook with the egg yolk. Cook this mixture until 80°C. Make sure you're stirring continuously so it's not catching on the bottom of the pan. When it's reached the correct temperature, add the gelatine and mix well. Leave on the side, until the whipped cream is ready. In another mixing bowl, whisk the second batch of double cream to a soft peak stage taking care not to over-whisk or it will not combine properly with the other ingredients. Then fold the soft cream into the mix using a silicone spatula. Once all the ingredients are mixed well, pour this mousse into a piping bag. Pipe this mousse directly on top of the chocolate marquise, then smooth it off with a palette knife, making sure there are no air bubbles. Allow to set.

Next, move on to the **hazelnut ice cream**. Preheat the oven to 160°C (140°C fan/Gas Mark 3). Scatter the hazelnuts over a baking tray and roast in the oven for 8–9 minutes. You're looking for a nice golden colour. When roasted, leave to cool on the side. When the hazelnuts are cool, roughly chop them and leave them in a container for later. Heat the cream and milk in a pan until nearly boiling. Whisk together the egg yolks and sugar in a small bowl. Pour a little of the hot cream over the eggs and whisk together. Add the remaining cream mix and the hazelnut praline. Pour the egg mix into the pan and gently cook for 8–10 minutes until thick enough to coat the back of a spoon. Set a medium bowl over another bowl of iced water. As soon as the custard has thickened, strain into a bowl. Add the chopped hazelnuts and blend the custard together. Place this ice cream in the bowl over ice to cool, then pour into a Pacojet container and freeze. Once frozen, re-blitz in the Pacojet and place back in the freezer until ready to plate.

For the **lemon jelly**, add the water, sugar and lemon juice to a medium pan. Bring to the boil and pour over the lemon balm leaves. Allow to infuse for at least 2 hours. Add the limoncello to the liquid and mix well. Strain the liquid through a sieve and weigh all the liquid. For each 100ml of lemon liquid, set the jelly with ¾ gelatine leaf. Ideally, you want 400ml, so 3 gelatine leaves to set this jelly. Fill a mixing bowl with water, add the 3 gelatine leaves to the water and allow to bloom. Bring 200ml of the lemon liquid to the boil and add the squeezed-out gelatine to the mixture. Pour in the other 200ml of lemon liquid and stir, making sure all the gelatine is dissolved. Allow to cool. When it's cooled completely, pour this jelly on top of the malt mousse and place back into the fridge to set. So, you should now have four layers of ingredients set and ready in your fridge before assembling.

"I first started to learn the craft of pastry while working in the pastry section, under the watchful eyes of Chris and James Tanner, when I worked at their restaurant Tanners in Plymouth. It was during this time I developed my love of working with pastry. I believe that having pastry skills gives you a broader range of overall knowledge in the kitchen. This chocolate marquise dish is a twist on the recipe I learned during my time with the Tanner brothers."

Assembly and Plating Up

First, take the coffee curd from the fridge and allow to come up to room temperate. Remove the large, layered ring mould from the fridge. Pull the square ring up and off the dessert. If it does not easily pull, try using a small blowtorch around the ring moulds to loosen them. Alternatively, should you not have or want to use a blowtorch, use a hot knife around the edge. You can trim off any rough edges after getting the ring mould off. Using a hot knife, slice the layered mousse into 1.2cm-thick pieces. From a single slice you should get two portions. Ideally, you want them to be 8cm long. Pipe four nice peaks of the coffee curd onto the cake, then add the halved roasted hazelnuts in between the coffee curd. Take the sorbet from the freezer and, using a hot spoon, rocher or quenelle the sorbet onto the malt mousse. Finish each dessert with 4 lemon balm leaves. Enjoy!

For the blackout coffee sponge

25g unsalted butter, softened
195g caster sugar
72g whole egg
95g plain flour
45g cocoa powder
2g bicarbonate of soda
4g baking powder
115ml brewed coffee (about 2 shots of espresso – I use the Angel's own blend)
22ml full-fat milk
82g crème fraîche

For the chocolate marquise

145g good-quality dark chocolate (70% cocoa)
72g unsalted butter
60g egg yolk
72g caster sugar
225ml double cream
3 tbsp cocoa powder

For the coffee curd

50g espresso
75g unsalted butter
7g caster sugar
50g good-quality dark chocolate (70% cocoa)
40g egg yolk

For the first stage of malt mousse

115ml double cream
20g malt extract syrup
28g malt powder (I use Ovaltine)

For the second stage of malt mouse

160g white chocolate
3g bronze gelatine leaves
30g egg yolk
112ml double cream

For the hazelnut ice cream

180g hazelnuts
300ml double cream
300ml full-fat milk
3 egg yolks
100g light soft brown sugar
1 tsp hazelnut praline

For the lemon jelly

200ml tap water
100g caster sugar
75ml lemon juice
½ bunch of lemon balm, leaves picked
25ml limoncello
3 bronze gelatine leaves

To garnish

24 roasted hazelnuts, halved
24 micro lemon balm leaves

Equipment

Stand mixer with a whisk attachment
Silicone mats
8 square mousse rings (I use the De Buyer stainless steel square pastry ring)
Piping bags
Temperature probe
Hand-held electric whisk
Chinois or fine sieve
Stick blender
Pacojet or ice-cream churner

93 Spring

'Chocolate Bar' Poached Cherries | Salted Almond

Serves 8

First, make the **cherry insert**. Mix the pectin and the 6g caster sugar in a bowl. You need to mix these together before adding into the liquid, so it doesn't become lumpy. In a medium saucepan, add the cherry purée, liquid glucose and 32g caster sugar and bring to the boil. Once boiling, add the Disaronno along with the sugar and pectin mixture. Place back on the heat and bring to the boil, making sure you're always whisking the purée. Pour the purée into a measuring jug, then into the 1cm sphere silicone moulds. Place the moulds into the freezer to set. The cherry inserts will then go in the centre of the chocolate caramel mousse. When frozen, pop the cherry inserts out of the moulds and cut in half. We will use two pieces per chocolate mousse. These can be made in advance and will last in the freezer for up to 1 month.

For the **chocolate caramel mousse**, start by soaking the gelatine in cold water. When the gelatine has bloomed, squeeze out any excess water and keep in a container until needed. Fill a medium pan halfway with water and place on the heat. Place the milk chocolate in a mixing bowl and place on top of the pan with the water to gently melt. With a stand mixer, whisk the egg yolk until you have a thick sabayon. While the egg yolk is whisking, add the sugar to a medium pan. Put this on the heat and start to make the caramel. We're looking for a dark caramel, but without it burning. Add the 127ml cream to the caramel and allow to cook out. The caramel will boil, then settle down once the cream is mixed in. It should look like a glossy caramel sauce. Pass the caramel through a fine sieve to make sure no sugar pieces are left. Before adding the gelatine to the caramel, make sure it is still hot enough for the gelatine to dissolve in it. Mix the gelatine into the caramel using a spatula. While the eggs are still whisking, slowly add the caramel to the sabayon and continue whisking on full. The milk chocolate should now be melted. Add it slowly to the sabayon and mix until fully combined. In a separate bowl, add the remaining 450ml cream and whisk to soft peaks. You don't want to over whisk the cream, as it will not mix in properly and may spilt the mousse. You now want to gently fold the whisked cream into the chocolate. Do this by folding a third of the whisked cream into the chocolate at a time. Gently fold the mousse with the cream until they are fully incorporated. Pour the mousse into piping bags ready to pipe into our silicone moulds.

Pipe the chocolate mousse into the silicone mini loaf moulds, making sure to only fill halfway up. Place two pieces of the cherry insert in the middle of each mousse. Pipe more chocolate mousse to cover the inserts. Smooth off the mousses with a palette knife and place a piece of baking paper over the top. Now put them into the freezer to firm up on a flat surface. They must be completely frozen before you spray them.

For the **cherry gel**, add the water, sugar and cherry purée to a saucepan. Bring to the boil, then add the agar-agar. Continue boiling for another 2 minutes, then pour into a container.

Cover and allow to set. Once firmly set, transfer the mixture to a blender and blend until smooth. Pass the gel through a chinois and then into a piping bag. Keep the bag in the fridge until required. You can make this in advance, and it will last for up to 3 days.

Next, on to the **salted almond ice cream.** Preheat the oven to 170°C (150°C fan/Gas Mark 3½). Scatter the almonds over a baking tray and roast in the oven for 8–9 minutes. You are looking for a nice golden colour. When roasted, set aside to cool. Once cool, roughly chop the almonds and leave them in a container to use later. Heat the cream, liquid glucose and milk in a pan until nearly boiling. Whisk together the egg yolks and sugar in a small bowl. Pour a little of the hot cream over the egg yolk mixture and whisk together. Add the remaining cream, along with the sea salt, and pour in the egg mix. Then return the mixture to the saucepan, and gently cook for 8–10 minutes until thick enough to coat the back of a spoon. Set a medium bowl over another bowl of iced water. As soon as the custard has thickened, strain into a bowl. Add the chopped almonds to the mixture and blend the custard together. Place this ice cream into the bowl which is on top of the iced water to cool down before putting into a Pacojet container. Pour this ice cream into the Pacojet container and freeze. Once frozen re-blitz into the Pacojet and place back in the freezer until ready to plate.

For the **chocolate ganache,** place the milk and cream in a small saucepan and slowly bring to the boil. Remove from the heat and pour the hot cream over the egg yolk and whisk. Put the pan back on the heat and slowly cook the cream. Using a thermometer, cook until it reaches 82°C and the mixture coats the back of a spoon. When the egg yolk is cooked, pour the mixture over the chocolate chips, and slowly mix in. You want to do this in three batches, so the chocolate does not become too hot. Once fully combined, put into a piping bag and pipe into the quenelle moulds. Put into the fridge to set. You can make the ganache in advance and it will last in the fridge for up to 5 days.

To prepare the **poached cherries**, wash the cherries under cold water. Cut the cherries into half and use a Parisienne scoop to remove all the stones. Now put the cherries into a container. Add the red wine, port, vinegar and sugar to a medium pan. Bring the liquid to the boil, then add the mustard seeds and star anise. Cover with cling film and allow to cool. We want the star anise and mustard seeds to infuse in the liquor. Allow 30 minutes for the infusion to take place. Once infused, remove the cling film, place the pan back on the heat and bring to the boil. Once boiled, remove from the heat and pass the liquid through a fine sieve. Pour the sieved liquid over the cherries and allow to cool completely. Ideally you want to do this on the day you serve the dessert, as the cherries won't hold their shape well. Keep in the fridge until ready to plate up.

With all the other elements prepared, now make the **chocolate cocoa spray**. Put the chocolate and cocoa butter into a mixing bowl. Fill a medium pan three-quarters full with water and put it on a medium heat. Now place the mixing bowl on top, making sure it does not touch with the water. The chocolate should now gently melt. Keep an eye on it, making sure the water does not boil. Using a stick blender, blend the chocolate and cocoa butter until completely mixed. Once mixed, set the bowl aside until required.

Put the melted chocolate mixture into a chocolate sprayer, making sure the correct attachment is on the sprayer. Turn out all the mousses onto a silicone mat, making sure there is space between them all. Spray the mousses evenly, taking care there is an even covering. Once sprayed, place them back in the freezer to firm up and freeze again. Ideally this needs to be done in the morning or a few hours before serving.

Assembly and Plating Up

Take out the chocolate caramel mousses and pipe three dots of the cherry gel onto the top of each one. Add a poached cherry to the top of each mousse and three pieces of the chocolate Aero. Place one piece of the chocolate ganache to the side of the mouse. Take out the almond ice cream and place one Rocher spoon of almond ice cream next the chocolate ganache and put a toasted almond on the top. Serve immediately.

For the cherry insert

6g pectin NH
6g plus 32g caster sugar
218g Morello cherry purée
16ml liquid glucose
37g Disaronno

For the caramel mousse

3 gelatine leaves
230g milk chocolate
90g egg yolk
65g caster sugar
577ml double cream

For the cherry gel

150ml tap water
50g caster sugar
350ml cherry purée
6g agar-agar

For the salted almond ice cream

60g blanched almonds
300ml double cream
50g liquid glucose
300ml full-fat milk
120g egg yolk
120g caster sugar
2.5g Maldon sea salt

For the chocolate ganache

72ml full-fat milk
172ml double cream
50g egg yolk
100g dark chocolate chips (I use Callebaut 54.5%)
125g dark chocolate chips (I use Callebaut 70%)

For the poached cherries

200g fresh cherries
100ml red wine
100ml ruby red port
75ml raspberry vinegar
75g caster sugar
1 tsp black mustard seeds
1 star anise

For the chocolate cocoa spray

250g dark chocolate (70% cocoa)
125g cocoa butter (I use Callebaut)

To garnish

70% Aero chocolate bar
8 toasted almonds

Equipment

1cm silicone sphere moulds
Piping bags
8 silicone mini loaf moulds for caramel mousse (I use the Silikomart Mini Loaf Cake Mould)
Blender
Chinois or fine sieve
Pacojet
8 silicone quenelle moulds
Parisienne scoop
Chocolate sprayer
Silicone mat

"Chocolate and cherries are classic flavours that work very well with the creamiest salted almond ice cream. This dessert has been a showstopper in the restaurant and is even more so with a dark chocolate Aero."

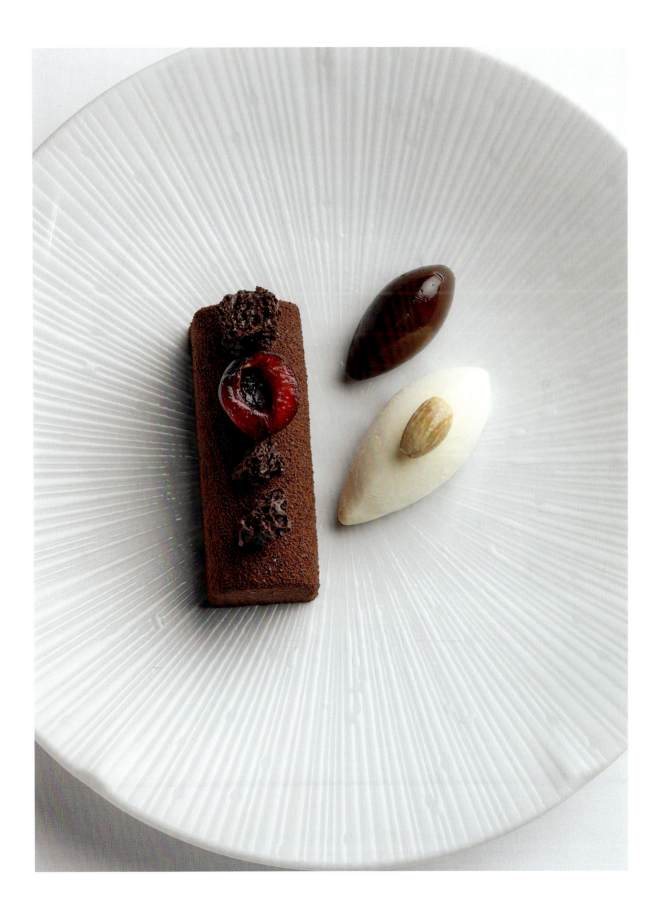

SUMMER

June – August

Canapés

Cod Brandade | Malt Vinegar Jam

Crab Tartlet | Grapefruit | Smoked Caviar

Amuse Bouche

Tomato And Peach Gazpacho | Natural Almonds

Starters

Cured Salmon | Watermelon Salsa | Oyster

Milk-Cured Duck Liver | Salted Peach | Sauternes

Sea Bream | Gooseberry Dashi | Buttermilk | Borage

Crab Risotto | Lemon | Sea Vegetables

Mains

Tomato Millefeuille | Ricotta | Artichokes | Smoked Tomato Jam

Ruby Red Beef Fillet | Caramelised Onion | Horseradish Buttermilk | Red Wine Jus

Roasted Turbot | Baby Gem | Broad Bean | Makrut Lime Butter Sauce

Pre-desserts

Calamansi | Lime Curd | Fennel Rice Crisp

Cucumber | White Chocolate Curd | Lime

Desserts

Yuzu Cream | Toasted Coconut Meringue | Mandarin | Vanilla Sorbet

'Peach Melba' Smoked White Chocolate Ice Cream

Raspberry Cannelloni | Macadamia Nut | Tarragon Ice Cream

The Angel Petit Four

Espresso Fudge Chocolate Domes

Serves 4

Cod Brandade | Malt Vinegar Jam

Begin by first preparing the **cod brandade**. Preheat the oven to 180°C (160°C fan/Gas Mark 4). Wash and dry the potatoes. With a fork, pierce each one 3–4 times. Put them onto an oven tray and sprinkle over a generous handful of the sea salt. Bake in the oven for 45 minutes–1 hour until soft. Once soft when pressed, remove them from the oven and allow to cool for 5 minutes.

After 5 minutes they should still be warm, but safe to handle. Cut them in half and scoop out the insides into a bowl. Next, you need to get the potato into a fine mash state. This can be achieved with a moulin or ricer or by passing the potato through a sieve. If you use the moulin/ricer, spoon portions of the potato in and work it through into a bowl. If you use a sieve, place it on top of a bowl and then spoon in portions of the potato and work it through the sieve using the back of a tablespoon or spatula. Whichever method you use, the result should be a smooth riced potato. Finally, add a few drops of the olive oil and mix through the potato with a fork. Set aside.

With a sharp knife, cut the cod into segments about 1cm square. Then, into a medium saucepan, pour the milk followed by the double cream. Stir to ensure they come together. Now add the cod pieces and stir so they are evenly spread across the saucepan. Next, add the thyme, rosemary, the lemon zest, the sprig of dill and a generous pinch of salt and pepper. Stir the ingredients together and then place the saucepan on a low heat. Continue to stir occasionally, giving the mixture time to warm through until it begins to lightly bubble. Stay with the saucepan during this process as you must not let the mixture get to the point where it boils. When it starts to bubble, remove the saucepan from the heat and allow the mixture to cool.

Once cooled, pass the cod through a chinois and keep the milk liquid. Add the cod to the potato and fold together with the spatula. Season with a pinch of salt and pepper. With your hands, complete the mixing process. You can add some of the remaining liquid if needed to bind them together. Next, take out 15g of the mixture and shape into a ball. Repeat this process until the mixture has been used. Place the balls on a tray, cover with a sheet of cling film and set aside. If you are preparing them up to a day before cooking, store the tray in the fridge.

Next, prepare the **malt vinegar jam**. To a small–medium saucepan, add the malt vinegar and sugar. Place the saucepan on a medium heat, then stir the mixture while adding the agar-agar. Keep stirring to ensure the powder fully dissolves and until the liquid starts to boil. Boil for a further 2–3 minutes. At this point, remove the saucepan from the heat, pour the mixture into a container and put aside to set. It will set faster if stored in the fridge.

While the mixture is setting, put the caraway seeds in a small pan. Toast them on a low–medium heat for 2–3 minutes. You will soon get wonderful aromatic smells. After a maximum of 3 minutes, remove the pan from the heat and allow the seeds to cool.

Once the malt vinegar jam has set to a firm jelly, spoon it into a blender, followed by the toasted caraway seeds. Blend on the high setting for a couple of minutes until you get a smooth gel. Over a bowl, pass the gel through the chinois (or sieve) using a ladle. This will keep in the fridge for up to a couple of weeks.

You are now ready to make the **split pea batter**. Using the blender, blitz together the green and yellow split peas until they become a fine powder. In a large mixing bowl, add the flour, beer, table salt and 15g of the split pea powder. Whisk the ingredients together until they form a light batter. You are looking for one with a consistency that is not too runny or thick. A good example of the perfect consistency would be tempura batter.

The cod balls need to be fried. If you do not have a fryer, they can be cooked in a large saucepan.

Get the oil to a temperature of 180°C and keep it there. Dip the cod balls into the batter and then deep-fry them for about 2 minutes until golden brown. Transfer them carefully from the oil to a plate. Allow a couple of minutes for the oil to drain off. Also, if the jam has been stored in the fridge, remove it a good 30 minutes before plating up so it comes to room temperature.

Assembly and Plating Up

First, put a mix of whole green and yellow split peas onto the plates as a base, then place a ball on top. We usually serve one ball per person as canapés in the restaurant. To finish the plate, drop on one or more dots of the jam. I recommend using a piping bag to get nice, neat beads of jam on each plate and give the dish that extra special look to finish it off.

" For me, this little canapé is an excellent example of how you can make the perfect take on a French classic using the finest of Devon's ingredients.

All three elements to create this dish can be prepared up to a day in advance of the frying stage. The jam can be kept in the fridge for up to a couple of weeks. If you want to make this dish with an alternative fish, then hake, brill and pollock work equally as well, just make sure you use skinned fillets. "

For the cod brandade

2 medium Maris Piper potatoes

200g cod loin fillet, skinned

125ml full-fat milk

100ml double cream

1 sprig of lemon thyme

1 sprig of rosemary

Zest of ½ lemon

¼ sprig of dill, chopped

Maldon sea salt and black pepper

Extra virgin olive oil

Oil, for frying (quantity depending on appliance)

For the malt vinegar jam

200ml malt vinegar

200g caster sugar

6g agar-agar

4g caraway seeds

For the split pea batter

50g green split peas

25g yellow spilt peas

125g gluten-free flour

300ml beer (we like Devon Pilsner)

3.5g table salt

Equipment

Moulin or ricer

Chinois or fine sieve

Blender

Deep-fat fryer (optional)

Temperature probe (optional)

Crab Tartlet | Grapefruit | Smoked Caviar

Serves 6

Begin by making the **gram flour tartlets**. First, add the plain flour, gram flour and salt to a mixing bowl. Put the olive oil, egg yolk and water into a jug, mix together and then pour into the flour mixture. Start to knead the dough and mix all ingredients well. Allow the dough to rest for 1 hour in the fridge. Preheat the oven to 180°C (160°C fan/Gas Mark 4). Sprinkle some flour onto a work surface and gently roll out the pastry until 3mm thick. Spray the tart cases with baking spray and then line 6 cases with the pastry. Place another tart case inside and push down. Place the tart cases on a baking tray and bake in the oven for 15–20 minutes until golden brown. Leave to cool and take out the tart cases.

For the **mayonnaise**, add the egg yolks, lemon juice and mustard to a mixing bowl and mix well. Gradually add the rapeseed oil to emulsify, while mixing with a stick blender. As it thickens, add a little more oil if needed. Add a pinch of salt. Keep in the fridge until ready to mix in the crab. The extra will keep in the fridge for 1–2 weeks.

To make the **pickle liquid**, add all the ingredients to a saucepan. Bring to the boil and allow to infuse. Pass the herbs and spices through a muslin cloth and then into a squeezy bottle.

To make the **grapefruit jelly**, start by cutting away the pith from the grapefruit. Then cut into small pieces. Add the grapefruit to a medium pan, followed by the lime juice, water, sugar and mint. Bring to the boil and then allow to infuse. Pass the grapefruit liquid through a fine sieve. Measure out 300ml and add 1.5g of kappa carrageenan. Bring to the boil, skim off any excess and allow to set in a 150ml container. Once set, dice into small squares.

The last element to prepare is the **crab filling**. Put the white crab into a mixing bowl, add the chives, mayonnaise, pickle liquid and seasoning. Mix together and it is now ready to add to the tart cases.

Assembly and Plating Up

Add white crab filling to each pastry case, add three pieces of grapefruit jelly and finish the tart off with three dots of smoked caviar. Dress the tart with kohlrabi shoots.

Equipment

12 x 10cm fluted tart cases
Baking spray
Stick blender
Muslin cloth
Squeezy bottle
Fine sieve

For the gram flour tartlets

110g plain flour, plus extra for dusting
70g gram flour
3g table salt
20ml extra virgin olive oil
15g egg yolk
55ml cold tap water

For the mayonnaise

2 egg yolks
2 tsp lemon juice
1 tsp Dijon mustard
220ml rapeseed oil

For the pickle liquid

100ml white wine vinegar
100g caster sugar
1 star anise
5g fennel seeds
1 sprig of thyme

For the grapefruit jelly

250g peeled red grapefruit
25ml fresh lime juice
25ml tap water
50g caster sugar
1 sprig of mint

For the crab filling

25g picked white crab meat
1 tsp chopped chives
8g mayonnaise (see above)
5ml pickle liquid (see above)
Salt, to taste

To garnish

Smoked caviar (I use Exmoor Caviar)
Kohlrabi shoots

"This tasty little canapé showcases Brixham crab at its best, freshly picked from the shell and prepared just before it is delivered to the Angel. The sweet, rich flavour of crab is perfectly balanced with the smokiness and saltiness of the caviar."

Tomato And Peach Gazpacho | Natural Almonds

Serves 4

To make the **gazpacho**, cut the tomatoes and peaches into small pieces and put them into a large mixing bowl. Next, add the cucumber, garlic and shallot to the mixture. Follow by adding the vinegar, sparkling water and lemon juice. Mix well, then add the salt, sugar, olive oil and basil leaves. Cover the bowl with cling film and allow the ingredients to marinate in the fridge for a few hours. Blend the mixture until smooth and pass through a fine sieve. Add extra olive oil and salt if needed, then add the pre hy and mix. Keep the gazpacho in the fridge to ensure it remains chilled until you want to serve it.

Assembly and Plating Up

Make sure that the cups or bowls you use for serving are chilled. I like to serve the chilled gazpacho with a garnish of blanched almonds.

> " A simple recipe for tomato and peach gazpacho. It is a cooling and refreshing cold soup served with almonds and perfect for the summer season. "

For the gazpacho

1kg tomatoes on the vine

4 ripe yellow peaches

1 cucumber, deseeded

1 garlic clove, finely sliced

1 banana shallot, finely sliced

30ml verjus

500ml sparkling water

Juice of 1 lemon

5g Maldon sea salt, plus extra if needed

10g caster sugar

50ml extra virgin olive oil, plus extra if needed

6 large fresh basil leaves

12g pre hy (see page 46)

24 natural blanched almonds

Equipment

Blender

Fine sieve

Cured Salmon | Watermelon Salsa | Oyster

Serves 6

Begin preparing the **pickled mustard seeds** by bringing a pan of water to the boil. Add the mustard seeds and cook for 1 minute. Remove and refresh the mustard seeds under cold water. Repeat this three times. Place the seeds in the fridge. Moving on to the pickle liquor, start by adding the vinegar, water and sugar to a pan and bring to a simmer until the sugar is dissolved. Add the mustard seeds to the pickle and set aside to infuse. This can be made in advance and kept in the fridge for at least a week.

To prepare the **cured salmon**, firstly prep the salmon fillet. You will need to skin the salmon by first making an incision at the tail end into the skin. Allow enough space to grip the skin with your fingers so you can hold the skin tightly while you are running your knife though as close to the skin as you can. Once the skin is removed, you can clean up the fillet before curing. In a mixing bowl, add the salt, sugar, lemon zest, dill and the coriander and fennel seeds. Mix well, then pour onto the salmon, covering the whole surface area. Place in the fridge for 3 hours to cure. Once cured, wash under cold running water for 5 minutes to remove the excess salt. Pat dry with kitchen paper or J cloth. Once dried, set a water bath to 40°C. Prior to cooking the salmon, sprinkle the seaweed across the skin side, then roll up in cling film to keep the shape and vacuum pack. Now place into the water bath and cook for 25 minutes. Once cooked, remove from the water bath and straight away put into an ice bath to cool and halt any further cooking. Once cool, keep in the fridge for several hours to firm up before cutting it into portions. Your portions should each weigh between 40g and 50g. Once portioned up, put them all into a vacuum pack and seal. The salmon can be cured in advance and lasts up to 3 days in the fridge.

To make the **salmon fritters**, begin by making a smoked béchamel sauce. Bring the milk to the boil in a small saucepan. Place another pan on the heat and melt the smoked butter. Add the flour to the butter and gently mix. Continue whisking until a paste forms, then cook for a further 2–3 minutes. Add the milk to the roux, stirring as you go, until you get a smooth sauce. Cook the sauce for 10 minutes on a low heat, stirring continuously until the sauce has thickened. Add both the Parmesan and Cheddar. Cook for a further 5 minutes. Season the sauce with salt and pepper. Place a piece of baking paper on top and place in the fridge. This can be made in advance the day before and kept in the fridge. Cut the cured salmon into a small dice, then add the smoked béchamel sauce until combined. Chop the dill and add to the salmon fritter mix. Using a spatula, mix all ingredients together and roll into 12g balls. Next, on to the coating of the salmon fritters. Lay out three mixing bowls, one with the flour, one with the eggs and one with the breadcrumbs. Place the salmon fritters into the flour with a slotted spoon, then dust off the fritters and put into the egg mixture. Coat the balls evenly with the egg and put into the breadcrumbs. Roll the fritters in the bowl, making sure the breadcrumbs are stuck to the fritters. Roll each fritter in your hands and put into the fridge ready to fry later.

To make the **watermelon salsa**, peel off the outer skin of the watermelon and all the white underlayer. Once all the outer has been removed, cut the watermelon into 3cm-wide pieces and vacuum pack at the strongest setting to compress the watermelon. Remove from the vacuum pack and cut in half. Put aside one half for the watermelon balls, and slice the other half as thinly as possible and begin to brunoise as finely as you can. Add half of the pickled mustard seed dressing and let it sit for 20 minutes. Once done, strain off the watermelon as there will be a lot of excess water. Brunoise the shallot and chiffonade the dill. Now mix the watermelon, shallot, remaining pickled mustard seed dressing and dill together. You should make the salsa a day before you want to use it and keep in the fridge.

For the **oyster mayonnaise**, first shuck the oysters and remove from their shells. Keep the shells for later. Reserve the oyster liquor. Rinse the oysters. Blend together the oysters, egg yolks and lemon juice. Add half of the oyster liquor and the fresh mustard. Blend on high speed for 20 seconds. Gradually add the rapeseed oil to the oysters. You need to add the oil slowly, otherwise it will split. Once all the oil is added, season with the sea salt and cayenne pepper. Pass through a fine sieve. Place in a small squeezy bottle and put straight into the fridge. This must only be made on the day you want to serve the dish.

For the **watermelon balls**, take out a piece of the reserved compressed watermelon and, using a melon baller, scoop out as many small balls as you can. Keep these balls in the fridge until later when needed for plating. These need to be done on the day of serving.

Assembly and Plating Up

Place the cured salmon into a water bath at 45°C for 20 minutes. Make sure the fryer is turned on to 180°C for the salmon fritters. Take the reserved oyster shells, place them into a pan of water and bring to the boil. This will clean the shells and get rid of any dirt or muscle. Leave to dry. Add 2 teaspoons of watermelon salsa to each shell and place on a bed of sea salt. On six more plates, dress five watermelon balls per plate with a little olive oil and a pinch of sea salt. Take the salmon from the water bath and carefully take it out of the bag. Remove the cling film from the salmon and glaze it with some olive oil. Place a piece of salmon onto each plate at 11 o'clock. Add the dressed watermelon balls to the plates, keeping a little even distance between them. Take the oyster mayonnaise from the fridge and place one big dot on the lefthand side of the plate, then add three more small dots around the watermelon balls. Sprinkle the fennel pollen over the oyster mayonnaise. Drop the salmon fritters into the fryer and cook until golden brown. When nicely coloured, season with sea salt and place on top of the watermelon salsa. Finally, add the sea fennel and sea purslane leaves over the mayonnaise and salmon and you are ready to go.

For the pickled mustard seed dressing

25g mustard seeds, soaked overnight

100ml white wine vinegar

100ml tap water

100g caster sugar

For the cured salmon

500g salmon fillet (from a 3–4kg whole salmon – I use Loch Duart salmon)

250g table salt

250g caster sugar

Zest of 2 unwaxed lemons

25g dill

5g coriander seeds

6g fennel seeds

20g smoked dulse seaweed (we get ours from Wellocks)

For the salmon fritters

250ml full-fat milk

20g smoked butter

25g plain flour

50g Parmesan, grated

50g Cheddar, grated

10g dill

Sea salt and black pepper, to taste

For the coating

50g plain flour

2 eggs, beaten

150g fine dried breadcrumbs

For the watermelon salsa

1 large watermelon

1 banana shallot

8g dill

For the oyster mayonnaise

2 oysters (I use Porthilly oysters), plus 4 additional oyster shells to serve

2 egg yolks

10ml lemon juice

2g fresh Dijon mustard

350ml rapeseed oil

A pinch of sea salt

A pinch of cayenne pepper

To garnish

300g Maldon sea salt

20ml olive oil

Fennel pollen (we get ours from Wellocks)

24 sea fennel leaves

32 sea purslane leaves

Equipment

Water bath

Vacuum pack bags

Blender

Fine sieve

Squeezy bottle

Melon baller

Deep-fat fryer

"This fresh and elegant cured salmon dish is a staple at the Angel. It comprises some explosive flavours, which work together in surprising harmony."

Serves 6

Milk-Cured Duck Liver | Salted Peach | Sauternes

The **milk-cured liver** should be made first as the livers need to be marinated overnight. After marinating, it will need to be cooked in a water bath and rolled. So, allow at least a day in advance to prepare this. In a large pan, add the water, cream, Sauternes, crème de pêche liqueur, fruit peels and salts. Bring to the boil, then add the thyme and rosemary. Next, add the ice cubes to the cream mixture and allow to cool. In a separate mixing bowl, add the deveined duck livers. Once the liquid has cooled, whisk together, making sure that all ingredients are thoroughly mixed. Now pour the mixture over your duck livers. Cover the duck livers with cling film and leave in the fridge for a minimum of 12 hours. We usually do this overnight.

The following day, remove the livers from the liquid and pat dry with kitchen paper. You can now discard the liquid. Place the livers in a vacuum pack bag and seal on high to remove all the air. Set the water bath to 35°C and cook the livers in it for 3½ hours. When the duck livers are coming to the end of cooking, set up an ice bath. Half-fill a pan with ice cubes and cover with tap water. When the 3½ hours cooking time is up, place the livers, still in the vacuum pack bag, into the ice bath. Allow the livers time to harden up and the fat solids will become firm. Over a J cloth, remove the livers from the vacuum pack bag and scrape off any yellow fat with a spoon, allowing the flesh to be seen. Lay out two sheets of cling film on a work surface and smooth them down. Put the duck livers on to the cling film and roll tightly in the cling film to form a ballotine. It should be around 6cm in diameter, depending on the size of your duck liver. Place it in the fridge to firm up and set.

You can make the **salted peach chutney** up to a day before it is needed. Add all the ingredients to a large saucepan. Place on a high heat and bring to the boil. Once boiling, reduce the heat to low and simmer until reduced to a thick and sticky mixture. Transfer to a food processor and blitz on high for 2 minutes until smooth. You can add a splash of water if it is too thick to blend. Pass through a chinois or fine sieve and refrigerate in an airtight container until needed. Transfer to a piping bag or squeezy bottle when ready to plate up.

Another element you can make in advance is the **peach and Sauternes jelly**. Pour the water into a large saucepan, then add the dried apricots, mandarins, Sauternes and tea. Place on a high heat and bring to the boil. Leave to cool completely and infuse for about 2–3 hours. Once infused, pass through a chinois. Pour 600ml of the strained liquid into a saucepan and add the peach purée. Add the vegetable gel, place the pan on a high heat and bring to the boil. Remove from the heat and pour into a flat tray. Put aside to chill and set. Once set, cut out a piece the jelly with a ring cutter, ideally one which is the same size as your cooked duck liver. The set jelly can be prepared 2–3 days before serving but must be kept in the fridge, covered with cling film.

To make the **thyme crackers**, add all the dry ingredients to a stand mixer. Start the mixer on a medium speed and pour in the water and olive oil until you have a dough. Remove the dough from the mixer, put it into a bowl, cover with cling film and allow to prove for 30 minutes at room temperature. Once the 30 minutes is up, put the bowl into the fridge for a further 30 minutes to finish proving. Once the second stage of proving has ended, preheat the oven to 160°C (140°C fan/Gas Mark 3). Remove the dough from the fridge and place it on a lightly floured surface. Roll out the dough into a strip which will go through a pasta machine. Set the machine to ten and pass the dough through it. Reduce the setting by two and roll through again. Repeat this process, reducing the thickness by two each time until you have passed the dough through on the 0 setting. Place the crackers on an oven tray, brush with olive oil and sprinkle with salt. Bake in the oven for 8–9 minutes until golden brown. When cooked, remove from the oven and allow to cool. These crackers last up to 2 days in a lidded container kept a room temperature.

Our final element to prepare is the poached peach **garnish** for the plate. Cut each peach in half and remove the stone. Now cut each portion into three pieces so you have a total of six slices from each whole peach. Put the pieces into a vacuum pack bag, then drizzle them with olive oil and a good pinch of salt. We want the peaches to lightly poach in their own juices and marinate. Cook them in the water bath at 85°C for 8–9 minutes. Once cooked, remove from the water bath and set aside, still in the vacuum pack bag, so they can cool naturally at room temperature.

Assembly and Plating Up

Slice the duck liver ballotine into 2cm-thick pieces. Place a halved piece of peach and Sauternes jelly on top of the liver, covered with a piped dot of the salted peach chutney and the edible flowers. Next to this, pipe a good dot of chutney onto each plate. Break up the thyme crackers and place one on each plate, topped with small pieces of the poached peach and smoked duck, with small dots of the peach chutney in between. Now enjoy.

For the milk-cured liver

175ml tap water
130ml double cream
50ml Sauternes
20ml crème de pêche liqueur
3 slices orange peel
3 slices grapefruit peel
4.5g pink salt
25g table salt
2 sprigs of thyme
2 sprigs of rosemary
150g ice cubes
500g ethically farmed duck livers, deveined (I use Mr. Duck)

For the salted peach chutney

250g white peaches
75g dried apricots
1 shallot, sliced
100g demerara sugar
125g peach purée
100ml apple cider vinegar
3 lemon thyme leaves
2 Granny Smith apples, peeled, cored and chopped
Pinch of saffron
300ml bottled freshly squeezed orange juice
Maldon sea salt, to taste

For the peach and Sauternes jelly

300ml tap water
75g dried apricots
2 mandarins
125ml Sauternes
10g apricot and peach tea leaves
200g peach purée
14g vegetable gel (I use MSK)

For the thyme crackers

200g plain flour, sifted, plus extra for dusting
5g table salt
6g fresh yeast
10g thyme leaves
75ml tap water
25ml olive oil

To garnish

6 yellow peaches
Olive oil
300g smoked duck breast
12 marigold flowers
12 viola flowers
Sea salt

Equipment

Vacuum pack bags
Water bath
Food processor
Chinois or fine sieve
Piping bag or squeezy bottle
5cm ring cutter
Stand mixer
Pasta machine

"This dish has become a firm favourite in the restaurant. Throughout the year, we change the flavours to reflect seasonality. The milk-cured duck liver is served differently from other livers and has a more subtle flavour, which goes very well with the salted peach chutney."

Serves 4

Sea Bream | Gooseberry Dashi | Buttermilk | Borage

To prepare the **cured sea bream**, first prepare the fillet of sea bream. If you have a good fishmonger, ask them to remove the skin for you. If you need to skin the bream yourself, begin by making an incision at the tail end into the skin. Allow enough space to grip the skin with your fingers so you can hold the skin tightly while you are running your knife though as close to the skin as you can. Once the skin is removed, clean up the fillets and remove any bloodline away from the flesh. In a mixing bowl, add the salt, sugar, lemon zest and juice, dill and orange zest and juice. Mix well, then pour over the bream, making sure to cover the whole surface area. Place in the fridge for 20 minutes to cure. Once cured, wash under cold running water for 5 minutes to remove the excess salt. Pat dry with kitchen paper or J cloth. Put the fillets into a container, cover with cling film and keep in the fridge until you are ready to plate up.

You can make the **gooseberry purée** up to a day before it is needed. Add all the ingredients to a large saucepan. Place on a high heat and bring to the boil. Once boiling, reduce the heat to low and simmer until the liquid has reduced to a thick and sticky mix. Transfer to a food processor and blitz on high speed for 4 minutes until smooth. If it is too thick to blend, add a splash of water. Pass through a chinois or fine sieve and refrigerate in an airtight container until needed. Transfer to a piping bag or squeezy bottle when ready to use.

For the **dashi liquid**, in a medium saucepan, add the pear juice, water and dashi powder. Bring to a simmer. You do not want the liquid to boil. Once the dashi granules have melted and completely dissolved, remove from the heat and allow time to cool.

To make the **buttermilk dashi**, mix 100ml of the dashi liquid with the buttermilk. Season with the verjus and some white soy sauce. Add salt, sugar, and lemon juice to taste. Pour into a squeezy bottle and keep in the fridge until required. It must be kept cold and only removed from the fridge when you are plating up.

Prepare the **garnish**, by slicing the radishes very thinly and putting them immediately into iced water. Now slice the gooseberries to the same thickness and keep them in a container at room temperature.

Assembly and Plating Up

Slice the cured sea bream into thin slices. You want four slices per bowl. Place six dots of the gooseberry purée onto the bream. Put the sliced radishes and gooseberries in between the dots. Garnish with the borage and the sea vegetables. Pour 50ml of the buttermilk dashi into the side of each bowl and split the sauce with borage oil. Finish each dish with some chive flowers.

For the cured sea bream

2 x 300–400g fillets of sea bream (we get ours from Flying Fish)

100g table salt

100g caster sugar

Zest and juice of 2 unwaxed lemons

12g dill

Zest and juice of 1 unwaxed orange

For the gooseberry purée

250g white gooseberries

1 shallot, sliced

100g demerara sugar

125g pear purée

100ml apple cider vinegar

3 lemon thyme leaves

2 Granny Smith apples, peeled, cored and chopped

300ml pear juice

For the dashi liquid

250ml pear juice

250ml tap water

8g dashi powder

For the buttermilk dashi

100ml dashi liquid (see above)

100ml buttermilk

10ml verjus

White soy sauce, to taste

Lemon juice, to taste

Salt, to taste

To garnish

½ bunch of different coloured heritage radishes

8 white gooseberries

12 borage leaves

8 sea purslane leaves

8 sea fennel leaves

Borage oil (see page 278)

12–16 chive flowers

Equipment

Food processor

Chinois or fine sieve

Piping bag (optional)

Squeezy bottle(s)

"*This dish is a favourite with our customers. It has the unique taste of dashi and goes really well with the fresh gooseberries and buttermilk. A perfect dish to start for our diners who have chosen the tasting menu.*"

Serves 6

Crab Risotto | Lemon | Sea Vegetables

For the **shellfish oil**, preheat the oven to 160°C (140°C fan/Gas Mark 3). Add the shells to a large roasting tray and roast in the oven for 15 minutes. Add the roasted shells to a large pan along with the rapeseed oil. Put the pan on a medium heat to warm the shells and oil. Stir to make sure all the shells are coated with the oil. Stir them together and then remove from the heat. Cover the pan and keep it at room temperature for a day so the ingredients have time to infuse. The next day, remove the cover and put the pan back on the heat. Start at a medium heat and after a minute turn it up to high. Cook on a high heat for another minute, then remove from the heat and drain the oil from the shells into a bowl, through a muslin cloth. Keep the oil in a jar in the fridge for up to 2 weeks.

To make the **crab and langoustine bisque**, preheat the oven to 180°C (160°C fan/Gas Mark 4). On a large gastro tray, roast the crab bones together with the langoustine heads and claws for 15–20 minutes. Meanwhile, add the oil, carrot, celery, fennel and shallots to a pan. Once the ingredients have softened, add the tomatoes. Cook out until you have a jammy consistency. Then add the tomato purée and bay leaf and cook down. You want to have a good deep red colour in the purée before adding the brandy. Once you are happy with the colour, add the brandy and burn off the alcohol. Then add in the white wine and reduce the liquid by half. Once reduced, add the roasted bones and top up with water so the shells are just covered. Bring to the boil, then add the tarragon. Simmer the stock for 45 minutes. Remove from the heat and leave to rest for 10 minutes. Once rested, gradually pass the stock through a chinois and then a double layer of muslin cloth into another pan. Place the pan on a medium heat and reduce by three-quarters. Once reduced, add the butter and cream, if needed, to create a good foamy consistency. Keep in the fridge for 3 days or freeze the bisque for up to a month.

Now make the **preserved lemon gel**. In a medium saucepan, add the sugar, lemons and water. Bring to the boil, then pour into a blender and blitz on a high setting until you have a smooth gel. With a spatula, transfer the contents from the blender back into a saucepan on a medium heat. While constantly whisking, add the agar-agar. Then, still gently whisking, cook for 4 minutes. Pour the mixture into a dish, cover with cling film and place in the fridge to set. You can make the gel up to a day in advance of serving the dish. Once it has set, use a spatula to put it into a blender. Blitz on the high setting and add the saffron. After a couple of minutes blitzing, pass the mixture through a chinois or sieve. Once sieved, pour it into a squeezy bottle or piping bag. You can prepare the gel up to a day in advance of serving, but it must be kept in the fridge.

Now on to cooking the **risotto rice**. Make sure you have your cooking timer ready to set. Fill a medium pan with the water and bring to the boil. While the water is boiling, place a large pan on the heat. Add the unsalted butter and melt it. As soon as it has melted, add the shallots and cook out, making sure they do not start to colour. Once they have softened and become translucent, add the risotto rice and turn up the heat. Toast off the rice for 2 minutes with the shallots and butter. By now, the water in the other pan should be boiling. Pour it over the risotto rice and stir. Bring the rice to the boil, then turn down the heat and set your timer for 5 minutes. It is very important that the rice is cooked for only 5 minutes. During the cooking time, continually stir the rice. When the 5 minutes is up, strain the rice in the steamer tray and keep the liquid. Once strained, put the rice in a blast chiller or fridge to cool down. Keep both the rice and liquid in the fridge until you are ready to plate.

Assembly and Plating Up

In a medium pan, add the risotto rice and some of the reserved cooking liquid to just cover the rice. Place on the heat and gently reheat the rice. You don't want to over-stir the rice because you will break the grains. Let the liquid reduce over the rice until you cannot see it. Then add some of the crab and langoustine bisque until the rice is covered. When this has been absorbed into the rice and you cannot see the liquid, add the crème fraîche and Parmesan. Finish by adding the crab meat and some seasoning. If you need to add a little more bisque to moisten the rice, you can. Add a drop of lemon juice, chopped chervil and flat-leaf parsley, and then spoon into your bowls. Finish the risotto by placing the preserved lemon gel and sea purslane on top and spoon over a good amount of crab bisque. Complete the dish with a drizzle of the shellfish oil and serve.

For the shellfish oil

500g langoustine or shrimp shells

120ml rapeseed oil

For the crab and langoustine bisque

2kg langoustine heads and claws

1kg crab bones and claws

Oil, for frying

3 carrots, roughly chopped

2 celery sticks, roughly chopped

1 fennel bulb, roughly chopped

2 shallots, roughly chopped

5 tomatoes, chopped

2 x 400g tins of puréed tomatoes

1 bay leaf

50ml brandy

250ml white wine

2 litres tap water

35g tarragon leaves

100g unsalted butter (optional)

100ml double cream (optional)

For the preserved lemon gel

125g caster sugar

125g preserved lemons

400ml tap water

9g agar-agar

1g saffron

For the risotto rice

500ml tap water

120g unsalted butter

2 banana shallots, brunoised or finely diced

75g arborio rice

To finish

30g crème fraîche

25g Parmesan, finely grated

250g white crab meat (I use locally caught Brixham crab)

Lemon juice, to taste

15g chopped chervil

15g flat-leaf parsley

Salt and pepper

To garnish

35-40 sea purslane leaves

Equipment

Chinois or fine sieve

Muslin cloth

Blender

Squeezy bottle or piping bag

"This dish is the perfect showcase for the best crab in the South-West. It is also something Joyce Molyneux was very passionate about. She would only buy in the very best and freshest shellfish from the local fishermen and would then go on to use every piece. No part of any shellfish would go to waste. It is an ethos which I am very happy and proud to be keeping today."

Serves 6

Tomato Millefeuille | Ricotta | Artichokes | Smoked Tomato Jam

Start with the **smoked tomato jam**. Finely chop the tomatoes. Sweat down the shallots, garlic and spices in a pan. Add the tomato paste and roast off. Deglaze the pan with the vinegar and then add the tomatoes and sugar. Cook the jam down until it has a good consistency and then finish off with the lime juice. Season with salt and pepper. Blend until smooth and pass through a fine sieve. Keep in a squeezy bottle in the fridge for up to 2 weeks.

Then move on to the **tomato fondue**. Take a large saucepan, fill with water, lightly salt and place on a high heat. Bring to a rolling boil. While it is heating up, prepare the plum tomatoes. Using a sharp paring knife, make two light incisions into the skin, in an X shape, at the bottom of the tomatoes. Prepare an ice bath for the tomatoes and have a spider/tongs/sieve to hand for getting the tomatoes in and out of the boiling water. Dunk the tomatoes in the boiling water, two or three at a time, for about 5 seconds. You should be able to see the skin peeling back from the incision. After dunking, immediately plunge the tomatoes into the ice bath and repeat the process for all the tomatoes. Allow to cool completely for 5–10 minutes and then take the tomatoes out of the ice bath.

Peel the skin from the tomatoes with a paring knife and cut into quarters, removing the core and seeds. Dice the tomato petals and keep in a container until needed. In a large saucepan, add the olive oil and place on a medium heat. Sweat the shallot until translucent and then add in the tomatoes, garlic and thyme leaves. Now add a couple of pinches of rock salt and sugar, mix well, then cook on a medium-low heat for 2–3 hours, stirring occasionally. You will know when the tomatoes are cooked as they will have released all their liquid and have reduced right down. Add more olive oil if the fondue looks too dry. Season to taste with more salt and sugar, then transfer to a container. After they have cooled to room temperature, place in the fridge until required. They will keep for 3 days.

Next, move on to the **confit tomatoes**. Begin by peeling the tomatoes using the same process you undertook for plum tomatoes for the fondue. Once they are all peeled, make the confit tomato liquor. Add the olive oil, water, rock salt, lime juice, garlic and basil to a suitable container and whisk well. Then add the peeled tomatoes to the liquor, cover and leave at room temperature for 4 hours. Once the 4 hours are up, remove the tomatoes from the liquor and drain with kitchen paper or J cloths. Cover and refrigerate until required. You need to prepare them on the day you are serving the dish.

To prepare the **baby artichokes**, fill a large pan with water and ice cubes, then squeeze the juice from all the lemons in. Then put the lemon skins into the water. Remove the green outer leaves from the artichokes to expose the pale yellow leaves inside. Using a knife, trim an inch off the top of the baby artichokes. Remove the outer layers with a peeler. Now trim them into a circular shape. Ideally you want to take off the tough layer of the stem and the underside from the heart. Once you have a nice, round heart, put it in the lemon iced water. Prepare all the baby artichokes this way. Once all the artichokes have been prepared, using a serrated knife, trim off the top of the artichokes and place back into the water. You are now ready to cook them. Using a pan on a medium heat, sweat the mirepoix (shallot and carrot), coriander seeds, thyme, and rosemary. Add the water and oil, then the artichokes. Bring to a simmer, then place a sheet of baking paper over the top and cook on a low heat for 10–15 minutes.

To prepare the **artichoke salad filling**, scoop out the middle of the artichokes, dice them finely and place into a mixing bowl. Dress in lemon oil, then add the chopped herbs, salt and pepper. Now put the mixture into a piping bag.

For the **puff pastry**, preheat the oven to 200°C (180°C fan/Gas Mark 6). Roll out the puff pastry on a silicone mat to form a 30cm square. Lift onto a baking sheet, cover with baking paper, then place a flat baking sheet or tray on top. Now put a heavy baking dish on top of the sheet or tray. Bake for 15–20 minutes until golden. Once the pastry has cooled, cut it into 8 x 4cm rectangles. Keep at room temperature so they are ready for building the millefeuille.

To make the **whipped ricotta**, place the ricotta in a small mixing bowl. Add the lemon zest, salt and pepper. Mix the ingredients together and then put into a piping bag.

Assembly and Plating Up

To make your crispy capers, squeeze out any excess liquid, then deep fry at 160°C for 30–40 seconds.

To assemble, lay out three rectangles of puff pastry. On one layer, add a layer of tomato fondue. Next, pipe the artichoke salad filling and a thin layer of the smoked tomato jam on another layer of pastry, and place on top of the tomato fondue. On the third layer of pastry, place four confit tomatoes, four big dots of whipped ricotta, a few dots of tomato jam, some crispy capers and some celery cress. Next, fry your artichoke shells in a pan with the butter, then fill with the tomato fondue and some sliced baby tomatoes. On each plate, add a millefeuille, an artichoke shell, a slice of baby tomato, a confit tomato, two dots of jam and two dots of whipped ricotta.

For the smoked tomato jam

1.2kg tomatoes on vine
2–3 shallots, finely chopped
1 tsp smoked paprika
½ tsp cinnamon
½ tsp chilli powder
2 cloves garlic, crushed
Zest and juice of 1 lime
200g tomato paste
120ml apple cider vinegar
120g light brown sugar
Salt and pepper

For the tomato fondue

1kg plum tomatoes
100ml extra virgin olive oil, plus more if needed
1 shallot, brunoised or finely diced
1 garlic clove, crushed
4 sprigs of thyme, leaves picked
Rock salt and sugar

For the confit tomatoes

2 x 100g punnets of cherry tomatoes (ideally one red and one yellow)
100ml extra virgin olive oil
250ml tap water
10g rock salt
20ml fresh lime juice
2 garlic cloves, sliced
10 basil leaves

For the baby artichokes

3 unwaxed lemons
12 baby violet artichokes
1 banana shallot, brunoised or finely diced
1 carrot, peeled and roughly chopped
1 tsp coriander seeds
4 sprigs of thyme
4 sprigs of rosemary
500ml tap water
120ml extra virgin olive oil
100g unsalted butter

For the artichoke salad filling

350g cooked baby artichokes (see above)
Lemon oil (see page 50)
20g chopped chives
20g chopped dill
Salt and black pepper, to taste

For the puff pastry

600g rolled French puff pastry (I use Maître André)

For the whipped ricotta

200g buffalo ricotta
Zest of 1 unwaxed lemon
Salt and black pepper, to taste

To garnish

20g lilliput capers
1 bunch micro celery cress
Baby tomatoes, sliced

Equipment

Fine sieve
Piping bags
Blender

“This savoury millefeuille is layered with seasonal heritage tomatoes and artichokes. It works perfectly with the whipped ricotta and crispy capers.”

Serves 6

Ruby Red Beef Fillet | Caramelised Onion | Horseradish Buttermilk | Red Wine Jus

Start with the **caramelised onion purée**. First, cut the onions in half, cut off the tops and bottoms, then peel away the outer skin. Finely slice the onions as thinly as you can (this is called julienne). Place a large pan on a high heat and add the rapeseed oil. Now put in the sliced onions with the sprigs of thyme and sweat them until all the moisture has gone and the natural sugars start to caramelise them. The onions should have a nice golden brown colour. Then add the unsalted butter and allow the onions to caramelise further until they have a dark golden brown colouring. Then pour in the double cream, stir and cook out for a minute. Transfer the onions and cream to a blender. Blitz until you have a smooth purée. Season with salt and pass through a fine sieve. Allow to cool and transfer the purée into a piping bag. This can be made in advance and will last in the fridge for up to 3 days.

You can also make the **pickled petit onions** in advance. First, soak the onions in hot water, which will make them easier to peel. Using a paring or a turning knife, slice a very thin piece of the root off and peel off the skin. Prepare all the onions this way, then place a pan of lightly salted water on a high heat and bring to the boil. While you wait for the water to boil, add the tap water, vinegar, sugar, bay leaf, fennel seeds, coriander seeds and star anise to a medium pan, then bring it to the boil on a medium heat. Whisk frequently to ensure that the sugar totally dissolves while the water is heating up to boiling point. Once it has boiled, turn the heat down to low so the liquor remains warm until you need it. Once the other pan of water has come to a boil, reduce the heat to a simmer and blanch the petit onions. Cook them for 2–5 minutes until they have softened, then remove from the water. Place the cooked onions into a container and then cover with the warm pickle liquor. Close the container lid or cover with cling film. Leave to cool for 2–3 hours. Once cooled to room temperature, put the onions and liquor into a vacuum seal pickling jar. They will keep in the fridge for up to 2 weeks.

Next, make the **truffle pommes purée**. First, preheat the oven to 180°C (160°C fan/Gas Mark 4). Place the potatoes on a baking tray and cover with sea salt. Cook in the oven for 1¼ hours. Depending on the size of the potatoes, they may need more cooking for the insides to become soft. Once cooked, remove the potatoes from the oven and cut them in half. Scoop out the soft potato and put it through a moulin or ricer. Place a pan on a medium heat and add the butter. Once it has melted, add the potato and begin to beat with a whisk until incorporated. In another pan, warm the milk and then slowly add it to the potatoes, using a whisk until you get the desired light, fluffy consistency. Season with salt and pepper to taste. Then add the truffle oil and the grated Wiltshire truffle. After gently mixing them in with a whisk, spoon the potato mixture into piping bags and keep warm.

Now move on to the wonderful **beef fillet**. Cut the fillet into six portions and place into vacuum pack bags. Cook in the water bath at 58°C for 20–25 minutes. Once cooked, remove the beef from the water bath and rest the meat in the bags for 10 minutes. Remove the fillets from the bags, season on all sides with salt and pepper, then sear them in a very hot pan on all sides. Rest for 5–10 minutes. In a hot pan, add the butter and rosemary, along with a couple of pinches of sea salt. Foam the butter and then add in the rested fillets. Baste the beef in the hot butter, keeping it moving all the time, so it warms through but does not cook. Rest for another 2 minutes before carving and plating.

To prepare the **shimeji mushrooms**, prep them by cutting off most of the stem. Cut to about 1cm from the head of the mushroom. Prep all the mushrooms this way and put them in a mixing bowl. Place a frying pan on a medium heat, add the diced shallots and start to sweat them. When they become translucent and have not started to colour, add the mushrooms. Once they start to colour a little, add the lemon juice and olive oil. Season with sea salt and remove the pan from the heat. Keep the mushrooms in the warm pan, off the heat, until needed for plating up.

On to the **horseradish buttermilk**. Put all the ingredients into a mixing bowl and whisk them together. Season with salt, sugar and lemon juice to taste. Transfer the mixture into a piping bag and keep in the fridge until needed.

To make the **red wine sauce**, pour the red wine jus into a saucepan on a medium heat and reduce by three-quarters. Once reduced, whisk in the butter and set aside ready for plating up.

The final element to prepare is the **spinach**. Place a pan on a high heat. Once warm, add the butter and a pinch of salt. Now add the spinach and allow it to wilt for a couple of minutes. Stir occasionally so it is coated with the melted seasoned butter. Drain onto kitchen paper and serve immediately. Use a tablespoon to ball the spinach into small parcels for each plate.

Assembly and Plating Up

Make sure your plates are warm before plating up. Place three three halves of petit onions in a semicircle on the plate. In between the onions, add the pickled mushrooms. Place a large dot of the caramelised onion purée inside the circle and around the mushrooms. Add the spinach parcels to the lefthand side, then place the hot beef fillet on top. Finish the dish by dotting on the horseradish buttermilk (1 big teaspoon) in the middle of the onions, drizzling a few drops of the nasturtium oil on top. Serve the truffle pommes purée on a small (warm) side plate with the truffle grated over it, and individual small jugs of the red wine jus. I hope your guests enjoy this dish as much as ours do.

For the caramelised onion purée

5 large Spanish white onions

3 tsp rapeseed oil

2 sprigs of thyme

250g unsalted butter

100ml double cream

Table salt, to taste

For the pickled petit onions

250g raw petit silverskin onions

100ml tap water

100ml white wine vinegar

100g caster sugar

1 bay leaf

1 tbsp fennel seeds

1 tbsp coriander seeds

1 star anise

For the truffle pommes purée

1.5kg Pierre Koffmann potatoes

200g unsalted butter

300ml full-fat milk

20g fresh Wiltshire truffle

10g white truffle oil

Maldon sea salt and black pepper

For the beef fillet

1 medium centre cut beef fillet

100g butter

4 sprigs of rosemary

Maldon sea salt and black pepper

For the pickled shimeji

150g punnet of shimeji mushrooms

1 banana shallot, brunoised or finely diced

10g lemon juice

50ml olive oil

Maldon sea salt

For the horseradish buttermilk

500ml fresh buttermilk

50g horseradish crème

100ml full-fat crème fraîche

10g caster sugar

Lemon juice, to taste

Pinch of Maldon sea salt

For the red wine sauce

700ml red wine jus (see page 279)

50g unsalted butter

For the spinach

200g bag of baby leaf spinach

50g unsalted butter

Maldon sea salt

To garnish

Nasturtium oil

10g fresh Wiltshire truffle, grated

Equipment

Blender

Fine sieve

Piping bags

Vacuum seal jar

Moulin or ricer

6 vacuum pack bags

Water bath

"Local farmer Tim Johnson at Stokes Marsh Farm in nearby Coulston, Wiltshire, supplies most of our beef from his outstanding Aberdeen Angus and Hereford crossed herds. Tim prides himself on giving his cattle the best possible quality of life and everything that the cattle eat is grown on the farm. Stokes Marsh Farm is working towards being completely sustainable: all their organic waste is quickly turned into natural fertiliser and the energy released is turned into electricity which provides the farm with power.

Pommes purée is a classic French side dish that was made by the late French chef Joël Robuchon. It has an irresistibly rich silky-smooth texture, comprising a generous amount of butter that is stirred into the potato and then beaten together with milk. The perfect accompaniment to the beef fillet."

Roasted Turbot | Baby Gem | Broad Bean | Makrut Lime Butter Sauce

Serves 6

Start with the **tomato fondue**. Take a large saucepan or stock pot, fill with water, lightly salt and place on a high heat. Bring to a rolling boil. While it is heating up, prepare the plum tomatoes. Using a sharp paring knife, make two light incisions into the skin, in an X shape, at the bottom of the tomatoes. Prepare an ice bath for the tomatoes and have a spider/tongs/sieve to hand or some utensil for getting the tomatoes in and out of the boiling water. Dunk the tomatoes in the boiling water, two or three at a time, for about 5 seconds. You should be able to see the skin peeling back from the small incision. After dunking, immediately plunge the tomatoes into the ice bath and repeat the process for all the tomatoes. Allow to cool completely for 5–10 minutes and then take the tomatoes out of the ice bath.

Peel the skin from the tomatoes with a paring knife and cut into quarters, removing the core and seeds. Dice the tomato petals and keep in a container until needed. In a large saucepan, add the olive oil and place on a medium heat. Sweat the shallot until translucent and then add in the tomatoes, garlic and thyme leaves. Now add a couple of pinches of rock salt and sugar, mix well, then cook on a medium-low heat for 2–3 hours, stirring occasionally. You will know when the tomatoes are cooked as they will have released all their liquid and have reduced right down. Add more olive oil if the fondue looks too dry. Season to taste with more salt and sugar, then transfer to a container. After they have cooled to room temperature, place in the fridge until required. They will keep for 3 days.

Next, move on to the **confit tomatoes**. Begin by peeling the tomatoes using the same process you undertook for plum tomatoes for the fondue. Once they are all peeled, make the confit tomato liquor. Add the olive oil, water, rock salt, lime juice, garlic and basil to a suitable container and whisk well. Then add the peeled tomatoes to the liquor, cover and leave at room temperature for 4 hours. Once the 4 hours are up, remove the tomatoes from the liquor and drain with kitchen paper or J cloths. Cover and refrigerate until required. You need to prepare them on the day you are serving the dish.

For the **white asparagus**, first make the cooking liquor. Add the butter, water, salt, sugar and lemon juice to a pan, then place on a medium heat until the butter has melted and the mixture begins to simmer. Turn off the heat. Peel the asparagus carefully, turning as you peel to keep the natural cylindrical shape of the asparagus. Once peeled, bring the cooking liquor to the boil and place the asparagus into the liquid. Once the asparagus has been added, immediately remove the pan from the heat and cover with a cartouche. Leave for 20 minutes and then check the asparagus. If the asparagus hasn't softened enough, repeat the process by bringing the liquid back to the boil and turning the heat off again. Check again after 10 minutes. Once cooked, remove the asparagus from the liquid and transfer to a chopping board. Cut off the hard and woody part of the asparagus from the bottom. Now cut each asparagus spear into four pieces: cut horizontally in half, then cut each half vertically again, in half. You will use one half-tip and one half-stem per portion. Refrigerate until needed.

For the **reduction**, add all the ingredients to a pan and bring to a boil, then take off the heat, cover in cling film, then leave it to infuse. Once cooled, place in fridge.

For the **tomato essence**, the day before it is needed, cut the cherry tomatoes in half and put the pieces into a mixing bowl. Add all the dry ingredients, except the salt and sugar, and mix. Then blitz the cherry tomatoes in a food processor. Pour the tomato mixture into a large pan and add the sparkling water, lemon juice, salt and sugar. Line a colander with muslin and place it on top of a bowl. Pour in the liquid and place in the fridge. Leave for a day until needed, to allow time for all the impurities to come out.

To prepare the **buttered gem lettuce**, remove the outer leaves of the lettuce and cut off the root. Cut into quarters, then remove the core of hard, crunchy leaves. You should have four bunches of leaves that are pliable enough to roll and chiffonade. Just before you start cooking, chiffonade the leaves as finely as possible and keep in a container ready to use when plating up. Also, make sure you have the chives, broad beans and some diced butter to hand so you can cook them just before you plate the dish.

With all the other elements prepared, you now need to brine the **turbot**. Cover the turbot in the brine and transfer to the fridge for 25 minutes. Pat dry with kitchen paper or J cloths. Make sure the turbot is as dry as possible, so you get the best possible sear when cooking it. Once thoroughly dried, put back into the fridge until you start cooking.

For the **tomato and lime makrut butter sauce**, first add the reduction, lemongrass, fish stock and essence to a medium pan, bring to a boil and reduce the liquid by half. Once reduced, remove from the heat, and stir in the cream. Put back on a low heat and bring to a simmer. Reduce further until you have just a quarter left of the original liquid. Take off the heat and emulsify the cold cubed butter into the mixture with a stick blender for best consistency. Once fully emulsified, add the tomato fondue, ponzu and lime juice to season.

The final task before moving on to the assembling and plating up is to warm and salt the confit tomatoes. Remove them from the fridge and sprinkle with rock salt. Place in a warm environment or heat up gently in the oven at 75°C (55°C fan/Gas Mark as low as possible) for 10 minutes.

Assembly and Plating Up

First, make sure the tomato and lime butter sauce is warm and ready to be brought back to the heat when you need it. Bring to a simmer in a medium pan and then turn the heat down to low. In a separate frying pan, add a few cubes of butter and enough water to cover the bottom of the pan, about 1cm deep. Heat gently until the butter has melted, then turn the heat off. You will use this to heat and glaze the white asparagus.

Have a large non-stick pan ready for the turbot. Place the pan on a medium heat and add a splash of rapeseed oil. You will turn the heat up to high just before you add the fish.

In a small pan, heat up the tomato fondue. If it gets dry, add a splash of water.

The final pan and element to finish is the buttered gem lettuce. Place a pan on a high heat and add 2–3 cubes of the butter. Once they start melting, add the broad beans. Sauté quickly on a high heat, without burning the butter, then add the lettuce. Season generously with a heavy pinch of salt, then stir quickly, mixing the broad beans and salt right through. Once wilting, remove the lettuce from the heat, then add the chives and mix again, making sure to check your seasoning. Drain on kitchen paper or J cloth and bring to the plates.

Now take the pan with the butter and water in and turn up the heat to maximum. Once it is boiling, add the white asparagus and sauté in the emulsion for 20–30 seconds. If the emulsion reduces too much, add a splash of water. This will glaze and reheat the cooked white asparagus. Transfer to a side plate or tray.

Now turn up the heat on the non-stick fish pan and place in all of the fish fillets, skin-side down. Cook for about 3 minutes until golden and crisp. Add the butter and allow it to melt and foam. Spoon the foaming butter over the fish and remove from the heat. Add some water to deglaze the pan. Leave the fillets in the pan to finish the cooking process through residual heat.

To plate, start with the buttered lettuce. Take a spoon and ball it, as well as you can, into a nice sphere. Place on each plate, slightly offset to the left of the centre. Put the fish, skin-side up, next to the buttered lettuce, with another piece of buttered lettuce on top. Place one stem piece of white asparagus next to the fish with a confit tomato on top. Quenelle a nice portion of tomato fondue and place between the asparagus and the fish. To complete the dish, you can then garnish with any sea vegetables you like. Take to the table and pour over the tomato and lime butter sauce at the table, for that little added touch of theatrical pleasure and presentation.

For the tomato fondue

1kg plum tomatoes

100ml extra virgin olive oil, plus extra if needed

1 shallot, brunoised or finely diced

1 garlic clove, crushed

4 sprigs of thyme, leaves picked

Rock salt and sugar

For the confit tomatoes

2 x 100g punnets of cherry tomatoes (ideally one red and one yellow)

100ml extra virgin olive oil

250ml water

10g rock salt, plus extra for sprinkling

20ml fresh lime juice

1 garlic clove, crushed

10 basil leaves

For the white asparagus

200g unsalted butter, plus a few cubes for glazing

400ml tap water

16g table salt

16g caster sugar

20ml fresh lemon juice

4 white asparagus spears

For the reduction

3 shallots, finely sliced

400ml dry white wine

200ml white wine vinegar

225ml tap water

50g tarragon

50g flat-leaf parsley

50g dill

For the tomato essence

600g cherry tomatoes on the vine

1 celery stick, finely chopped

1 banana shallot, finely chopped

½ fennel bulb, chopped

1 garlic clove, crushed

Pinch of cayenne pepper

10g basil leaves

20g tarragon leaves

200ml sparkling water

Juice of 1 unwaxed lemon

8g table salt

12g caster sugar

For the buttered gem lettuce

1 baby gem, thinly sliced

20g chives, finely chopped

50g broad beans, shelled

75g unsalted butter, diced

Salt, to taste

For the turbot

4–6kg turbot, cut into 6 fillets (I buy mine from Flying Fish)

Fish brine (see page 272)

Rapeseed oil, for cooking

100g unsalted butter

For the tomato and makrut lime butter sauce

125ml reduction (see above)

1 lemongrass stick

50ml fish stock (see page 273)

500ml tomato essence (see above)

250ml double cream

250g cold, smoked salted butter, cubed

2 tsp tomato fondue (see above)

50ml tomato ponzu (I buy mine from Wellocks)

Lime juice, to taste

To garnish

Sea vegetables of your choice (optional)

Equipment

Food processor

Muslin cloth

> " This dish showcases its ingredients at their ultimate best and it's one of my all-time favourites at the Angel. The tomato ponzu goes perfectly with the smokiness of the butter sauce. I use Flying Fish, the best supplier in the South-West for my fish, as Johnny and his team are so passionate not only about the quality of the fish but also how they source it. I have been using Flying Fish for over 10 years now and they are quite simply the best fishmonger in the land. "

Calamansi | Lime Curd | Fennel Rice Crisp

Serves 8

Start by making the **calamansi sorbet**, which can be prepared a few days in advance. Add the water and calamansi purée to a medium saucepan. Then add the caster sugar and sorbet stabiliser to a mixing bowl. Mix thoroughly with a spoon, otherwise you will end up with lumps in your sorbet. Once mixed, pour into the saucepan containing the water and purée. Bring to the boil, whisking continuously. Allow to cool. Once cooled, transfer the liquid to a measuring jug. Add the Greek yoghurt and blend the mixture together with a stick blender. Gently pour it into 8 of the silicone moulds, filling the moulds to the top. Place a piece of baking paper over the top and put straight into the freezer, making sure they are laid on a flat surface.

Making the **lime curd** begins by placing the lime juice, butter and sugar into a saucepan. Bring to the boil and remove from the heat. Put the egg yolk into a ThermoMixer and temper the yolks. Add the mixture from the saucepan and cook until it reaches 83°C. Pour over the white chocolate pieces, stir to ensure an even mix and then allow to set. Once set, transfer to a piping bag. This can be kept in the fridge for at least a week.

For the **puffed fennel rice**, preheat the oven to 160°C (140°C fan/Gas Mark 3). Combine all the ingredients in a medium baking tray. Bake in the oven for 9 minutes, or until golden brown. Halfway through the cooking process, turn the rice and the seeds with a spatula, making sure all the honey and maple syrup covers the rice. When it's cooked, pour the rice out onto baking paper and allow to cool completely. When cooled, add to a container and keep in the fridge for up to 4 days.

Now make the **white chocolate dip**. Put the white chocolate and cocoa butter into a mixing bowl. Place a medium pan of water on the heat and put the mixing bowl over the pan. The chocolate will now gently melt. Make sure the water does not boil and the mixing bowl does not come into contact with the water. Once the mixture has melted, add the Power Flowers or food colouring, and using a stick blender, blend the chocolate until completely combined. Once mixed, set the bowl aside until required. You can make the dip in advance and keep it in a covered container in the fridge for a couple of days. However, it is best when made and used on the day of serving. If made in advance, you will need to warm it through first before using.

Assembly and Plating Up

Remove the sorbet from the freezer and allow to stand at room temperature for 2–3 minutes so it can soften a little. Pop a portion out of the mould and put a cocktail stick through one end, through the flat surface side and gently dip into the white chocolate dip, making sure it covers the sorbet. Once coated all over, place on parchment paper to set. It will set quickly. Repeat for the remaining sorbet. Once set, place them onto your serving plates. Pipe the lime curd on the middle of the calamansi sorbet, then add a nice piece of the puffed fennel rice crisp on top. Serve immediately.

> " Calamansi is a variety of citrus fruit commonly called the golden lime. This pre-dessert is perfect for the summer months and goes very well with the anise taste of fennel. A combination which works so well together. "

For the calamansi sorbet

110ml tap water
125ml calamansi purée (I source mine from Wellocks)
110g caster sugar
25g sorbet stabiliser
100ml Greek yoghurt

For the lime curd

50ml fresh lime juice
75g unsalted butter
50g caster sugar
40g egg yolk
75g white chocolate

For the puffed fennel rice

25g puffed cereal (I use Rice Krispies)
25g sunflower seeds
25g pine nuts
6g fennel seeds
10g runny blossom honey
15g maple syrup

For the white chocolate dip

65g white chocolate pieces (I use Callebaut)
40g cocoa butter (I use Callebaut)
2 White Power Flowers or 4g white food colouring

Equipment

Stick blender
8 silicone pomponette moulds
ThermoMixer
Piping bag
Cocktail sticks

Serves 12

Cucumber | White Chocolate Curd | Lime

First, make the **cucumber and lime granita**. Cut the cucumbers in half and remove the seeds with a spoon. Use a grater to remove the skin. Squeeze the cucumbers through a muslin cloth to get out as much juice as possible. Keep the juice and discard the pulp left in the muslin. Pour 150ml of the juice into a bowl and keep the remaining juice until required later. Pour the water, sugar and liquid glucose into a saucepan, then bring it to the boil, stirring until the sugar dissolves. Remove from the heat and allow to cool. Once cooled, add the cucumber juice along with the lime zest and juice. Stir in the Greek yogurt. Once combined, pour into a container, cover and freeze until required.

Add a little alcohol-free gin to the remaining cucumber juice. Taste, then add a little honey or more gin if you want to reduce the acidity a little and raise the flavour of the botanicals in the gin. Do not be tempted to use alcoholic gin, as it will totally ruin the balance of the dish.

To make the **white chocolate curd**, place the water, butter and sugar into a saucepan. Bring to the boil and remove from the heat. Put the egg yolk into a ThermoMixer and temper the yolk. Add the mixture from the saucepan and cook until it reaches 83ºC. Pour over the white chocolate pieces, stir to ensure an even mix and then allow time to set. Once set, transfer to a piping bag.

The final step is to make the **cucumber balls**. Peel the cucumber and discard the skin. Using a melon baller, gently scoop out the cucumber and place into a mixing bowl. You want to use as much of the cucumber as you can. Put the balls into some of the remaining gin-flavoured cucumber juice (you need to keep back a little to finish the dish) and allow them to infuse.

Assembly and Plating Up

Pipe three peaks of the white chocolate curd onto a small dish. Place a few infused cucumber balls between the curd, along with 2 tablespoons of the cucumber juice. Finish with a good amount of the cucumber and lime granita. Serve straight away.

> "This is a wonderful summer palate cleanser. The unusual combination of ingredients works surprisingly well."

For the cucumber and lime granita

2 large cucumbers
70ml water
85g caster sugar
25g liquid glucose
Zest and juice of 1 lime
100ml Greek yoghurt
Alcohol-free gin (I use Pentire's Seaward)
Honey, to taste

For the white chocolate curd

50ml water
75g unsalted butter
50g caster sugar
40g egg yolk
75g white chocolate pieces (I use Callebaut)

For the cucumber balls

1 cucumber
30ml gin-flavoured cucumber juice

Equipment

Muslin cloth
ThermoMixer
Piping bag
Melon baller

Summer

Serves 10

Yuzu Cream | Toasted Coconut Meringue | Mandarin | Vanilla Sorbet

Begin by preparing the **spiced biscuit crumb**. Preheat the oven to 160°C (140°C fan/Gas Mark 3). First, add the cubed butter and both sugars to a stand mixer. Using the paddle attachment, beat the butter and sugar to a creamy consistency. Add the honey, cinnamon, mixed spice and salt. Now work with the paddle for a further 2 minutes. Next, add the bicarbonate of soda and both flours, then mix slowly. You want all the ingredients to be completely combined. Spread this mixture onto a silicone mat and cook in the oven for 12–15 minutes until dark brown. Remove from the oven and allow to cool. Once the biscuit you have made is cold, put it into a food processor. Mix until reduced to a very fine crumb. In a small saucepan, add the rest of the butter and melt it. Gradually add the melted butter into the spiced biscuit until evenly combined. With a palette knife, spread the spiced biscuit into the square mould, making sure it's perfectly flat. Place in the fridge to set.

For the **yuzu crème**, first place a saucepan on a medium heat. Add the yuzu purée and bring to the boil. Then whisk in the agar-agar and keep whisking on the heat for a further 2 minutes. Remove from the heat, then add the gelatine leaf and allow to melt. In a mixing bowl, add the eggs and sugar. Pour the yuzu purée mixture over the eggs and sugar. Place the pan back on a low heat, then gradually add the cubed butter. Make sure the butter is added slowly, otherwise the mixture will split. The yuzu crème will look thick and glossy. Once all the butter is combined, add the yuzu mixture to the square mould over the top of the spiced biscuit. Place into the fridge to set completely.

To make the **mandarin gel**, add the water, sugar and mandarin purée to a saucepan and bring to the boil. Now add the agar-agar and boil for a further 2 minutes. Pour into a container and allow to set. Once firmly set, put into a blender and blend until smooth. Pass the gel through a chinois and put into a piping bag. Store the gel in the fridge until required.

With the **coconut and vanilla sorbet**, start by adding the water, coconut purée and vanilla bean paste to a medium saucepan. In a mixing bowl, add the sugar and sorbet stabiliser, then mix with a spoon. Make sure they are completely mixed, otherwise you will get lumps in your sorbet. Pour into the saucepan with the water and coconut purée. Bring to the boil, whisking continuously. Then whisk in the stabiliser mixture, pour into a Pacojet and allow to freeze. Once frozen, blitz in the Pacojet and put into a container. Place in the freezer until ready to plate. If you don't have a Pacojet, you can use an ice-cream churner, in which it would normally take up to 45 minutes.

Making the **mandarin jelly** begins with adding the mandarin purée, water and sugar to a small saucepan. Bring to the boil, then add the gelatine. Bake spray the takeaway-style containers to ensure the jelly will not stick when removing. You want 1 leaf of gelatine to every 100ml of liquid. When the gelatine has mixed in, pour the mixture into the containers, making sure there is 150ml in each one. Allow to set in the fridge. Once set, place some baking paper over the top, flip over the containers and place on a flat work surface. Lift off the containers and dice the jelly into cubes. Place the cubed jelly into a container, cover and store in the fridge until required.

To make the **coconut meringue**, preheat the oven to 90°C (70°C fan/Gas Mark ¼). Add the egg whites and vinegar to a stand mixer with a whisk attachment fitted. Whisk gradually until you have soft peaks. Then start adding the sugar, bit by bit, until all the sugar is fully dissolved into the egg whites. Continue whisking until you have stiff peaks and can no longer feel any grains of sugar in the mixture. Add the cornflour and whisk again. Line a baking tray with a silicone mat, pour on the meringue and smooth out with a palette knife until you have a thin, even layer. Sprinkle the coconut evenly across the meringue. Bake in the oven for 1¼ hours, or until the meringue is crisp on top but not colouring (thicker shapes may take slightly longer). Allow to cool completely on the tray, then peel off the shapes or snap the sheet into shards.

Assembly and Plating Up

With a small knife, gently remove the yuzu crème from the mould. Next, using the ring cutter, place the ring on top of the yuzu crème and push down. Using a spatula to help, take the crème and place on a plate. Push the metal ring down and the yuzu crème will come away from the ring cutter. You should have one nice circle of yuzu crème on the lefthand side of the plate. Repeat for the remaining plates, and top each circle with a few shards of coconut meringue. Place three pieces of cubed mandarin jelly around the right-hand side of the crème. Pipe three dots of mandarin purée on the plate in between the jelly. Add 1 teaspoon of spiced crumb on the righthand side of the plate, ready for the sorbet. Remove the sorbet from the freezer and spoon a quenelle onto the crumb. To complete plating, add some micro lemon balm, just a few pieces, to add a little extra sharpness.

> "This dessert was the first of many summer desserts I have put on the Angel's menu. The flavour of yuzu is tart and fragrant, closely resembling that of grapefruit, with overtones of mandarin orange. This complex, layered taste is exactly what makes yuzu so special. All the elements which are stored in the fridge or freezer until needed can be made a day in advance."

For the spiced biscuit crumb

165g unsalted butter, cubed, plus 75g for cooking
70g light soft brown sugar
55g caster sugar
21g runny blossom honey
1g ground cinnamon
1g mixed spice
1g table salt
2g bicarbonate of soda
170g plain flour
60g wholemeal flour

For the yuzu crème

135g yuzu purée
1.5g agar-agar (I use MSK)
½ bronze gelatine leaf
135g eggs
135g caster sugar
175g cold unsalted butter, cubed

For the mandarin gel

150ml tap water
50g caster sugar
350g mandarin purée (I use Boiron)
6g agar-agar

For the coconut and vanilla sorbet

55ml tap water
250g coconut purée (I use Boiron)
1 tsp vanilla bean paste
55g caster sugar
12g sorbet stabiliser

For the mandarin jelly

300g mandarin purée
50ml tap water
50g caster sugar
3 bronze gelatine leaves

For the coconut meringue

4 egg whites
1 tbsp white wine vinegar
240g caster sugar
2 tbsp cornflour
70g desiccated coconut

To garnish

Micro lemon balm

Equipment

Stand mixer with paddle and whisk attachments
Silicone mats
Food processor
20cm square mould (I use a De Buyer stainless-steel square pastry ring)
Blender
Piping bags
Pacojet or ice-cream churner
Baking spray
3 takeaway-style containers
3cm ring cutter (I use a Vogue round plain pastry cutter)
Chinois

Serves 6

'Peach Melba' | Smoked White Chocolate Ice Cream

To make the **vanilla olive oil**, whisk together the oil and vanilla seeds. Pour into a squeezy bottle and store at room temperature until needed – this can be kept for up to 4 weeks.

To make the **peach and raspberry centres**, add the raspberry and peach purées to a pan with 32g of caster sugar and the lemon juice, then bring to the boil. In a separate mixing bowl, add the 6g of caster sugar and pectin and mix together well so there are no lumps in the mixture. Add the pectin mixture to the purées and whisk the mixture for a further 2–3 minutes, making sure it comes to the boil again. Pour the liquid into a measuring jug and then into individual pomponette moulds. Allow to cool, then put in the freezer until needed.

For the **peach mousse**, place a medium pan on the heat and fill three-quarters of the way up with water. Place a mixing bowl on the top and add the white chocolate. Gently melt the white chocolate; you don't want it to burn. Once melted, remove from the heat. Soak the gelatine in ice-cold water until it's bloomed. In another pan, add the peach purée and bring to the boil. Then add the bloomed gelatine and whisk together. In a large mixing bowl, add the double cream and whisk to semi-peaks. Now add the peach purée and peach flavouring compound to the melted chocolate and, using a stick blender, blitz the purée, compound and chocolate together. Gently fold in the whipped cream and transfer the mixture to a piping bag. Half-fill the mini loaf moulds with the peach mousse and place the raspberry insert in the middle of each. Fill up the remaining moulds with the peach mousse and smooth off with a palette knife. Place a piece of baking paper on the top and put in the freezer to set.

To make the **white chocolate crémeux**, put the gelatine into a small bowl of ice-cold water and allow to bloom. Place the milk and cream into a pan and bring the boil. Take off the heat. Whisk the eggs together. Pour the milk and cream mixture over the eggs and whisk. Put this back on the heat and stir continually until the custard is cooked. Squeeze the water out of the gelatine and stir into the custard until completely dissolved. Set aside. Pour the custard over the white chocolate and, using a stick blender, blitz the mixture until very smooth. Pass through a fine sieve, place into a piping bag and reserve in the fridge until needed.

For the **smoked white chocolate ice cream**, place a medium pan on the heat and fill three-quarters of the way up with water. Place a mixing bowl on the top and add the white chocolate. Gently melt the white chocolate; you don't want it to burn. Once melted, remove from the heat. Cling film the mixing bowl with the chocolate and pierce a hole on the top. Fill a smoking gun with smoking chips. Turn it on and light the chips to start the smoking gun off. Allow the wood chips to smoulder for no more than 30 seconds before you apply the smoke to the food. All the heat is contained in the smoking chamber, so the smoke that's released is cool. Smoke the white chocolate for 15 minutes and let it take on the smoke without getting too intense, just sufficient enough to deliver a light smoky taste. Keep the chocolate covered with cling film until cooled. While the chocolate is cooling, set up an ice bath ready to cool the ice cream once it has cooked out. Whisk together the egg yolk and sugar in a bowl. In a medium pan, add the cream and milk and bring to the heat. Pour this liquid over the egg yolk and whisk in well. Pour the cream mixture over the chocolate and hand blend in. Once blended, put the mixture into a large pan and gently cook (using the temperature probe to keep a check on the temperature) to 82°C, stirring continuously until it coats the back of a spoon. Once up to temperature, pass through a chinois and leave to cool in a bowl over the ice bath. Pour into Pacojet containers and then blitz with the Pacojet or place in containers in a freezer if you do not have a Pacojet. The ice cream can be made up to a week in advance but must be kept frozen.

Begin making the **peach gel** by adding the water, sugar and peach purée to a saucepan. Bring to the boil, then add the agar-agar and peach flavouring compound. Continue boiling for another 2 minutes, then pour into a container. Cover and allow to set. Once firmly set, transfer it to a blender and blend until smooth. Pass the gel through a chinois and then put it into a piping bag. Keep the bag in the fridge until required. You can make the gel up to 3 days in advance if it is stored in the fridge.

With all the other elements prepared, now make the **white chocolate cocoa spray**. Put the chocolate and cocoa butter into a mixing bowl. Fill a medium pan three-quarters full with water and put it on a medium heat. Now place the mixing bowl on top, making sure it does not touch with the water. The chocolate should now gently melt. As it melts, add the white Power Flowers. Keep an eye on it, making sure the water does not boil. Using a stick blender, blend the chocolate and cocoa butter until completely mixed. Once mixed, set the bowl aside until required.

Put the white chocolate cocoa spray into the chocolate sprayer, making sure the correct attachment is on the sprayer. Turn out all the peach mousses onto a silicone mat, making sure there is space between them all. Spray the mousses evenly, taking care there is an even covering over each one. Once sprayed, place them back in the freezer to firm up and freeze again. Ideally, this needs to be done during the morning or a few hours before serving.

Assembly and Plating Up

Once the mousses have set, remove them from the moulds and allow time for them to defrost. I usually take mine out on the morning of the day I want to serve them.

With everything prepared, you are now ready to plate up and serve. Remove the peach gel and white chocolate crémeux from the fridge and the smoked white chocolate ice cream from the freezer.

Place a mousse on the lefthand side of each plate and add six dots of white chocolate crémeux on top. Add three peach balls between the dots to form a line. Add a fresh raspberry to each plate, and two dots of the peach gel. Finish with a rocher of smoked white chocolate ice cream along with a tempered chocolate disc, a few segments of frozen and dehydrated raspberries, and a drop of vanilla oil. Serve straight away.

For the vanilla olive oil

50ml olive oil
½ tsp vanilla seeds

For the peach and raspberry centres

90g raspberry purée
125g peach purée
32g plus 6g caster sugar
32ml fresh lemon juice
6g Pectin NH
15g liquid glucose

For the peach mousse

137g white chocolate
2g bronze gelatine leaves
70g peach purée
190ml double cream
3g peach flavouring compound

For the white chocolate crémeux

1 gelatine leaf
100ml full-fat milk
100g double cream
80g eggs
180g white chocolate

For the smoked white chocolate ice cream

220g white chocolate
50g egg yolk
50g caster sugar
125ml double cream
250ml full-fat milk

For the peach gel

150ml water
50g caster sugar
350g peach purée
6g agar-agar
2g peach flavouring compound

For the white chocolate cocoa spray

250g white chocolate
125g cocoa butter (I use Callebaut)
2 white Power Flowers

To garnish

18 yellow peach balls
6 raspberries
6 tempered chocolate discs (see page 280)
6 frozen raspberries
dehydrated raspberries

Equipment

Hand-held electric whisk
24 cavity pomponette mould (I use the Pavoni Formaflex 24 Cup Pomponette Mould)
Stick blender
9 cavity silicone mini loaf mould
Piping bags
Food smoking gun
Temperature probe
Chinois or fine sieve
Pacojet
Blender
Chocolate sprayer
Silicone mat
Squeezy bottle

"Peach Melba is an all-time classic desert. It was created by the renowned French chef Auguste Escoffier while he was head chef at London's Savoy Hotel. He first made it in the 1890s for Australian soprano Nellie Melba. The dish is a perfect example of a summertime dessert, combining the beautiful, sweet richness of in-season peaches with the sharpness of the raspberries. This well-balanced combination of fruits is finished off with a twist. At the Angel, I serve it with smoked white chocolate ice cream. I hope my take on a peach Melba would find approval from the great man himself."

Serves 4

Raspberry Cannelloni | Macdamia Nut | Tarragon Ice Cream

For the **raspberry gel**, add the water, sugar and raspberry purée to a saucepan. Bring to the boil, then add the agar-agar. Continue boiling for another 2 minutes, then pour into a container. Cover and allow to set. Once firmly set, transfer it to a blender and blend until smooth. Pass the gel through a chinois and then into a piping bag. Keep the bag in the fridge until required. You can make this in advance and it lasts up to 3 days.

I make the **tarragon ice cream** in a ThermoMixer. However, you can make this in a pan and gently cook out to 83°C. Add the milk, cream, sugar and egg yolk to the ThermoMixer, then blitz on full speed. Turn down to speed setting 3 and gently cook the ice cream, turning the temperature up slowly to 83°C. This usually takes 5-10 minutes. Once the custard is ready, add the tarragon and allow to infuse. Place the custard over a bowl of ice-cold water to cool. When cold, using a stick blender, gently blend the tarragon and vanilla pod into the ice cream and pass through a fine sieve. Put the ice cream into the freezer.

To prepare the **pâte de brick**, preheat the oven to 170°C (150°C fan/Gas Mark 3½). In a small saucepan, melt the butter and maple syrup together. Measure out the pastry sheets to 14 x 8cm and lay out on a lightly floured chopping board. Brush over the maple butter. Wrap the pastry around copper tubes and cook on a cooling rack in the oven for 8 minutes. When golden brown, allow to cool for a few minutes and take the pastry off the tubes. You need two pieces per serving.

Begin preparing the **raspberry mousse** by adding the egg whites to a stand mixer and whipping them to semi-peaks. While whisking, in a medium saucepan, add the sugar and water, then heat the liquid to 121°C. Once this temperature has been reached, pour it into the whipped eggs. Beat until cool. Gently melt the gelatine in a small saucepan and add to the raspberry purée. Fold the egg meringue through the purée. In another mixing bowl, whip the cream to soft peaks and gently fold into the purée. Mix thoroughly and add into two piping bags. Keep in the fridge until ready to pipe into the pastry tubes.

Now make the **set macadamia milk**. Preheat the oven to 170°C (150°C fan/Gas mark 3½). Place the macadamia nuts on a tray and roast in the oven for 6-7 minutes until golden brown. Add the milk to a medium pan and gently heat to a low simmer. Add the nuts and gently infuse. Allow the milk to cool. Using a stick blender, blend the nuts into the milk and pass through a fine sieve. Weigh the milk mixture out to 500ml, add the agar-agar and gently bring to the boil, then place into a container. Cover and allow to cool in the fridge. Add the set milk to a blender and blend until smooth. Pass through a fine sieve and spoon the mixture into a squeezy bottle. Put in the fridge until needed.

Assembly and Plating Up

Fill the pastry tubes with the raspberry mousse. Place two tubes on each plate and pipe both the set macadamia milk and raspberry gel over the top of each one. Add two dots of raspberry gel and one dot of macadamia milk on the right of the plate and garnish with three pieces of roasted macadamia. Add a quenelle of tarragon ice cream and then place a few pieces of tarragon shoot on the ice cream and on the pastry tubes. Add the edible flowers if using.

> " This dessert is special one for me. It is one I made with Hywel Jones at Lucknam Park and when I competed in *MasterChef: The Professionals* in 2016. The flavours are unique and somewhat different for a dessert. "

For the raspberry gel
150ml tap water
50g caster sugar
350g raspberry purée
6g agar-agar

For the tarragon ice cream
330ml full-fat milk
80ml double cream
100g caster sugar
100g egg yolk
¼ sprig of tarragon
1 vanilla pod, deseeded

For the pâte de brick
100g unsalted butter
50g maple syrup
Plain flour, for dusting
170g feuille de brick pastry sheets (I get mine from Wellocks)

For the raspberry mousse
2 egg whites
38g caster sugar
60ml tap water
5g bronze gelatine
250g raspberry purée
150ml double cream

For the set macadamia milk
100g macadamia nuts
600ml full-fat milk
7g agar-agar

To garnish
Roasted macadamia nuts, chopped
12 tarragon shoots
Edible flowers (optional)

Equipment
Blender
Chinois or fine sieve
Piping bags
ThermoMixer (optional)
Stick blender
8 10cm x 1.5cm copper tubes
Stand mixer with whisk attachment
Temperature probe
Squeezy bottle

Espresso Fudge Chocolate Domes

Serves 24

To make the **espresso fudge**, line the tin with greaseproof paper. Put all the ingredients into a large, heavy-bottomed pan and melt over a low heat until the sugar dissolves, then bring to the boil, stirring constantly. Boil for 20–30 minutes, still stirring constantly. The mixture will turn golden and needs to reach 112–116°C. This is the soft-ball stage (i.e. when a bit is dropped into cold water it will hold its shape). Once the fudge has reached this stage, remove from the heat and allow to cool for 5 minutes. Then beat using a hand-held electric whisk for 5–8 minutes. The fudge will thicken and lose its shine. Pour into the prepared tin and allow to cool and crystallise overnight. Do not put in the fridge.

For the **dark chocolate domes**, using a glass cloth, polish the chocolate moulds. Decorate the moulds using edible gold leaf and coloured cocoa butter. To line the moulds, temper the dark chocolate (see page 280). Fill the moulds completely with the chocolate, then tap the moulds firmly on the work surface to remove any air bubbles. Turn the moulds over, allowing the excess chocolate to run out into a large bowl. Save the excess chocolate to cap the domes the next day. While still inverted, tap the moulds gently to produce a thin shell, then scrape the top and sides of the moulds to remove excess chocolate. Place face down on a silicone sheet for 2 minutes to prevent any chocolate pooling in the base of the shells. Turn the chocolate-lined moulds right way up, then allow to crystallise in a cool, dry place overnight (not the fridge, which has too much moisture).

Assembly and Plating Up

Wearing disposable, powder-free gloves, roll teaspoon-sized pieces of fudge into balls and gently press into the set chocolate domes. To cap the chocolates, pour the reserved tempered chocolate over the fudge-filled moulds. Scrape off the excess chocolate. I use an angel feather transfer sheet at this stage to decorate the base of the domes, but this is completely optional.. Crystallise in a cool, dry place overnight before turning out the chocolates from the moulds. The chocolates can be stored in airtight containers in a cool place for up to 2 weeks.

For the espresso fudge

250g unsalted butter, softened
397ml condensed milk
125ml full-fat milk
50g golden syrup
750g granulated sugar
60ml (4 shots) espresso (I use the Angel's own blend)

For the dark chocolate domes

24-carat edible gold leaf
Coloured cocoa butter
500g good-quality dark chocolate (70% cocoa)

Equipment

30 x 20cm tin
Temperature probe
Hand-held electric whisk
Glass cloth
24 30mm semi-sphere polycarbonate chocolate moulds
Silicone sheet
Disposable gloves

> *"This petit four is one of our signature chocolates and is very unique to the Angel. I use the Angel's own coffee, which we blend ourselves. It is the perfect match for the sweet and delightful fudge."*

AUTUMN

September – November

Canapé

Artichoke | Lovage Tartlet

Amuse Bouche

Red Cabbage Gazpacho | Olive Oil

Starters

Jerusalem Artichoke Ravioli | Serrano Ham | Roasted Chicken Consommé

Mushroom Tartlets | Cep Custard | Wiltshire Truffle | Garlic Chive Cress

Mains

Roasted Pigeon | Glazed Salsify | Cocoa Nib | Hazelnut

Oat Crusted King Oyster | Mushrooms | Salt Baked Celeriac | Mushroom Foam

Dartmouth Pie

Pre-desserts

Cassis | Fermented Redcurrants | Lemon Thyme | Orange Blossom Sorbet | Crème Fraîche | Grapefruit | Cocoa Granola

Desserts

Roasted Coffee Parfait | Mascarpone | White Chocolate Granita

Blackberry Millefeuille | Crème Fraîche Sorbet

Nut Butter Brûlée | Nashi Pear | Pine Nut Ice Cream

Serves 4

Artichoke | Lovage Tartlet

First, prepare the **baby artichokes**. I cook them à la barigoule, as in the red mullet recipe on page 64. Fill a large pan with water and ice cubes, then squeeze the lemons in. Once all the juice has been squeezed from the lemons, add the skins to the water. Pull off the green outer leaves of the artichokes to expose the pale yellow ones insides. Using a knife, trim an inch off the top of the baby artichokes. Peel the outer layers away with a peeler. Now trim each artichoke into a circular shape. Ideally you want to take of the tough layer of the stem and the underside from the heart. Once you have a nice, round artichoke heart, put it in the water. Prepare all the baby artichokes this way. Then, using a serrated knife, trim off the tops of the artichokes and place back into the water. You are now ready to cook the baby artichokes. In a pan on medium heat, sweat off the mirepoix, coriander seeds, salt and pepper. Add the tap water, wine, thyme and rosemary and then the baby artichokes. Bring to a simmer, then place a sheet of baking paper over the top and gently cook on a low heat for 10–15 minutes.

To make the **Jerusalem artichoke purée**, half-fill a pan with water and lemon juice. Peel the artichokes, and place them in the water and lemon juice until ready to slice. Then thinly slice them, add to a clean pan and cover them with the milk and cream. Cook the artichokes on a low heat for 12–15 minutes until soft. Once soft, strain them in a colander. After the liquid has thoroughly drained away, put them in a blender and blend until smooth. Season the blended artichokes with salt and allow to cool completely. When cooled, pour the purée into a squeezy bottle and keep in the fridge until needed. The purée can be made up to 3 days advance as long as it is kept in the fridge.

Prepare the **lemon oil** by pouring the lemon juice and olive oil into a bowl. Whisk, then add the sugar and salt to taste. Put into a container for use later. This can be made in advance and will last up to 1 week in the fridge.

For the **artichoke salad**, scoop out the middle of the cooked artichokes (the heart), finely dice them and add to a mixing bowl. Dress the diced artichokes with lemon oil, then add the chopped herbs, salt, and pepper.

Begin making the **tart cases** by preheating the oven to 160°C (140°C fan/Gas Mark 3). Use the small ring cutter to cut out the spring roll pastry. For each tart case, you want to cut two pieces of pastry. Melt the butter in a pan on a low heat. Brush the melted butter over one side of each piece of the pastry. Then fold the pastry inside the tart case moulds. Place another circle of pastry inside and push down. Put the tart case moulds onto a baking tray and cook in the oven for 8 minutes until the pastry is golden brown. Remove them from the oven and take out of the moulds. Carefully dry the pastry on a J cloth and allow to cool.

The final element is the **lovage mayonnaise**. Put the egg yolks and lemon into a mixing bowl, then whisk together. Gradually add in the lovage oil and whisk until you have a thick mayonnaise. Season with salt, and a little more lemon juice to taste. Put the mayonnaise into a piping bag. This can be made up in advance and kept in the fridge for 1–2 weeks.

Assembly and Plating Up

Pipe the Jerusalem artichoke purée onto the bottom of each tart case. Put the artichoke salad on top of the purée. Now add five dots of the lovage mayonnaise and finish off with the bronze fennel and sea purslane flowers.

For the baby artichokes

Juice of 3 unwaxed lemons

4 baby artichokes (300–350g each)

125ml extra virgin olive oil

1 carrot, peeled and roughly chopped

1 celery stick, roughly chopped

1 tsp coriander seeds

1 tsp Maldon Sea salt

500ml tap water

250ml dry white wine

4 sprigs of thyme

4 sprigs of rosemary

Pepper

For the Jerusalem artichoke purée

Juice of 1 lemon

500g Jerusalem artichokes

150ml full-fat milk

150ml double cream

Maldon sea salt

For the lemon oil

25ml lemon juice

75ml olive oil

50g caster sugar

Salt, to taste

For the artichoke salad

350g cooked baby artichokes (see above)

Lemon oil (see above)

20g chopped chives

20g chopped dill

Salt and pepper, to taste

For the tart cases

160g spring roll pastry (25 sheets per packet)

40g unsalted butter

For the lovage mayonnaise

2 egg yolks

12ml lemon juice, plus extra to taste

350ml lovage oil (see page 278)

Salt, to taste

To garnish

Bronze fennel leaves

12 purslane flowers

Equipment

5cm ring cutter

4 tart cases (I use 7.5cm mini fluted tart case moulds)

Pastry brush

Piping bags

Blender

Squeezy bottle

" Lovage is a unique flavour: it tastes like celery but is a bit sweeter with a stronger flavour. It has hints of anise and parsley and goes well with the variations of artichoke and lemon. "

Serves 4

Red Cabbage Gazpacho | Olive Oil

To make the **gazpacho**, cut the cabbage into quarters and remove the heart. Now cut the cabbage into thick slices and put them into a mixing bowl. Add the apple, cucumber and olive oil. Make sure your juicer is set up. Now pass the mixture through the juicer until the cabbage, apple and cucumber are completely juiced. Put the juice into a bowl, then add the verjus. Use a stick blender to mix all the ingredients together. Finally, add the lemon juice, salt, sugar, pre hy and crème fraîche and taste. Add a little more seasoning if you are not completely happy with the balance of flavours. Pass the gazpacho through a double muslin cloth into another bowl. Cover with cling film and place in the fridge until needed. I make this on the day I want to use it.

Assembly and Plating Up

Make sure the dishes you use for serving are chilled and the gazpacho is cold before plating up. Pour the red cabbage gazpacho into a small dish and add a few drops of olive oil and your chosen herb oil to finish.

> " Joyce Molyneux made a fantastic recipe of red cabbage that was served in the Carved Angel alongside her game dishes. I wanted to showcase her recipe in a cold gazpacho with a twist. "

For the red cabbage gazpacho

1 red cabbage (350–400g)
1 Granny Smith apple, cored and chopped
1 cucumber, peeled and chopped
15ml olive oil, plus extra to serve
50g verjus (I use Minus8)
Lemon juice, to taste
Caster sugar, to taste
7g pre hy (see page 46)
20g crème fraîche
Maldon sea salt, to taste

Equipment

Juicer
Stick blender
Muslin cloth

To garnish

Olive oil
Herb oil (see page 278)

Jerusalem Artichoke Ravioli | Serrano Ham | Roasted Chicken Consommé

Serves 6

Begin by making the **double chicken stock**. Preheat the oven to 180°C (160°C fan/Gas Mark 4). Place the chicken wings on a large oven tray and roast in the oven for about 30 minutes until golden brown. Remove from the oven, drain off the fat, then set aside. While the wings are cooking, in a large saucepan on a medium heat, add the shallots, carrots, mushrooms, leeks, celery, rosemary and thyme. Allow a couple of minutes for them to start roasting off, then add the garlic. You want the vegetables to be dark in colour. Deglaze the pan with the vinegar and wine. for about a minute, then add the white soy sauce. Reduce the heat to low and simmer until most of the liquid has evaporated. Now add the roasted wings and the chicken stock. Continue simmering gently for 2 hours, skimming the liquid when necessary. After 2 hours, skim once more, remove from the heat and set aside to let the contents infuse for 1 hour. Now strain the liquid through muslin into a bowl, cover with cling film, then put in the fridge to set. Once chilled, there will be a layer of fat on top. Scrape this off, cover again with cling film and then place the remaining clear liquid back into the fridge until required.

For the **roasted chicken consommé**, add the double chicken stock, egg whites and minced chicken breast to a large saucepan and whisk. Add the diced vegetables and a good pinch of table salt. Bring the stock to the boil. Keep stirring continuously and reduce to a simmer. Stop stirring and watch for the mixture to coagulate and form a raft on top of the stock. A small hole will start to form in the centre. Make it bigger with a spoon. Continue to simmer gently for 45 minutes. Turn the heat off and let it stand for a few minutes. Using a ladle, spoon out the consommé and pass through a sieve lined with a muslin cloth. Season and leave to cool. Place in the fridge ready to heat when needed.

To make the **pasta**, start by placing the eggs, egg yolks and a drizzle of olive oil into a mixing bowl. Whisk all the ingredients together and add a pinch of salt. Pour this mixture into a measuring jug and leave to one side. Set up a food processor, I usually use a robot-coupe in the restaurant but a food processor or a stick blender with all attachments will work. Put the flour into the food processor with a quarter of your egg mixture. Blitz the dough to large crumbs: they should come together to form a dough when squeezed. If it feels too dry, gradually add more egg mixture until it comes together. Empty the dough onto a floured surface and begin to knead the dough together for 2–3 minutes until it has a nice and smooth finish. Wrap the dough in cling film and put into the fridge to rest for at least 45 minutes. Bring the pasta dough out of the fridge and cut in half. Set up a pasta machine and feed the dough through the widest setting. Repeat this process with the dough, narrowing the rollers one notch at a time until you have a smooth sheet of pasta. On the lowest setting, feed the sheet through twice until it's semi-transparent. Using a 5cm ring cutter, cut out the pasta sheets and place them to a tray. Keep covered until needed.

Next, prepare the **artichoke filling**. Preheat the oven to 180°C (160°C fan/Gas Mark 4). In a roasting tray, add the Jerusalem artichokes, the oil and a pinch of salt and pepper. Mix well, then roast in the oven for about 40 minutes. They may take a bit longer depending upon the size of the artichokes. You are looking for them to be soft in the middle. Once cooked, remove from the oven and leave to cool slightly for 5–10 minutes. Using a small, serrated vegetable knife, cut the artichokes in half vertically, then scoop out the insides with a teaspoon and keep to one side.

Now make the **Mornay cheese sauce**. Bring the milk to the boil in a small saucepan. Place another pan on the heat and melt the butter. Add the flour and continue whisking until a paste forms. Continue cooking for a further 2–3 minutes. Add the milk to the roux, stirring as you go, until you get a smooth sauce. Cook the sauce for 10 minutes on a low heat, stirring continuously until the sauce has thickened. Add both the Parmesan and Cheddar. Cook for a further 5 minutes. Season the sauce with salt and pepper. Add some cheese sauce to the artichoke filling and mix well.

In a small pan, add the artichoke filling and roughly an equal amount of Mornay sauce. Over a medium-low heat, combine well, season with salt and pepper, then add the chopped chives. Once you are happy with the seasoning, transfer to a piping bag and store in the fridge. You can make the sauce up to 3 days in advance as long as it is stored in the fridge.

The final task is to make the ravioli. Start by brushing the egg wash over one side of the pasta discs. Place a 25g ball of artichoke mixture into the centre of half the discs. Now cover them all with the remaining discs. Make sure the filling is not spilling out and there is a rim around each ravioli. Press the two sheets together to seal in the filling, making sure no air is trapped inside. With the pastry cutter, trim off any excess dough.

Assembly and Plating Up

To begin, make sure to have your consommé hot and ready. Half-fill a large saucepan with water and add a couple of pinches of salt. Bring it to the boil, then carefully add the ravioli. While the ravioli is cooking, place your Serrano ham under a low grill to gently caramelise. Cook the ravioli for 4 minutes and then remove them from the water. Place onto a plate or tray lined with kitchen paper or J cloth to absorb any excess water. Place one ravioli into the centre of each bowl, add the crispy Serrano ham and the hazelnuts. Finish the ravioli with the consommé and a sprinkling of garlic shoots.

" This ravioli goes really well with the roasted chicken consommé, a beautiful clear stock. It is elegantly served with hazelnuts and Serrano ham to complete a perfectly balanced dish. "

For the artichoke filling

6 medium Jerusalem artichokes, cleaned
1 tbsp rapeseed oil
10g chives, finely chopped
Table salt and black pepper, to taste

For the Mornay cheese sauce

250ml full-fat milk
20g unsalted butter
25g plain flour
50g Parmesan, grated
50g Cheddar, grated
Salt and pepper

To garnish

6 slices of Serrano ham
24 hazelnuts
Micro garlic chives

For the double chicken stock

4kg chicken wings, cut into small pieces
2 shallots, sliced
2 large carrots, peeled and diced
150g button mushrooms, sliced
2 leeks, sliced
2 celery sticks, sliced
2 sprigs of rosemary
2 sprigs of thyme
3 garlic cloves, crushed
50ml sherry vinegar
200ml white wine
75ml white soy sauce
2.5 litres chicken stock (see page 274)

For the roasted chicken consommé

750ml double chicken stock (see above)
3 egg whites
1 chicken breast, minced
½ head of celery, diced
1 carrot, peeled and diced
½ shallot, diced
Table salt, to taste

For the pasta

3 medium eggs
2 medium egg yolks
Extra virgin olive oil
280g 00 flour, plus extra for dusting
Table salt
1 medium egg, for egg wash

Equipment

Muslin cloth
Sieve
Food processor or stick blender
Pasta machine
5cm ring cutter
Piping bag

Serves 6

Mushroom Tartlets | Cep Custard | Wiltshire Truffle | Garlic Chive Cress

First, make the **mushroom ketchup**. Chop the chestnut mushrooms as finely as possible. Bring a large saucepan to a medium heat, pour in the oil, then add the shallot. Sweat down until the shallot is translucent. This will only take a couple of minutes. Now add the mushrooms. Stir with a wooden spoon so the shallot does not stick to the bottom of the pan. Add a pinch of salt, then turn up the heat to high, stirring every few minutes, until the mushrooms have released all of their moisture and are a dark brown colour. Next, add the sugar and sherry vinegar. Stir thoroughly and cook out the vinegar. It will take about 5 minutes for the mixture to thicken and become glossy. At this point, add the cream and reduce by half. If the cream starts boiling, reduce the heat. Once you have a thick mixture, remove from the heat and transfer to a blender. Blend on high, slowly adding the chilled butter. Add the water as required so the mixture does not become too thick. You are looking for a smooth, glossy consistency. Pass through a chinois or fine sieve, then season with salt to taste. The ketchup can be stored in the fridge for 3 days.

For the **mushroom velouté**, heat the oil in a large pan. Add the mixed mushrooms and shallot and gently fry until golden brown, allowing the moisture from the mushrooms to cook out. Add the butter. Then add the garlic and thyme. Add the dried mushrooms, followed by the sherry vinegar, and deglaze the pan. Once deglazed, add the chicken stock and slightly reduce. Finish the velouté by adding the double cream, bringing to the boil and then transferring to a blender. Blend the mushroom velouté until smooth and pass through a fine sieve. Season with salt and pepper, making sure the consistency is not too thick. Add a little hot water and mix in well if it does thicken too much. Place over a bowl of ice to cool down. Keep in the fridge until required. It will keep well for up to 3 days.

Prepare the **mushroom set** by pouring 600ml of the mushroom velouté into a small pan. Add the kappa carrageenan and gently bring to the boil. Once boiling, pour into the half-sphere moulds and allow to cool. Keep in the fridge until needed. You can make this up to 3 days in advance as long as it is kept in the fridge. Make sure that when you are ready to plate up, it has been removed from the fridge and come up to room temperature.

Make the **mushroom essence** a day before serving the dish. Put in the mushrooms in a food processor and blend until you have fine duxelles. Remove and place in a pan, cover with the water and bring to a boil. Add in the garlic, rosemary and thyme. Reduce the heat to a light simmer and then cook for a further 30 minutes. Allow time to cool, before storing overnight in the fridge. During the following day, bring the mushroom essence back up to the boil and then pass through a fine sieve with a double layer of muslin cloth to remove all impurities. Once strained, set aside until required.

Next, prepare the **cep stock**. Bring a pan up to a medium heat. Add the rapeseed oil, leek, carrot, celery and shallots. Sweat down until translucent, making sure they do not colour. Add the mushroom essence and bring to the boil. Then add the dried ceps and sherry vinegar. Grate 5–10g truffle into the stock and add the bay leaves and dried morels. Finish the stock with sugar and salt to taste. Bring the stock to a light simmer for 1 hour and then sit for 30 minutes. Pass through a fine sieve with double layer of muslin.

To make the **cep jelly**, measure out 600ml of the cep stock and pour into a pan. Add the vegetable gel and gently bring to the boil. Skim off any bubbles from the mixture and use a flat metal tray to set the jelly. With a ring cutter, cut out the jelly and place twelve jelly pieces into a container. Cover with a lid or cling film and keep these and the remaining jelly in the fridge until needed. You can make this element up to 3 days in advance.

To make the **tartlet cases**, preheat the oven to 180°C (160°C fan/Gas Mark 4). Unroll the pastry and cut it into 7cm squares. Lightly spray the fluted tart cases with baking spray and push a square of pastry into each one. Do not push too hard, as this could make the pastry stick. You then want to place an additional tart case on top of each pastry, so that it is between two tart cases. Put the tart cases onto a baking tray, then place another baking tray on top of the tart cases. Weigh the cases down with a couple of heavy pots or pans on top. Bake in the oven for 14 minutes. Remove the top baking tray from the tart cases and you will be able to see the overlapping pastry and judge if they are cooked by their colouring. They should have a nice, golden brown colour, not too pale. If they need longer, continue cooking until they have achieved the right colour. Once cooked, remove from the oven and leave to cool completely for about 30 minutes.

The final element to is the **pickled shimeji mushrooms**. First, cut off most of the stem so they measure 1cm from the head of the mushroom. Put them into a mixing bowl. Place a frying pan on a medium heat, add the shallot and start to sweat it. When it becomes translucent and has not started to colour, add the mushrooms. Once they start to colour a little, add the lemon juice and olive oil. Season with salt and remove the pan from the heat. Keep the mushrooms in the warm pan, off the heat, until needed for plating up.

Assembly and Plating Up

Place a cep jelly on the bottom of each plate. Fill each tart case with mushroom velouté, followed by the mushroom set and a piece of cep jelly. Add dots of mushroom ketchup around the tart. Finish off with the pickled shimeji mushrooms and morels. A generous amount of shaved Wiltshire truffle along with a sprinkling of the two types of cress complete the dish and you are ready to serve.

> *"These mushroom tarts showcase a rich mushroom flavour throughout the dish. It's one of my favourites, using a variety of mushrooms and Wiltshire truffle."*

For the mushroom ketchup

250g chestnut mushrooms
50g rapeseed oil
1 shallot, finely sliced lengthways
25g soft light brown sugar
25ml sherry vinegar
125ml double cream
50g cold unsalted butter, cubed
100ml tap water
Maldon sea salt, to taste

For the mushroom velouté

50g rapeseed oil
500g mixed wild mushrooms, sliced
1 banana shallot, brunoised or finely diced
50g unsalted butter
2 garlic cloves, sliced
2 sprigs of thyme
20g dried morels
20g dried ceps
25ml sherry vinegar
300ml chicken stock (see page 274)
100ml double cream
Salt and black pepper, to taste

For the mushroom set

600ml mushroom velouté (see above)
2.7g kappa carrageenan

For the mushroom essence

1.5kg button mushrooms
1 garlic clove, crushed
2 sprigs of rosemary
2 sprigs of thyme
750ml tap water

For the cep stock

1 tbsp rapeseed oil
1 leek, diced
1 carrot, peeled and diced
2 celery sticks, diced
2 shallots, finely sliced
Mushroom essence (see above)
25g dried ceps
20ml sherry vinegar
Wiltshire truffle, plus extra to garnish
2 bay leaves
25g dried morels
Sugar and salt, to taste

For the cep jelly

600ml cep stock (see above)
14g vegetable gel (I use MSK)

For the tartlet cases

600g rolled French puff pastry (I use Maître André)

For the pickled shimeji mushrooms

200g punnet of shimeji mushrooms
1 banana shallot, brunoised or finely diced
10ml lemon juice
50ml olive oil
Maldon sea salt, to taste

To garnish

24 dried morels
Garlic chive cress
Celery cress

Equipment

Blender
Chinois or fine sieve
6 4cm x 2cm half-sphere moulds
Muslin cloth
Food processor
5cm ring cutter
12 fluted tart cases
Baking spray

Serves 4

Roasted Pigeon | Glazed Salsify | Cocoa Nib | Hazelnut

Start with the **pickled petit onions**. Soak the onions in hot water before you prep them, as this will make them easier to peel. Using a paring or turning knife, slice a very thin piece of the root off and peel the skin off. Work your way through the onions and peel them all. Once they are all peeled, place a pan of lightly salted water on a high heat and bring to the boil. While you wait for the water to boil, in another saucepan, add the water, vinegar, sugar, bay leaf, star anise, fennel and coriander seeds and bring to the boil, whisking it every couple of minutes so that the sugar dissolves. When it has boiled, turn down the heat to low to keep warm until you need it. After the other pan of water has come to the boil, drop the heat a little to a simmer and blanch the petit onions in it. Cook them for 2–5 minutes until softened, then remove from the water. Place the cooked onions into a container, cover with the warm pickle liquor, then cover with cling film. Leave to cool for 2–3 hours. Once cooled to room temperature, vacuum seal or place them into a jar, ensuring they are all submerged in the liquor. They will keep in the fridge for 2 weeks.

To prep the **squab pigeons**, preheat the oven to 180°C (160°C fan/Gas Mark 4). Heat a frying pan with the oil. Clean and truss the squab pigeons, season with salt and pepper and brown the birds in the hot pan until golden on all sides. Add the butter to the pan and baste the birds. Then put the thyme and rosemary into the pigeon cavities. Place the pigeons in the oven and cook 4–5 minutes. Once cooked, remove from the oven and allow to rest on a cooling rack. To finish the pigeons, carefully carve the breasts off the carcasses and trim away any excess fat. Leave the breasts on a flat oven tray ready to warm up before serving. Keep a carcass, as it will be used to make the sauce.

For the **braised pigeon filling**, put the duck fat into a pan. Gently bring to the heat and add the garlic, thyme and rosemary. Now add the pigeon legs and cook slowly on a low heat for at least 1 hour. You want the meat to gently fall off the bone. When the pigeon legs are cooked, allow them to cool in the duck fat. Once they have cooled, pick the meat off the legs and place into a mixing bowl. Keep this to one side until the ox cheek has been cooked.

Preheat the oven to 150°C (130°C fan/Gas Mark 2). In a separate ovenproof pan, heat the rapeseed oil and place in the ox cheek. Colour the cheek until golden brown and evenly coloured all over. Add the celery, carrot, shallot and bay leaves. Roast off the vegetables until they have a nice golden brown colouring. Then pour in the red wine and reduce the liquid by half. Once reduced, add both stocks and bring to the boil. Once boiling, remove from the heat, then put into the oven and cook the ox cheek for 3–4 hours until very tender and soft. Allow the ox cheek to cool in the liquor. When the cheek is cold, drain off the liquid and place the cheek into the same mixing bowl as the cooked pigeon legs. Mix both meats together with a spoon and add a little of the drained liquor to the picked meats. Season the mixture. This will be reheated later to fill the tart cases.

Next, move on to the **cocoa oats**. Preheat the oven to 160°C (140°C fan/Gas Mark 3). On a baking tray, add all the ingredients and mix very well with your hands. Squeeze the oats together and make sure everything is well incorporated. Bake in the oven for 25–30 minutes. Take the tray out every 5 minutes and mix quickly with a spoon. Once they are cooked and golden brown, remove from the oven, allow to cool, then transfer to a container with a lid. Store at room temperature until required. They will keep for 2 days.

For the **pigeon sauce**, preheat the oven to 180°C (160°C fan/Gas Mark 4). Roast the chopped pigeon wings until a nice golden brown. This usually takes 20–25 minutes. Add the pigeon carcass, juniper berries and star anise to the red wine jus in a saucepan. Bring the sauce to a simmer, add the thyme and allow to infuse for an hour or so. Pass through a fine sieve and leave to warm up later when plating.

For the **tart cases**, preheat the oven to 160°C (140°C fan/Gas Mark 3). Using the small ring cutter, cut out the spring roll pastry. For every tart case you need two sheets of pastry. Put the butter into a pan and place on a low heat to gently melt. Brush the melted butter over the pastry and then gently fold a sheet of pastry inside each tart case mould. Place another sheet inside and push down. Put the tart cases on a baking tray and cook in the oven for 8 minutes. The tart cases should be golden brown. Once cooked, remove from the oven and dry the tart cases on a J cloth.

Next, make the **chocolate and hazelnut emulsion**. Preheat the oven to 180°C (160°C fan/Gas Mark 4). Scatter the hazelnuts over a roasting tray and roast in the oven for around 8–12 minutes until a lovely golden caramel colour. In a medium saucepan on a low–medium heat, warm the cream, chocolate, cocoa nibs and coconut milk. Stir with a silicone spatula, so that the chocolate melts and combines. Once the hazelnuts are roasted, add them to the saucepan and continue to simmer for 20–30 minutes until the liquid becomes dark. Be careful not to have the heat too high, or it will split. Transfer to a blender and blend on maximum speed for 5 minutes. You may wish to add some water while blending to let the emulsion down, if too thick. The finished product should be not too thick and run off a spoon steadily. Season with salt, lemon juice and sugar until you are happy with the finished product. This can be kept vacuum sealed, or in a container with cling film pushed over the surface to prevent a skin forming. It will keep in the fridge for up to 2 days.

Now get the **glazed salsify** ready. To begin, half-fill a large pan with ice and water, then slice and squeeze the lemon into the iced water. Now you want to wash the salsify, to ensure there is no loose dirt on the skin. Once washed, gently peel the salsify, turning between each cut so you keep the cylindrical shape and don't create any flat edges. Put each piece of peeled salsify into the iced water to prevent it from turning brown. Once the salsify are all peeled, cut them down into 8cm-long portions. Place your salsify into vacuum pack bags, along with the coconut milk and coffee beans. Vacuum seal the bags and then steam for 8–15 minutes. The length of cooking time will depend upon the thickness of the salsify pieces. You want them to be soft, but not so overcooked that they break. Once they begin to feel soft in the centre, remove from the steamer and leave to cool in the bag. If you are worried they may be slightly too cooked, quickly cool them over a bowl of ice. If you do not have a steamer, you can instead poach the bag in simmering water. Once cooked, they need to be kept in the bag until required. Once cool, place the bags in the fridge. They will keep for 2 days.

To **garnish**, prepare the cavolo nero leaves. First, make sure they are clean by washing them under cold tap water and then patting dry with kitchen paper. Simply strip each leaf from the stem with a knife. Store the leaves in a lidded container or one covered with cling film until required.

Assembly and Plating Up

First, prepare the emulsion to cook the cavolo leaves. Place a small pan on a medium heat, then add the butter, water and salt. Cook until the butter has melted and the water is simmering. Using either a stick bender or a whisk, mix thoroughly together and emulsify. Reduce the heat to low so the emulsion remains warm until needed.

In a frying pan on a high heat, heat some oil and then put in the salsify. Season with a couple pinches of table salt and then evenly colour the salsify all over. Keep the pan and salsify moving so that it doesn't burn. Once you have a nice colour, add the butter and a splash of water to the pan. Shake the pan to create an emulsion and glaze the salsify. Remove from the pan and place onto the plates straight away. If you need to, cook in the oven at 180°C (160°C fan/Gas Mark 4) for 3 minutes to bring back up to temperature before plating. I use one or two salsify sticks per portion.

Gently heat the chocolate and hazelnut emulsion in a small saucepan on a low-medium heat, taking care not to split with too much heat. Add some water if needed to bring to the right consistency; it should run off a spoon smoothly but still be thick enough to leave a coat. Spoon some onto the centre of each plate and create a circle with the back of the spoon.

Take out 5-10 pickled petit onions and slice them in half. Cook them in a preheated oven at 180°C (160°C fan/Gas Mark 4) for 1 minute and dress lightly with some olive oil. If you have a blowtorch, then torch the pickled onions for some colour after cooking. Arrange a few petit onion halves per plate on top of the emulsion.

Just before plating, bring the small pan of butter/water emulsion back to a simmer and cook the cavolo leaves in it for 1-2 minutes. Once cooked, remove the leaves from the emulsion, drain them on kitchen paper and place on the plates.

Warm the braised pigeon filling in a pan and spoon into the cooked tart cases. Finish the tart cases off with a sprinkling of the cocoa oats over the top. Warm the pigeon breasts under the salamander or grill and place on top of the hazelnut and chocolate emulsion. Top one of the breasts per plate with more of the cocoa oats. Finish the dish with the pigeon sauce when served.

For the pickled petit onions

250g petit silverskin onions

100ml tap water

100ml white wine vinegar

100g caster sugar

1 bay leaf

1 star anise

1 tbsp fennel seeds

1 tbsp coriander seeds

Salt

For the squab pigeons

1 tbsp rapeseed oil

4 whole squab pigeons

Knob of butter

2 sprigs thyme

2 sprigs rosemary

Salt and pepper, to taste

For the braised pigeon filling

200g duck fat

3 garlic cloves, crushed

2 sprigs of thyme

2 sprigs of rosemary

8 pigeon legs, from the squab (see above)

1 tsp rapeseed oil

1 ox cheek, skinned

1 celery stick, finely diced

1 large carrot, finely diced

1 banana shallot, finely diced

2 bay leaves

100ml red wine

300ml veal stock (see page 275)

150ml chicken stock (see page 274)

For the cocoa oats

50g oats

10g maple syrup

1 tbsp cocoa powder

3g table salt

15g extra virgin olive oil

For the pigeon sauce

8 pigeon wings, from the squab (see above), chopped into small pieces

1 pigeon carcass, cooked

3 juniper berries

2 star anise

700ml red wine jus (see page 279)

2 sprigs of thyme

For the tart cases

160g spring roll pastry (25 sheets per packet)

40g unsalted butter

For the chocolate and hazelnut emulsion

45g hazelnuts

100ml double cream

50g dark chocolate (70% cocoa)

7g cocoa nibs

100ml coconut milk

Lemon juice, to taste

Salt and sugar, to taste

For the glazed salsify

1 unwaxed lemon

200g raw salsify (we get ours from Wellocks)

50g coconut milk

8g coffee beans (I use the Angel's own blend)

1 tbsp rapeseed oil

50g unsalted butter

Table salt, to taste

To garnish

6 small cavolo nero leaves

95g unsalted butter

500ml water

Table salt

Olive oil

Equipment

Fine sieve

3cm ring cutter

4 fluted tart cases

Blender

Vacuum pack bags

Steamer

Blowtorch (optional)

"This pigeon recipe showcases the bird in two different ways. You have the perfect gamey tender breast, along with a deep-filled fluted pigeon tart. It all works extremely well with the chocolate and hazelnut emulsion."

Serves 6

Oat Crusted King Oyster Mushrooms | Salt Baked Celeriac | Mushroom Foam

To make the **salt-baked celeriac fondants**, preheat the oven to 200°C (180°C fan/Gas Mark 6). In a large mixing bowl, add the flour, salt, rosemary and egg whites. Mix well with your hands, combining the egg whites through with your fingers. Once well mixed, slowly add the tepid water (it makes it easier to work the ingredients than cold water) until you have a dough. The dough should be firm but workable. Once you are happy with the consistency of the dough, remove it from the bowl and transfer to a lightly floured surface. Roll the dough out to about 1cm thick and place the celeriac in the centre. Wrap the celeriac in the dough, peel off any excess and roll with your hands into a ball, ensuring you have an even thickness all the way around. Any leftover salt bake dough can be wrapped tightly in cling film (or vacuum packed), then kept for 3 days in the fridge. You can salt-bake almost any vegetable you like. Place the balls onto an oven tray and bake for 45 minutes–1¼ hours. After 45 minutes, check the celeriac by poking with a wooden skewer or temperature probe. Once the skewer slides easily through, the celeriac is cooked. If you use a probe, you are looking for the centre to reach 64°C. Remove from the oven and leave to cool for 2–3 hours until room temperature. Once cooled, remove the celeriac from the salt-bake shell and cut into 1.5cm-thick slices. Using a ring cutter, cut a round from each strip. With a large celeriac, you may be able to get 2–3 rounds from one strip. Transfer your celeriac fondants to a tub, cover and refrigerate. These will keep well for 3 days. Save the excess celeriac trim to make the celeriac dice.

To make the **mushroom ketchup**, finely chop the chestnut mushrooms; the finer you can chop them, the faster they will cook down. Bring a large saucepan to a medium heat, pour in the oil, then add the shallot. Sweat down until the shallot becomes translucent and does not colour. This will only take a couple of minutes. Stir with a wooden spoon so the shallot does not stick to the bottom of the pan and burn. Now add the chopped mushrooms. Add a pinch of salt, then turn up the heat to high. Cook the mixture on a high heat, stirring every few minutes, until the mushrooms have released all of their moisture and are a dark brown colour. Next, add the sugar and sherry vinegar. Stir thoroughly and cook out the vinegar. It will take about 5 minutes for the mixture to thicken and become glossy. At this point, add the cream and reduce by half. If the cream starts boiling, reduce the heat. Once you have a thick mixture, remove from the heat and transfer to a blender. Blend on high, slowly adding the chilled butter. Add a little water as required so the mixture does not become too thick. You are looking to achieve a smooth glossy consistency. Pass through a chinois or fine sieve, then season with salt to taste. The ketchup can be stored in the fridge for 3 days.

Prepare the **sherry vinegar gel** by putting the sherry vinegar and sugar into a medium saucepan. Whisk constantly and bring to the boil. Then continue to whisk while you add the agar-agar. Whisk for a further 2 minutes at boiling point. Remove from the heat and pour into a container. The mixture will set at room temperature, place in the fridge to set more quickly. The larger the surface area of the container you use, the faster it will set. Once completely set, mix in a blender on high until smooth. Pass through a chinois and put in a piping bag or squeezy bottle. The gel can be kept in the fridge for up to a week.

For the **mushroom cream**, pour the rapeseed oil into a large saucepan. Bring up to a medium-high heat. Then put add the mushrooms and sweat them down with a pinch of sea salt. Cook the moisture out and continue to cook and stir until golden brown. Add half the butter, the rosemary, thyme and garlic cloves. Cook for a few more minutes until the mushrooms are crispy and still golden. Now drain any excess liquid from the mushrooms using a colander and put them into another pan. Add enough tap water to cover them. Bring to the boil and remove from the heat. Decant into a container, cover with cling film (or a lid) and refrigerate overnight. The following day, drain the mushrooms through a colander. This time, discard the mushrooms but keep the liquid. Put the liquid into a saucepan, bring to the boil and reduce by half. Add in the remaining 50g butter along with the double cream. Whisk thoroughly and season to taste with a pinch or two of salt. This cream can be kept in the fridge for 3 days.

To make the **celeriac 'pickle' dice**, remove all the skin from the celeriac left over from making the fondants. Cut into strips and then into 2–3mm pieces. If there is not sufficient celeriac left after making the fondants, you can make the dice from scratch. First, peel and dice a raw celeriac, then cook in boiling salted water for 2–3 minutes until soft (but not overcooked!). Using a sieve, remove from the pan and run under cold water to cool quickly. Now empty onto kitchen paper to dry. Once dried, put the celeriac into a bowl with the chives. Pour over the lemon juice, olive oil and truffle oil. Mix well and taste. Season to your liking and add a little more oil or lemon juice if needed. Transfer to a storage container and refrigerate until required. It will keep for up to 3 days in the fridge.

Begin making the **oat-crusted pastry** by putting the oats and kataifi pastry into a food processor (or blender). Now, blitz in 3–5-second bursts until you have crumbs, but not powder. The mixture should be stored in a covered container, in the fridge, until required. It will keep well for up to a week.

For the **king oyster mushrooms**, cut them through the middle into equal halves (you should have 18 halves). You are going to coat 12 halves of the mushrooms in the oat-crusted pastry, with the other six halves kept back for frying. To coat the mushrooms, put the flour, eggs and oat-crusted pastry in separate bowls. First, coat half of the mushrooms in the flour, then in the egg and finally the oat-crusted pastry. Set aside until required. With the remaining king oyster halves, using a pointed knife, score a diamond pattern on the flat sides. To achieve this, make diagonal cuts, not too deep, around the mushrooms until you have a diamond pattern. Place a frying pan on the heat, then add the rapeseed oil. Add the scored king oyster mushrooms and rosemary and fry for about 2 minutes until the mushrooms develop a good colour and crust. You may wish to push down on the mushrooms with a palette knife or spoon to make sure they colour evenly and do not curl up. Flip the mushrooms when done and colour on the other side. Remove the mushrooms from the pan and keep warm.

Next, deep-fry the coated king oyster mushrooms. Set a deep-fat fryer to 190°C. It should remain at this temperature throughout the frying process. With your oil at 190°C, carefully add the coated mushrooms and fry for about 1½ minutes. When the mushrooms start to float, turn them over and continue frying for another 1½ minutes. Remove from the fryer and drain on kitchen paper or a J cloth.

Assembly and Plating Up
First, spoon some mushroom ketchup onto each plate. Place a crispy king oyster piece on top, flat side facing up. On the flat surface, place some dots of sherry vinegar gel and lovage mayonnaise. Place another half of crispy king oyster opposite with some grated black truffle on top. Place the pan-fried king oyster between the other two, and shave truffle over the top using a Microplane. In the final corner of the plate, place a celeriac fondant with the celeriac 'pickle' dice on top.

Sprinkle the celeriac 'pickle' dice over the plates. With a stick blender, whip the mushroom cream into a foam. Spoon the foam over each plate, as generously as you like.

> "This is a very special dish using best-in-season king oyster mushrooms. Ours are supplied by Devon Forest Fungi, who are locally based in the seaside town of Dawlish. This is quite a complex, multi-element dish, but most elements can be prepared at least a day in advance, and it is guaranteed to impress any vegetarian or pescatarian guests with its deep umami flavours and range of textures."

For the salt-baked celeriac fondants

370g plain flour, plus extra for dusting

14g table salt

2 sprigs of rosemary, finely chopped

2 egg whites

62ml tepid water

1 celeriac

For the mushroom ketchup

250g chestnut mushrooms

3 tbsp rapeseed oil

1 shallot, finely sliced lengthways

25g soft light brown sugar

25ml sherry vinegar

125ml double cream

50g cold unsalted butter, cubed

100ml tap water

Maldon sea salt, to taste

For the sherry vinegar gel

200ml sherry vinegar

200g caster sugar

10g agar-agar

For the mushroom cream

2 tbsp rapeseed oil

500g white button mushrooms, finely sliced

100g unsalted butter

2 sprigs of rosemary

2 sprigs of thyme

3 garlic cloves, crushed

50ml double cream

Sea salt

For the celeriac 'pickle' dice

Leftover salt-baked celeriac or 1 small celeriac

25g chopped chives

15ml lemon juice, or more to taste

50ml extra virgin olive oil, or more to taste

25ml truffle oil

5g salt

For the oat-crusted pastry

120g whole or rolled oats

120g kataifi pastry or finely chopped filo pastry

For the king oyster mushrooms

9 king oyster mushrooms

100g plain flour

2 eggs, beaten

1 tsp rapeseed oil

2 sprigs of rosemary

To garnish

Lovage mayonnaise (see page 168)

25g black truffle (I use Wiltshire truffle)

Equipment

Temperature probe or skewer

6cm ring cutter

Blender

Chinois or fine sieve

Piping bag or squeezy bottle

Food processor

Deep-fat fryer

Stick blender

Microplane

Dartmouth Pie

Serves 8

For the **shortcrust pastry**, put the flour, salt and sugar into a stand mixer. Add the butter and mix until the flour and butter look like breadcrumbs. Gradually add the cold tap water to form a firm dough. Place the dough into a bowl, cover with cling film and allow to rest for at least 1 hour.

To make the **lamb filling**, preheat the oven to 140°C (120°C fan/Gas Mark 1). First, gently heat the lamb fat in a large ovenproof saucepan or casserole. Season the lamb with salt and black pepper. Add the diced mutton to the pan and brown the meat until golden. Add the spices and cook for a further 2–3 minutes. Add the shallots and celery. Then add the flour and stir, making sure all the lamb and vegetables are thoroughly coated. Now add the lamb stock and bring to the boil. Once the mixture has started to boil, add the orange zest and juice, prunes, raisins, apricots and garlic. Cook the lamb filling in the oven for 2–2½ hours until very tender. Taste the filling and adjust the seasoning if needed. Leave the lamb filling to cool. Once the mixture has cooled, put it into your pie dish.

Assembly and Plating Up

Preheat the oven to 200°C (180°C/Gas Mark 6). When the dough has rested and the pie filling has been cooked, gently roll out the pastry on a floured surface. Roll out the pastry as thin as you can to cover the pie in the dish. Egg wash the pastry. Re-roll the pastry trimmings and use alphabetical letter cutters to cut out DARTMOUTH PIE and add these pastry letters to the top of the pie. Make a hole in the centre to allow steam to escape. Cook for 25 minutes until golden brown. Reduce the heat and cook for a further 15 minutes. Serve immediately.

For the shortcrust pastry

300g plain flour, plus extra for dusting
Pinch of table salt
Pinch of caster sugar
250g cold unsalted butter, diced
120ml cold tap water

For the lamb filling

100g lamb fat
1kg mutton, diced
½ tsp ground coriander
½ cinnamon stick
5 allspice berries
2 banana shallots, brunoised or finely diced
2 celery sticks, diced
4 tsp plain flour
400ml lamb stock (see page 276)
Zest and juice of 1 unwaxed orange
150g prunes, pitted
100g golden raisins
100g dried apricots
2 garlic cloves, finely chopped
Maldon sea salt and black pepper

> "This is my take on the historic Dartmouth Pie, which was an absolute classic from Joyce Molyneux. It works perfectly with the spices and prunes, along with a twist with the inclusion of golden raisins. It was a real honour for me to make this recipe."

For assembly

2 egg yolks, for egg wash

Equipment

Stand mixer
5cm x 25.5cm pie dish
Alphabet cutters

Cassis | Fermented Redcurrants | Lemon Thyme

Serves 10

Making the **stock syrup** is very straightforward. Place the water and sugar into a medium pan and bring to the boil. Once boiling, remove from the heat and leave to cool. This will keep for 2 weeks stored in the fridge.

This process must be undertaken at least 8 days before anything else (apart from the stock syrup). To make the **fermented redcurrants**, first remove the berries from their stems and put them into a sterilised Kilner jar. Add water and salt, then stir and close the jar. Make sure the jar is sealed tight and store it at room temperature for a week at least. In the restaurant I tend to leave them for 2 weeks. After the week (or 2 if you have time), open the Kilner jar. Gently pour the berries into a sieve. Carefully place the sieved berries into a fresh clean Kilner jar, pour in the stock syrup and add the thyme. Seal the jar and place it in the fridge. Allow the berries at least 24 hours to infuse before using them.

While the redcurrants are fermenting, make the **cassis sorbet**. Add the water and blackcurrant purée to a medium saucepan. Add the sugar and sorbet stabiliser to a mixing bowl. Mix together thoroughly with a spoon, otherwise you will end up with lumps in your sorbet. Once mixed, pour into the saucepan containing the water and purée. Bring to the boil, whisking continuously, then add the cassis liqueur. Stir and remove from the heat. Allow to cool. Once cold, transfer the liquid to the measuring jug. Now pour it into the silicone moulds. Fill the moulds to the top. Place a piece of baking paper on top and put straight into the freezer, making sure they are laid on a flat surface.

For the **blackcurrant gel**, add the water, sugar and blackcurrant purée to a saucepan. Bring it to the boil, then add the agar-agar. Boil for another 2 minutes, then pour into a container. Cover and allow to set. Once firmly set, transfer it to a blender and blend until smooth. Pass the gel through a chinois and put into a piping bag. The bag can be stored in the fridge until required.

Now make the **white chocolate dip**. Put the white chocolate and cocoa butter into a mixing bowl. Place a medium pan of water on the heat and put the mixing bowl over the pan. The chocolate will now gently melt. Make sure the water does not boil and the mixing bowl does not come into contact with the water. Once the mixture has melted, add the white Power Flowers or white food colouring, and, using a stick blender, blend the chocolate until completely combined. Once mixed, set the bowl aside until required. You can make the dip in advance and keep it in a covered container in the fridge for a couple of days. However, it is best when made and used on the day of serving. If made in advance, you need to warm it through first before using.

Assembly and Plating Up

Remove the sorbet from the freezer and allow to stand at room temperature for 2–3 minutes so it can soften a little. Pop a portion out of the mould and put a cocktail stick through one end, through the flat surface side, and gently dip into the white chocolate dip, making sure it covers the sorbet. Once coated all over, place onto baking paper to set. It will set quickly. Repeat until all the sorbet is used. Once set, place them onto your serving plates. Pipe the blackcurrant gel on the plate first, then add your sorbet on top of the gel. Add a dot of blackcurrant gel on top of the coated sorbet and three fermented redcurrants.

In the restaurant, I usually add a white chocolate aero to this pre-dessert, however, this can only be made in a commercial kitchen as it requires a vacuum pack machine and an espuma gun.

"This pre-dessert celebrates our supplier Calancombe Estate. Their vineyards and winery are located in Modbury, just 20 miles from the restaurant. They are very well-known for their English sparkling wines and cassis liqueur. The wonderful cassis works exceptionally well with the redcurrants."

For the stock syrup

100ml tap water

100g caster sugar

For the fermented redcurrants

200g redcurrants

130ml tap water

1½ tbsp table salt

200g stock syrup (see above)

1 sprig of thyme

For the cassis sorbet

55ml tap water

125g blackcurrant purée (I use Boiron)

55g caster sugar

12g sorbet stabiliser (I use MSK)

15ml cassis liqueur

For the blackcurrant gel

150ml tap water

50g caster sugar

350g blackcurrant purée

6g agar-agar

For the white chocolate dip

65g white chocolate pieces (I use Callebaut)

40g cocoa butter (I use Callebaut)

2 white Power Flowers or 4g white food colouring

Equipment

2 Kilner jars

10 silicone pomponette moulds (I use the 24-cup Pavoni Formaflex mould)

Blender

Chinois or fine sieve

Piping bag

Sieve

Measuring jug

Stick blender

Orange Blossom Sorbet | Crème Fraîche | Grapefruit | Cocoa Granola

Serves 8

For the **crème fraîche cream**, place the cream, sugar and milk in a medium saucepan. In a separate mixing bowl, fill the bowl with water and add the bronze gelatine. Allow the gelatine to bloom. When it's ready, squeeze the excess water and place on a tray. Bring the cream mixture to the boil and add the gelatine. Allow to cool completely. Once cooled, add the crème fraîche and blend. Pour the cream into 8 dishes, weigh each dish to 50-60g. Place your dishes into the fridge to set.

Now on to the **orange blossom sorbet**, using a medium saucepan, pour in the water and orange juice. Mix well, place on a high heat and bring to the boil. Once boiling, turn off the heat. In another bowl, mix the sugar and stabiliser together. Then add the sugar and sorbet stabiliser to the pan and mix well. Turn on the heat again and bring back to the boil. Once boiling, add the orange blossom water and mix well. Transfer the mixture to a container over a bowl of ice water. Chill the sorbet for 20 minutes over ice and then put straight into the freezer until frozen. Churn the sorbet with a Pacojet, then transfer to the freezer until required later. The sorbet will keep well in the freezer for up to a month.

To make the **grapefruit curd**, pour the grapefruit juice into a saucepan. Place on a medium heat. The grapefruit juice needs to reduce by half and let the liquid slightly caramelise. You want to end up with 60ml reduced grapefruit juice. When the grapefruit juice has reduced by half, add the butter and sugar, then bring to the boil. Once boiling, remove from the heat. Put the egg yolk into a ThermoMixer and temper them. Once tempered, add them to the mixture in the saucepan and cook until it reaches 83°C. Pour over the white chocolate pieces, stir to ensure an even mix and then allow to set. Once set, transfer to a piping bag. This can be kept in the fridge for at least a week.

For the **cocoa oats**, preheat the oven to 160°C (140°C fan/ Gas Mark 3). Mix the oats, cocoa powder, olive oil, maple syrup and salt. Bake in the oven for 9 minutes, or until cooked. Place a piece of baking paper on the side and let the oats cool on it completely. Put into a sealed container until required. They will keep for up to 3 days.

Assembly and Plating Up
Firstly, remove the crème fraîche cream from the fridge and allow to come up to room temperature for 5-10 minutes. Remove the orange blossom sorbet from the freezer. Then add three big dots of the grapefruit curd on top of each crème fraîche cream. Next, using a rocher spoon, place a good scoop of the sorbet onto the cream. Finally, add two generous pinches of the cocoa oats.

For the crème fraîche cream
125ml double cream
50g caster sugar
15g full-fat milk
½ leaf bronze gelatine
125ml crème fraîche

For the orange blossom sorbet
110ml tap water
500ml fresh orange juice
105g caster sugar
25g sorbet stabiliser (I use MSK)
6ml orange blossom water

For the grapefruit curd
120ml grapefruit juice
75g unsalted butter
50g caster sugar
45g egg yolk
75g white chocolate, broken into pieces (I use Callebaut)

For the cocoa granola
75g fine oats
½ tsp cocoa powder
10ml olive oil
7g maple syrup
A pinch of Maldon sea salt

Equipment
Pacojet
ThermoMixer
Temperature probe
Piping bag with small nozzle

"This pre-dessert was one I served on the *Great British Menu*, using a model of the famous *Only Fools and Horses* yellow Supervan III car to serve it in."

Serves 6

Roasted Coffee Parfait | Mascarpone | White Chocolate Granita

To make the **coffee parfait**, set up a stand mixer with the whisk attachment. Weigh out the sugar and water into a medium saucepan. In a separate mixing bowl, fill the bowl halfway with water and add the gelatine. Allow the gelatine to bloom. Place the sugar and water mixture on the heat and cook to 118°C. This is the soft-ball stage (when a bit is dropped into cold water, it will hold its shape). Always use a thermometer to keep checking the temperature. Once the gelatine has bloomed, squeeze out the excess water and put onto a small tray, ready for the sugar. While the sugar is cooking, begin to whisk the egg yolk and vanilla in the mixer. This will double in volume and look like a thick sabayon. When the sugar reaches 118°C, pour the sugar mixture, coffee essence and espresso coffee onto the yolk mixture and continue to whisk until it is room temperature. Lightly whip the cream and mascarpone until at soft peak stage. Fold into the sabayon mixture and pour into piping bags. Pipe the parfait into the sphere moulds, place a piece of baking paper on the top and into the freezer. This can be made a few days in advance and needs time to freeze.

Start making the **chocolate coffee curd** by adding the espresso, butter and sugar to a small saucepan. Put the chocolate in one mixing bowl. In another mixing bowl, add the egg yolk and whisk. Then pour the hot espresso mixture over the egg yolk to temper it. Pour the whole mixture back into the saucepan and cook until it thickens, making sure to stir continuously as it cooks. You will know it is cooked when the mixture coats the back of a spoon. Pour this mixture over the chocolate, then mix well until everything has combined. Add the chocolate curd to a piping bag and place into the fridge. This curd will last up to 3 days. Before serving, it will need to come out of the fridge to be brought back up to room temperature.

For the **lemon gel**, add the water, sugar and lemon purée to a saucepan. Bring to the boil, then add the agar-agar. Continue boiling for another 2 minutes, then pour into a container. Cover and allow to set. Once firmly set, transfer it to a blender and blend until smooth. Pass the gel through a chinois and then into a piping bag. Keep the bag in the fridge until required. You can make this in advance and it lasts up to 3 days.

To prepare the **pâte de brick**, preheat the oven to 170°C (150°C fan/Gas Mark 3½). In a small saucepan, melt the butter and maple syrup together. Measure out the pastry sheets to 14 x 8cm and lay out on a lightly floured chopping board. Brush over the maple butter. Wrap the pastry around the ring moulds and cook on a cooling rack in the oven for 8 minutes. When golden brown, allow to cool for a few minutes and take the pastry off the tubes. You need two pieces per serving.

❝ This parfait looks very simple, but once you see the layers, you realise it's a flavour bomb. The coffee parfait pairs very nicely with the lemon gel and the white chocolate granita. ❞

To make the **whipped mascarpone**, place the mascarpone in a mixing bowl, add the sugar, lemon zest and juice and gently whip until stiff peaks form. Put into a piping bag and leave in the fridge until needed.

The final element is the **white chocolate granita**. Preheat the oven to 120°C (100°C fan/Gas Mark ½). Gently place the white chocolate pellets on a large baking tray. Gently cook in the oven for 45 minutes, stirring regularly. Using a wooden spoon, keep stirring the chocolate and it will begin to slowly caramelise. Once the chocolate has turned golden in colour, take it out of the oven and allow to cool. Place the chocolate in the freezer and let it harden. In a robot-coupe, add the ice cubes and blitz the ice until you have a fine granita. Then add the chocolate and allow to mix and melt. The chocolate will mix in with the ice. Place back into the freezer to firm up. The granita will last in the freezer for a few weeks.

Assembly and Plating Up

Place the two pieces of pastry on each plate. Add the roasted coffee parfait on the bottom. Pipe the coffee curd around the parfait. Now add five dots of lemon gel over the curd. Follow with three big dots of whipped mascarpone. Finish with the white chocolate granita on the top and serve.

For the coffee parfait

226g caster sugar
75ml tap water
1 gelatine leaf
160g egg yolk
1 vanilla pod (I use Zazou Emporium)
40ml coffee essence
20ml espresso coffee (I use the Angel's own blend)
300ml double cream
175ml mascarpone cream

For the chocolate coffee curd

50ml espresso coffee
75g unsalted butter, diced
7g caster sugar
50g good-quality dark chocolate (70% cocoa), broken into pieces
40g egg yolk

For the lemon gel

150ml tap water
50g caster sugar
350ml lemon purée
10g agar-agar

For the pâte de brick

100g unsalted butter
50g maple syrup
170g feuille de brick pastry sheets (we get ours from Wellocks)
Plain flour, for dusting

For the whipped mascarpone

200g mascarpone
25g caster sugar
Zest and juice of 1 lemon

For the white chocolate granita

450g white chocolate pellets
150g ice cubes

Equipment

Stand mixer and whisk attachment
Temperature probe
Electric hand-held whisk
Piping bags
6 4cm x 2cm sphere moulds
Blender
Chinois
12 4cm ring moulds
Robot-coupe

Serves 6

Blackberry Millefeuille | Crème Fraîche Sorbet

For the **puff pastry sheets**, preheat the oven to 200°C (180°C fan/Gas Mark 6). Roll out the puff pastry on a silicone mat to form a square about 30cm. Lift onto a baking sheet, cover with baking paper, then place a flat baking sheet or tray on top. Now put a heavy baking dish on top of the sheet or tray. Bake for 15–20 minutes until golden. Once the pastry has cooled down, cut it into 18 4 x 8cm rectangles. Keep at room temperature so they are ready for when you build the millefeuille.

To make the **blackberry gel**, first add the water, sugar and blackberry purée to a saucepan. Bring to the boil and then add the agar-agar. Continue boiling for another 2 minutes and then pour into a container. Cover and allow to set. Once firmly set, transfer the mixture to a blender and blend until smooth. Pass the gel through a chinois and then into a piping bag. Keep the bag in the fridge until required. You can make this in advance and it will last for up to 3 days.

Preparing the **crème fraîche sorbet**, can also be undertaken a few days in advance. Add the water to a medium saucepan. Next, add the caster sugar and sorbet stabiliser to a mixing bowl. Mix with a spoon. Ensure they are thoroughly mixed, otherwise you will end up with lumps in your sorbet. Once mixed, pour into the saucepan containing the water. Bring to the boil, whisking continuously. Remove from the heat and allow to cool. Once cooled, add the crème fraîche and mix well. Transfer the liquid to Pacojet containers and freeze. Churn the sorbet when ready to plate.

The next element is the **lime curd**. Begin by pouring the lime juice into a saucepan, then add the butter and sugar. Bring to the boil and remove from the heat. Put the egg yolk into a ThermoMixer and temper them. Add the tempered yolks to the saucepan and cook until the mixture reaches 83°C. Pour over the white chocolate pieces, making sure to stir so you get an even mix, then allow time to set. Once set, transfer to a piping bag. The lime curd can be kept for at least a week if stored in the fridge.

Prepare the **vanilla cream** on the day it will be used. Place the cream into a mixing bowl along with the vanilla. Whisk to semi peaks and place into a piping bag ready to pipe later. This needs to be freshly made as close to serving as you can.

> "A simple yet elegant dessert made with tasty blackberries and a twist of lime. A nice way to showcase the best of this particular fruit when it is in season."

Assembly and Plating Up

Paco the crème fraîche sorbet. Place three pastry rectangles next to each other per serving. Line one rectangle, which is the bottom layer, with 5 fresh, halved blackberries. Place another rectangle of pastry on top, then cover with a layer of vanilla cream. Finish by placing the last pastry rectangle on top and covering with a layer of lime curd, blackberry gel and lemon balm leaves. Next, zest over some lime. Finish off the dessert with a nice rocher of crème fraîche sorbet. Repeat with the remaining ingredients.

For the puff pastry sheets

600g rolled French puff pastry (I use Maître André)

For the blackberry gel

150ml tap water
50g caster sugar
350ml blackberry purée
6g agar-agar

For the crème fraîche sorbet

110ml tap water
105g caster sugar
25g sorbet stabiliser
500g crème fraîche

For the lime curd

100g lime juice (freshly squeezed or bottled)
150g unsalted butter
100g caster sugar
80g egg yolk
150g white chocolate, broken into pieces

For the vanilla cream

150ml double cream
1 tsp vanilla bean paste

To garnish

30 blackberries
Lemon balm leaves
1 lime

Equipment

Blender
Chinois or fine sieve
Piping bags
Pacojet
ThermoMixer

Nut Butter Brûlée | Nashi Pear | Pine Nut Ice Cream

Serves 6 – 8

First, make the **burnt butter brûlée**. Preheat the oven to 130°C (110°C fan/Gas Mark 1). Place the butter in a pan on a medium heat to noisette. Then, add in the vanilla and allow to infuse. Heat the cream and salt in a pan on a low heat. Keep warm until everything else is ready. Whisk together the egg yolk and light brown sugar. Slowly add 129g of the burnt butter to the cream. Allow the cream mixture to cool, then add the cream mixture to the egg yolk mixture and temper, then add the rum. Pour the brûlée into a suitably deep metal baking tray. Blind bake for 20 minutes. Then reduce the oven temperature to 110°C (90°C fan/Gas Mark ¼), add the tempered water to the tray and continue cooking until you have a perfect wobble. Allow to cool and place in the fridge. The brûlée will keep well in the fridge for up to 3 days.

For the **pear gel**, add the water, sugar and pear purée to a saucepan. Bring to the boil and then add the agar-agar. Continue boiling for another 2 minutes, then pour into a container. Cover and allow to set. Once firmly set, transfer it to a blender and blend until smooth. Pass the gel through a chinois and then into a piping bag. Keep the bag in the fridge until required. You can make this in advance and it will last for up to 3 days.

To make the **sugar tuile**, preheat the oven to 200°C (180°C fan/Gas Mark 6). Scatter the hazelnuts over a baking tray and roast in the oven for 6 minutes. Allow to cool ready for the caramel. Put the sugar, fondant icing and glucose in a pan. Place on a medium heat to caramelise. You are looking for a golden brown colour. Put the hazelnuts on a silicone mat and pour the caramel on top. Allow to cool completely. Blitz the hard caramel in a blender, then place into a sealed container. Line a baking tray with a silicone mat and sprinkle the caramel dust evenly over the tray. Bake in the oven at 200°C (180°C fan/Gas Mark 6) for 7–8 minutes until melted. Allow to cool, then gently pull off the tray. I cut the sugar tuile into shards to top the brûlée.

You can make **pine nut ice cream** a few days in advance. I make this in a ThermoMixer. However, you can make this in a pan and gently cook out to 83°C. Preheat the oven to 170°C (150°C fan/Gas Mark ½). Scatter the pine nuts over a baking tray and roast in the oven for 6 minutes. Allow to cool. Add the milk, cream, sugar, egg yolk and vanilla pod to the ThermoMixer and blitz on full speed. Turn down to speed setting 3 and gently cook the ice cream while turning the temperature up slowly to 83°C. This usually takes 5–10 minutes. Once the custard is ready, add the pine nuts and allow to infuse. Place the custard over a bowl of ice water to cool down. When cold, using a stick blender, gently blend the nuts into the ice cream and pass through a fine sieve. Put the ice cream into the freezer.

Assembling and Plating

Lightly toast the pine nuts for a few minutes in a small frying pan and allow to cool. Using ring cutters, cut out two different sized pieces of brûlée and place on each plate. Add a shard of sugar tuile to the top of each brûlée. Now add four slices of Nashi pear to each plate. Use the melon baller to scoop out 3 balls of Nashi pear per dish. Before placing them on the plate you can gently blowtorch them, if you wish to. Place the balls around the plate. Complete the plate with a rocher of pine nut ice cream on top of the pear and finish with the toasted nuts along with three dots of the pear gel.

> " This nut butter brûlée is simple to make, but so tasty with the burnt sugar tuile on top. It goes perfectly with the Nashi pear and pine nuts. "

Equipment

265 x 163mm metal baking tray (I use a GN1/4 stainless-steel gastronorm tray)
Blender
Chinois or fine sieve
Piping bag
Silicone mat
Stick blender
2cm and 3cm ring cutters
Thermomixer (optional)
'Melon baller
Blowtorch (optional)'

For the burnt butter brûlée

250g unsalted butter
1 vanilla pod, deseeded
1,220ml double cream
Pinch of Maldon sea salt
285g egg yolk
330g light soft brown sugar
40ml rum (I use Devon Rum Co honey spiced rum)
500ml tempered water

For the pear gel

150ml tap water
50g caster sugar
350ml pear purée
6g agar-agar

For the sugar tuile

20g hazelnuts
100g caster sugar
25g fondant icing
50ml liquid glucose

For the pine nut ice cream

100g pine nuts
330ml full-fat milk
80ml double cream
100g caster sugar
100g egg yolk
1 vanilla pod, deseeded

To garnish

1 Nashi pear, sliced
1 Nashi pear, for pear balls
10g pine nuts

WINTER

December – February

Canapé

Truffle Cheese Gougère

Amuse Bouche

Leek and Potato Velouté | Chive Gnocchi

Starters

Beetroot Tarts | Poppy Seed Goat's Cheese | Puffed Wild Rice | Celery Cress

Black Garlic Risotto | Sherry Vinegar | Crispy Quail Egg

Duck Ravioli | Bitter Orange | Cranberry | Duck Consommé

Mains

Venison Loin | Parsley Root | Pomegranate

Devonshire Lamb Loin | Brown Butter Artichokes | Sauce Picante

Roasted Line Caught Sea Bass | Caviar and Lettuce Cream

Pre-desserts

Apple Soufflé | Apple Syrup | Walnut and Maple Ice Cream

'The Black Penny'

Desserts

Chocolate and Bitter Orange | Pedro Ximénez | Roasted Pearl Barley

Chocolate | Coffee Curd | Lemon | Coffee Milk Sorbet

The Angel Petit Four

Toffee Apple and Cinnamon Chocolates

Serves 16

Truffle Cheese Gougère

First, prepare the **choux buns**. Place a large saucepan on a medium-high heat. Pour in the milk, followed by the water and butter. Warm until hot, but not boiling. Once warm, add the flour, salt and sugar. With a silicone spatula, stir the mixture until it becomes a smooth, thick roux. Be careful to ensure the mixture does not burn during the process. Once it has formed a roux, cook for a further 5 minutes, then place it in the bowl of a stand mixer. Using the beater attachment, mix on medium speed until the roux has cooled slightly – this should take 2–3 minutes. Then gradually add the eggs, still beating, until the choux pastry becomes glossy. If you see steam still coming off, do not be alarmed, as this is normal. Using a silicone spatula, scoop the mixture into a piping bag and set aside to rest.

Now make the **craquelin**. Add the butter to the stand mixer bowl. Make sure the butter is soft, or it will not combine properly with the other ingredients. Using the beater attachment, set the mixer on a slow speed and beat until the butter is smooth. Then increase the speed to medium and gradually start to add all the remaining ingredients. Beat on medium speed until you have a smooth mixture. Pour the mixture into the centre of a shallow baking tray lined with baking paper. Lay another sheet of baking paper on top, then evenly roll out the mixture as thinly as you can. Place into the freezer for 1 hour to set. Once set, take out of the freezer and leave for about 5 minutes to defrost a little. This will make it easier to cut. Using the 1.6cm ring cutter, cut out individual pieces and remove the excess mixture. Return the tray with the craquelin pieces to the freezer until required.

To make the **truffle cheese sauce**, melt the butter in a pan on a medium heat. Once melted, gradually add the flour, using a wooden spoon or spatula to combine the ingredients. It will start to thicken and make a roux. Then slowly add the milk and stir in until completely mixed. Season with pinches of salt and pepper. When you have a smooth roux, gradually stir in the Cheddar and Parmesan. Taste again and adjust the seasoning. Add your Wiltshire truffle and truffle oil. Allow to cool for about 10 minutes. Using your spatula, put the mixture into a piping bag. It is now ready to use for assembling the dish or can be kept in the fridge for up to 24 hours. Make sure when you are ready to use the mixture that it is up to room temperature – take it out of the fridge an hour before using.

Assembly and Plating Up

You are now ready to finish the cooking and assemble the dish. Preheat the oven to 160°C (140°C fan and low fan speed/Gas Mark 3). Pipe the choux buns, about 2.5mm wide, onto a silicone mat, allowing space between each one for the buns to expand. Place a piece of frozen craquelin on top of each bun. Bake for 8 minutes on low fan speed and then another 12 minutes on medium fan speed. Alternatively, bake at 160°C (140°C fan/Gas Mark 3) for 8 minutes, then at 170°C (150°C fan/Gas Mark 3½) for a further 12 minutes. Once cooked, remove from the oven and place on a wire rack to cool completely.

For the final cooking process, preheat the oven to 180°C (160°C/Gas Mark 4). With a small knife, make an incision on the bottom of each choux bun, then pipe some of the truffle cheese sauce inside each choux bun. You have now made what the French call a gougère. Place them onto a baking tray and cook in the oven for 5–6 minutes.

To serve, cut the gougères in half with a serrated knife and garnish with finely grated or shaved Parmesan.

> *"This truffle cheese gougère has become a favourite canapé here at the Angel. It is a French classic, which, when executed correctly, is guaranteed to please. The key to success is creating a perfectly seasoned filling and a well-cooked choux bun. The craquelin is a French-style savoury biscuit which adds crunch to an incredibly rich and indulgent gougère."*

For the choux buns

160ml full-fat milk
160ml tap water
210g plain flour, sifted
6g table salt
6g caster sugar
310g eggs (6–8 medium eggs)
150g unsalted butter

For the craquelin

95g unsalted butter, softened
70g Parmesan, finely grated
110g plain flour
38g soft light sugar
Pinch of table salt

For the truffle cheese sauce

50g unsalted butter
65g plain flour
500ml full-fat milk
125g mature Cheddar, grated
125g Parmesan, freshly shaved or grated
25g Wiltshire black truffle, shaved
White truffle oil, to taste
Table salt and black pepper, to taste

To garnish

Parmesan, finely grated or shaved

Equipment

Stand mixer and beater attachment
Piping bag
1.6cm ring cutter
Silicone mat

Leek and Potato Velouté | Chive Gnocchi

Serves 6

First, prepare the **leek and potato velouté**. Wash the leeks under cold water to remove any excess dirt. Remove the root at the bottom and the darker green tops. Slice all the light green parts of the leeks and the shallot very finely. Put the butter in a large pan and melt it. Once melted, add the shallot, garlic and thyme. Sweat them down, making sure they do not colour. Add the leeks and cook them down quickly to allow the moisture in the leeks to evaporate. Season with salt and pepper, then cook for a further few minutes. Now add the sliced potato and sweat down. Once sweated, pour in the chicken stock and bring to the boil. Then turn down the heat and cook for a further 8–10 minutes. Add the double cream and cook for another 3–4 minutes. Use a kitchen blender to blend all the velouté until smooth and then pass through a fine sieve. Season with salt and pepper if required and allow the velouté to cool down over ice. You can keep the velouté in the fridge for up to 3 days.

To make the **chive gnocchi**, preheat the oven to 180°C (160°C fan/Gas Mark 4). Place the potatoes on a baking tray and cover with sea salt. Cook in the oven for 1¼ hours. Depending on the size of the potatoes, they may need more cooking time for the insides to become soft. Once cooked, remove the potatoes from the oven and cut them in half. Scoop out the soft potato and put it through a moulin or ricer. Allow the potato to cool in the fridge. Once the potato is cold, weigh out 250g and put into a bowl. Add the pasta flour, egg yolk, Parmesan and chives, then mix thoroughly. Try not to overwork the gnocchi, as you want it to be light and fluffy. I always cook a small piece of gnocchi in the fryer at 190°C until golden brown to test the flavour. You can then add more seasoning to the mixture if required. Roll out the gnocchi into thin pillows, then cut the gnocchi into 1cm pieces and gently squeeze into pillow shapes. I normally serve three pieces per person. I always make gnocchi fresh each day before service. So, it is best to make your gnocchi on the day you want to serve the dish.

Assembly and Plating Up

Place the leek and potato velouté on a low heat to gently warm up. You can add a little water, if needed, should it have become too thick in the fridge. Deep fry the gnocchi at 190°C. Place the gnocchi into the fryer to cook and colour. Once the gnocchi are a nice golden brown, they are cooked and ready to serve. Put three pieces of gnocchi in each bowl and garnish with kale shoots. Froth up the velouté with a stick blender and gently pour on the righthand side of the bowl. A perfect little amuse-bouche to begin a dinner party with and get everyone wanting more!

For the leek and potato velouté

400g leeks

1 shallot

100g unsalted butter

1 garlic clove, finely sliced

2 sprigs of thyme

1 small potato, peeled and sliced

600ml chicken stock (see page 274)

150ml double cream

Salt and black pepper, to taste

For the chive gnocchi

3 large potatoes

62g 00 pasta flour

10g egg yolk

25g Parmesan, grated

20g finely chopped chives

Maldon sea salt

Salt and black pepper, to taste

Kale shoots, to garnish

Oil, for frying (quantity depending on appliance)

Equipment

Blender

Fine sieve

Moulin or ricer

Deep-fat fryer, or pan

"This is a perfect winter warmer. We serve it just before the starter as an amuse-bouche. The velouté works exceptionally well with a crispy chive gnocchi."

Serves 8

Beetroot Tarts | Poppy Seed Goat's Cheese | Puffed Wild Rice | Celery Cress

The **goat's cheese** can be made up to 2 days in advance. Place the cheese into a large mixing bowl. Grate the lemon's zest into your goat's cheese using the Microplane and then add the soaked poppy seeds. Try to make sure the seeds are as dry as possible before adding. Use a silicone spatula or a wooden spoon to beat it together and then add a pinch of salt to taste. Transfer to a piping bag and tie at the top. Store in the fridge for up to 2 days.

For the **tart cases**, preheat the oven to 180°C (160°C fan/Gas Mark 4). Begin by unrolling the puff pastry and cutting it into 7cm squares. Lightly spray the fluted tart cases with baking spray and push a square of pastry into each one. Do not push too hard, as this could make the cases stick. Then place an additional tart case on top of each pastry, so it is between two tart cases. Place the tart cases onto a baking tray and then place another baking tray on top of the tart cases. Weigh the cases down a bit by placing a couple of pots or pans on top. Bake in the oven for 14 minutes. Remove the top baking tray from the tart cases and you will be able to see the overlapping pastry and judge if they are cooked by the colour. They should have a nice golden brown colouring, not too pale. If they need longer, continue cooking until they look right. Once cooked, remove from the oven and leave to cool for about 30 minutes.

Once cooled, remove the top tart cases. They should just pop out, but you may need to use a small knife to loosen them. Once removed, using a Microplane or small serrated vegetable knife, trim off the overhanging pastry. Work around the top of the pastry case, and once finished, the case should pull out quite easily. If you cannot pull the pastry case out, try going over the edges of the case again with your knife or Microplane, as there will probably be some excess pastry keeping the case in place.

Make the **pickled golden beetroot** by combining the vinegar, water, sugar, olive oil, white wine, salt and coriander seeds in a small saucepan. Then add the fennel seeds, star anise and shallot. Place the saucepan on a moderate heat and bring to the boil, using a whisk to incorporate all the ingredients, especially the sugar. Once boiled, set aside to cool completely and allow the ingredients to infuse. Now take the golden beetroots and slice them finely on the mandoline. You want to have 2mm-thick slices. Put the slices onto a flat surface and use the ring cutter to get evenly sized discs. Put the slices into a small bowl or container. Place the pickle liquor back on the heat and re-boil. Once boiled, using the sieve or chinois, strain the pickle liquor over the golden beetroot discs. Cover with cling film and set aside to cool for 20 minutes. Once cooled, put them in the fridge for later use. You can keep them in the fridge for up to 3 days.

To make the **cooked pickled candied beetroot**, put the raw candied beetroots into a pan, cover with water and bring to the boil. Turn the heat down to a simmer and cook for about 2 hours. The cooking time is very much dependent upon the size of the beetroots. You want them to be soft, but not so soft that they will break too easily. You should be able to squeeze the beetroot and feel it is cooked without it falling apart. For the pickle liquor, start by pouring the apple juice, vinegar and white port or wine into a pan. Place on a high heat and bring to the boil, then immediately turn down the heat and simmer until the liquid has reduced by three-quarters. Once reduced, add the sugar, olive oil and pinch of salt. Whisk to ensure the sugar dissolves and cook for a further 10 minutes at the same heat level. Remove from the heat and set aside. Peel the skins off the cooked candied beetroots and slice into 5mm-thick pieces. Then, using the 1.6cm ring cutter, cut the beetroot slices and put your discs into a small bowl or container. Bring the pickle liquor to the boil again and pour over the beetroot discs. Cover and place in the fridge until plating up. They will keep in the fridge for up to 3 days.

Prepare the **beetroot tartare** by taking the cooked red beetroots and finely slicing them into 1cm pieces. Then finely dice them and put into a mixing bowl. The finer they are diced, the better, but be careful not to create a purée. You want texture in this mix. Now add the shallot, mayo, Tabasco, Worcestershire sauce and salt. Mix the ingredients together and taste. Add more salt if you wish. Once you are happy with the flavour balance, put the tartare into a piping bag and store in the fridge until required. The tartare will keep in your fridge for up to 3 days.

For the **beetroot purée**, first roughly chop your cooked beetroots into small pieces and place into a pan. Now add the remaining ingredients. Place on a medium heat and reduce the liquid until it becomes glossy and thick. Transfer the mixture into a blender and blend until smooth and shiny. Once you are happy with the consistency, pass through a sieve or chinois. Allow the purée to cool. Once cooled, place into a squeezy bottle or piping bag. It will keep in the fridge for up to 3 days.

The last element to prepare is the **puffed wild rice**. Pour the oil into a large saucepan and place on a medium heat. Use a temperature probe to check when it reaches 180°C (and maintain the heat). If you have a deep-fat fryer, set it to 180°C. Put the wild rice into the hot oil and cook until it puffs. Remove carefully with a slotted spoon and drain off the oil on kitchen paper or J cloths. In just a few seconds the rice will puff up, so do not go anywhere! Once cooked and drained, transfer the puffed rice to an airtight container. Store at room temperature for up to 2 days.

Assembly and Plating Up

Start by building the tarts. I would recommend doing this on a tray, so that any mess does not get on the plates. Once the tarts are assembled, they can be transferred to the plates prior to serving.

Take the fluted tart cases and pipe in a nice amount of the goat's cheese. Over the top, pipe on a generous amount of the beetroot tartare, creating a peaked top. Next, put five of the beetroot discs into each portion of the tartare. Arrange them as you wish to create an eye-pleasing look. Pipe a few small dots of beetroot purée in between the discs. Sprinkle puffed rice over the top of the tarts.

For the plates, we want to arrange a tight ring of 6-8 golden beetroot discs in the centre, leaving space in the centre for the tart. Put a generous dot of beetroot purée in the centre on which the tart will sit. Now sit the tarts on each plate and garnish with celery cress and any edible flowers if you like. Once happy with your plate, serve to your guests and enjoy.

> "This dish is an absolute classic and staple here at the Angel. Using locally grown beetroots, we adapt the beetroot tart as the seasons change. Combining the different textures of beetroot, which have been well balanced and seasoned, with the acidity and richness of the goat's cheese, creates one of our most iconic starters to date."

For the goat's cheese

200g goat's cheese (I use Driftwood)

1 unwaxed lemon

15g poppy seeds, soaked with cold water for at least 1 hour, then dried thoroughly using kitchen paper

Salt, to taste

For the tart cases

600g rolled French puff pastry (I use Maître André)

For the pickled golden beetroot

100ml white wine vinegar

100ml tap water

100ml white sugar

100ml extra virgin olive oil

100ml dry white wine

Pinch of sea salt

8g coriander seeds

2g fennel seeds

1 star anise

1 banana shallot, finely sliced

2 golden beetroots

For the cooked pickled candied beetroot

2 candied beetroots

300g cloudy apple juice

120ml white wine vinegar

130ml white port or fortified white wine

25g caster sugar

45ml olive oil

Salt, to taste

For the beetroot tartare

2 red beetroots, cooked

1 banana shallot, brunoised or finely diced

1 tbsp mayonnaise (of your choice)

½ tsp Tabasco sauce

1 tbsp Worcestershire sauce

Pinch of table salt

For the beetroot purée

150g red beetroots, cooked

125g beetroot juice

25ml white wine vinegar

100ml red port

75ml red wine

75ml cloudy apple juice

For the puffed wild rice

200ml rapeseed oil

20g wild rice (available from most supermarkets)

To garnish (optional, but recommended)

Micro celery cress

Edible flowers of your choice

Equipment

Microplane

Piping bag

16 fluted tart cases

Baking spray

Mandoline

1.6cm ring cutter

Chinois or fine sieve

Blender

Squeezy bottle (optional)

Piping bags

Temperature probe (optional)

Deep-fat fryer (optional)

Serves 6

Black Garlic Risotto | Sherry Vinegar | Crispy Quail Egg

Begin by making the **black garlic purée for the risotto**. Thinly slice just the whites of the leeks. Wash the leeks under cold running water. In a large pan, melt the butter and add the leeks and banana shallot. Cook the leeks on a high heat so all the liquid evaporates from the leeks. Add the potato and cook for 5 minutes. Now add the salt, the peeled black garlic, and the black garlic paste, then cook for a further 10 minutes. Pour in the tap water and double cream. Cook the leeks down further until they have no bite. Blitz the leeks in a blender and pass through a fine sieve. Leave to cool and place in the fridge until needed.

Next, move on to the **Granny Smith purée**. Gently wash the apples under cold water. Peel and core the apples, then slice them into very thin slices. Put the slices into a large pan and add the sugar. Now add the water and bring to the boil, stirring continuously. Simmer the apples for 5–10 minutes or until soft. You want no colour on the apples, as they should remain as white as possible. Using a blender, blend the apples to a thick purée. Pass through a fine sieve and put into a piping bag straight away. Allow the purée to cool in the fridge. It can be kept in the fridge for at least 2 days.

To make the **black garlic garnish**, in a mixing bowl weigh out 75g Granny Smith purée. Add the black garlic paste and white miso. Mix all three ingredients together and put into a piping bag. Leave this garnish in the fridge until needed. You can make this up to 3 days in advance.

Now on to cooking the **risotto rice**. Make sure you have your cooking timer ready to set. Fill a medium pan with the tap water and bring to the boil. While the water is boiling, place a large pan on the heat. Put the unsalted butter into this pan and melt it. As soon as it has melted, add the shallots and cook out, making sure they do not start to colour. Once they have softened and become translucent, add the arborio rice and turn up the heat. Toast off the rice for 2 minutes with the shallots and butter. By now, the water in the other pan should be boiling. Pour it over the risotto rice and stir. Bring the rice to the boil. Once boiling, turn down the heat and set your timer for 5 minutes. It is very important that the rice is cooked for only 5 minutes. During the cooking time, continually stir the rice. When the 5 minutes is up, immediately strain the rice in the steamer tray and keep the liquid. Once strained, put the rice in a blast chiller or fridge to cool. Keep both the rice and liquid in the fridge until you are ready to plate. The rice is cooked daily in the restaurant.

For the **sherry vinegar gel**, in a medium saucepan add the sherry vinegar along with the sugar. Whisk constantly and bring to the boil. Then continue to whisk while you add the agar-agar. Whisk for a further 2 minutes at boiling point. Remove from the heat and pour into a container. The mixture will set at room temperature, but place in the fridge to set more quickly. The larger the surface area of the container you use, the faster it will set. Once completely set, mix in a blender on high until smooth. Pass through a chinois and put in a piping bag or squeezy bottle. The gel can be kept in the fridge for up to a week.

To prepare the **quail eggs**, place a medium pan on the heat and fill it with water. In a bowl, add ice and cold water and have it ready for the eggs to go into once they have been cooked. Bring the water in the pan to the boil and gently place in the quail eggs. Cook the eggs for 2 minutes 15 seconds and then immediately put them into the cold water bath. Once they have cooled, peel the eggs. Put the flour, eggs and breadcrumbs in separate bowls. First, coat the quail eggs in flour, then in egg and finally in the breadcrumbs. Leave these in the fridge until required. To fry the eggs, heat a deep-fat fryer to 180°C and deep-fry the eggs until golden brown.

Assembly and Plating Up

In a medium pan, add the risotto rice and some of the reserved cooking liquid to just cover the rice. Place on the heat and gently reheat the rice. You don't want to over-stir the rice because you will break the grains. Let the liquid reduce over the rice until you cannot see it. Add the black garlic purée to the rice and mix in well. Now add in the crème fraîche, Parmesan and salt. Allow to reduce if too wet, then add the chervil and chives. Place the risotto in a bowl, then add dots of sherry vinegar gel and black garlic garnish. Finally, place two crispy quail eggs in the middle of each plate.

" This risotto is very easy to prepare and owes its delicate, yet peculiar, flavour to its main ingredients – black garlic and sherry vinegar. It goes perfectly with the crispy quail eggs. "

For the black garlic purée for the risotto
6 large leeks
150g unsalted butter
1 banana shallot, brunoised
1 potato, peeled and sliced
5g table salt
50g peeled black garlic (I use the South West Garlic Farm bulbs)
25g black garlic paste (I use the South West Garlic Farm bulbs)
100ml tap water
100ml double cream
75ml crème fraîche
75g Parmesan, finely grated
25g chervil, finely chopped
20g chives, finely chopped
Salt, to taste

For the Granny Smith purée
8 Granny Smith apples
1 tsp caster sugar
100ml tap water

For the black garlic garnish
75g Granny Smith purée (see above)
100g black garlic paste
15g white miso

For the risotto rice
500ml tap water
120g unsalted butter
2 banana shallots, brunoised or finely diced
75g arborio rice

For the sherry vinegar gel
200ml sherry vinegar
200g caster sugar
5g agar-agar

For the quail eggs
12 quail eggs
50g plain flour
2 eggs, beaten
70g fine dried breadcrumbs
Oil, for frying

Equipment
Blender
Chinois or fine sieve
Piping bags
Steamer tray
Squeezy bottle (optional)

Duck Ravioli | Bitter Orange | Cranberry | Duck Consommé

Serves 6

Begin by making the **duck stock.** Preheat the oven to 180°C (160°C fan/Gas Mark 4). Place the duck carcasses, duck wings and chicken wings on a large oven tray. Roast them for about 45 minutes until golden brown. Remove the tray from the oven, drain off the fat, then set aside. While the carcasses and wings are cooking, in a large saucepan on a medium heat, add the oil with the shallots, carrots, mushrooms, leeks, celery, rosemary and thyme. Allow a couple of minutes for them to warm through, then add the garlic. Stir and cook for a further couple of minutes. Deglaze the pan with the vinegar and wine. This should take just a minute, then add the white soy sauce. Reduce the heat to low and simmer until most of the liquid has evaporated. Now add the roasted bones and wings, along with the chicken stock. Continue simmering gently for 2 hours, skimming the liquid when necessary. After 2 hours, skim once more, remove the pan from the heat and set aside to enable the contents to infuse for 1 hour. Now strain the liquid through muslin into a bowl, cover with cling film, then put in the fridge to set. Once chilled, there will be a layer of fat on the top. Scrape this off, cover again with cling film and then place the remaining clear liquid back in the fridge until required.

To make the **brine** for the duck legs, in a large saucepan, add the water, salt and sugar. Place on a high heat and bring to the boil. Remove from the heat and allow to cool for 10 minutes. Then add the thyme, rosemary, bay leaves, garlic, star anise and orange peel. Stir the contents and allow them an hour to infuse.

After the hour, you are ready to brine the **duck legs.** Simply, place them in the brine and set aside in a cool place (but not the fridge) for 24 hours. Once brined, remove them from the liquid, wash under cold water, then pat dry with a J cloth or kitchen paper. Place them in a vacuum pack bag along with the rosemary, thyme, garlic and stock. Vacuum seal the bag and cook in a water bath at 85°C for 4 hours. Once 4 hours have passed, remove the duck legs from the bag, and then pick out the bones and shred them. It is important to make sure no bones are left in the shredded duck meat. Cover and chill until needed.

For the **pasta filling**, preheat the oven to 180°C (160°C fan/Gas Mark 4). Pierce and salt the potatoes and bake in the oven for 1 hour. Once they become soft to touch, remove from the oven and allow to cool for 10 minutes. Cut the potatoes in half, scoop out the insides and pass through a moulin or ricer into a bowl. Add the cream, milk, crème fraîche and Parmesan. With a spatula or wooden spoon, fold the ingredients together. Then fold in three-quarters of the shredded duck legs, followed by the parsley, plus pinches of salt and pepper to season. Once the mixture has fully combined, roll it into 35g balls and set aside. Cover with cling film or put in an airtight container and refrigerate. They will keep for 2 days.

To make the **duck consommé**, combine 700ml duck stock with the minced duck breast, egg whites, leek, carrot, onion, cranberries, orange zest, thyme and rosemary in a large mixing bowl. Add pinches of salt and pepper to season and then whisk until thoroughly mixed. Pour the liquid into a large, tall pan and place on a low heat. Gently bring to the boil while stirring with a wooden spoon. During this process, all the impurities will rise to the top. Leave to cook for a further 10 minutes. With a ladle, gently pour out the clear consommé into a fine muslin cloth, ladle by ladle. Making sure you're getting none of the scum from the top. Leave to cool ready to heat later when plating.

For the **spiced cranberry chutney**, take a medium saucepan and add the olive oil, orange, cranberries, apples, chilli, bitter orange purée, sugar, vinegar and shallots. Place the pan on a low heat and gently cook down the ingredients until you have a jammy consistency. Transfer the mixture to a food processor and blitz on a high setting for 30 seconds. Pass through a fine sieve and pour into a squeezy bottle. If you don't have a squeezy bottle, a piping bag will do. Keep in the fridge until required. This will keep well for at least a week.

Making fresh **pasta** is not difficult and the results are worth the effort. Begin by whisking the egg and yolks together with the olive oil in a bowl. Put the flour and salt into a stand mixer. Start to mix on a medium speed and slowly pour in the whisked eggs. Continue mixing until a dough has formed. On a work surface which has a light dusting of flour, place the dough from the mixer and knead it into a ball. Place the dough into a bowl, cover with cling film and allow to rest at room temperature for 30 minutes. Once rested, take the dough from the bowl and place it on a lightly dusted work surface. Now cut into four equal pieces. In turn, roll out each piece into a 10 x 8cm sheet and pass through a pasta machine. Start at setting ten and gradually keep rolling down through the machine, reducing the setting by two each time until at zero. Using the pastry cutter, cut out discs and place them on a tray covered with greaseproof paper. Once all the discs have been cut, cover the tray with cling film and refrigerate until you build the ravioli.

To make the **bitter orange gel**, using a medium saucepan, add the bitter orange purée, sugar and water. Place on a high heat and bring to the boil. Then gradually add the agar-agar using a whisk and cook at boiling point for a further 2 minutes. Remove from the heat and pour into a container. Allow to cool for 10 minutes and then place in the fridge to set. Once set, transfer the gel to a food processor and blitz on high for 2 minutes. Pass the liquid through a chinois or fine sieve into a bowl. Then pour into a squeezy bottle or a piping bag and refrigerate until needed. This will keep well for 3 days.

To **crisp the duck**, put the reserved shredded duck meat into a mixing bowl with the rice flour and mix well until the meat is thoroughly coated. Place the coated meat into a sieve and toss to remove any excess flour. In a large pan, or a fryer, heat the oil to 180°C and fry the duck until crispy and golden. Remove from the fryer and drain off the oil using kitchen paper or J cloths. Keep at room temperature until required.

Our final task is the to make the **duck ravioli**. Start by brushing beaten egg over one side of the pasta discs. Place a duck ball into the centre of each disc. Then cover them all with the remaining discs. Make sure the filling is not spilling out and there is a rim around each ravioli. Press the two sheets together to seal in the filling, making sure no air is trapped inside. With the pastry cutter, trim off any excess dough.

Assembly and Plating Up

To begin, make sure you have the consommé hot and ready. Heat it up in a saucepan and then reduce the heat so that it will be ready for when you want it. Also, make sure your plates are warm.

To plate, first squeeze a good amount of spiced cranberry chutney in the centre of each plate. Follow this with some smaller dots scattered around and then fill some of the empty space with small dots of the bitter orange gel. Half-fill a large saucepan with water and add a couple of pinches of salt. Bring it to the boil and then carefully add in the ravioli. Cook for 5 minutes, then remove them from the water. Place onto a plate or tray lined with kitchen paper or J cloth to absorb any excess water. Now place the ravioli in the centre of the plates, on top of the larger body of chutney. Garnish with some fresh cranberries and some toasted orange, if you're using it, some chutney and scatter over some crispy duck. Take to the table and pour over the consommé in front of your guests.

> "This heart-warming dish is a nod to Joyce Molyneux's game consommé. It is a pure Joyce classic, which she often served at the Carved Angel. Diners today still talk of fond memories of how much they enjoyed the dish when Joyce had it on the menu. This consommé is full of flavour, making use of the whole duck, and is beautifully balanced with the dried cranberry."

For the duck legs
4 duck legs
50g rosemary
50g thyme
3 garlic cloves, finely chopped or grated
100ml chicken stock (see page 274)

For the duck stock
6 duck carcasses, chopped into very small pieces
2kg duck wings, cut into small pieces
2kg chicken wings, cut into small pieces
Oil, for frying
2 shallots, sliced
2 large carrots, diced
150g button mushrooms, sliced
2 leeks, sliced
2 celery sticks, sliced
2 sprigs of rosemary
2 sprigs of thyme
3 garlic cloves, crushed
50ml sherry vinegar
150ml red wine
75ml white soy sauce
2.5 litres chicken stock (see page 274)

For the brine
1 litre tap water
100g table salt
100g caster sugar
3 sprigs of thyme
3 sprigs of rosemary
3 bay leaves
3 garlic cloves, crushed
3 star anise
Peel of 1 unwaxed orange

For the pasta filling
250g potatoes (I use Pierre Koffmann, but any floury potato will work)
75ml double cream
65ml full-fat milk
50ml crème fraîche
40g Parmesan, finely grated
2 sprigs of flat-leaf parsley
Maldon sea salt and black pepper

For the duck consommé
700ml duck stock (see above)
500g duck breast, minced
4 medium egg whites
1 leek, sliced
1 large carrot, sliced
½ onion, sliced
60g dried cranberries
Zest of 1 large unwaxed orange
Leaves of 1 sprig of thyme
Leaves of 1 sprig of rosemary
Maldon sea salt and black pepper

For the spiced cranberry chutney
Extra virgin olive oil
1 large orange, peeled and roughly chopped
300g dried cranberries
3 Granny Smith apples, roughly chopped
¼ red chilli, deseeded and finely chopped
600g bitter orange purée (I use Boiron)
200g demerara sugar
200ml white wine vinegar
1½ shallots, sliced

For the pasta
1 medium egg
2 medium egg yolks
Extra virgin olive oil
280g 00 flour, plus extra for dusting
5g table salt

For the bitter orange gel
350g bitter orange purée
50g caster sugar
150ml tap water
6g agar-agar

For crisping the duck
50g rice flour
1 litre rapeseed or vegetable oil

For the duck ravioli
1 medium egg, beaten

To garnish
A handful of fresh cranberries
Toasted orange (optional)

Equipment
Large oven tray
Muslin cloth
Vacuum pack bag
Water bath
Moulin or ricer
Food processor
Fine sieve
Squeezy bottle or piping bag
Pasta machine
5cm pastry cutter
Chinois (optional)
Deep-fat fryer or temperature probe

Serves 4

Venison Loin | Parsley Root | Pomegranate

You can make the **pomegranate purée** and the **red wine jus** up to a day before it is needed. Add all the ingredients to a large saucepan. Place on a high heat and bring to the boil. Once boiling, reduce the heat to low and simmer until reduced to a thick and sticky mixture. Transfer to a food processor and blitz on high speed for 5 minutes until smooth. You can add a splash of water if it is too thick to blend. Pass through a chinois or fine sieve and refrigerate in an airtight container until needed. Transfer to a piping bag or squeezy bottle when ready to plate up.

For the **parsley root purée**, peel the parsley root and cut it into small pieces. Add to a large saucepan and cover with the milk and cream. Add a good pinch of salt and the butter and thyme. Bring to a simmer and cook for 15 minutes until the root is tender. Once cooked, pass through a colander and transfer to a blender. Blend until smooth, adding more salt if needed, and pass through a fine sieve. This can be kept in the fridge for 3 days.

Next, get the **venison loin** ready to cook. Cut the loin into four portions. Vacuum seal the venison loins individually and set a water bath to 58°C. Cook the venison loins for 15–20 minutes. After 20 minutes, remove the venison from the water bath and rest the meat in the bags for 5 minutes. Remove from the bags, season on all sides with salt and pepper, then sear in a very hot pan on all sides. Rest for 5–10 minutes. In a hot pan, add the butter, rosemary and a couple of pinches of salt. Foam the butter and pour over the rested venison loins. Baste the venison and keep moving in the hot butter to make sure the meat is hot. Rest for another 2 minutes, before carving and plating.

Next, we move on to the **roasted parsley root garnish**. Preheat the oven to 180°C (160°C fan/Gas Mark 4). Cut the parsley roots in half and place into a hot pan. Season with salt and allow to get some colour. Roast in the oven for 4 minutes until tender. Add the butter and thyme and baste the parsley roots. Keep warm to ready to plate up.

Assembly and Plating Up

Heat up the red wine jus and the parsley root purée, then add a quenelle of purée to the top of each plate. Add a piece of roasted parsley root on the right-hand side of each plate, with four dots of pomegranate purée on top and four pomegranate seeds. Finish off with the venison on the left, topped with six pomegranate seeds. Serve with individual small jugs of the red wine jus.

For the red wine jus

600ml (see page 279)

For the pomegranate purée

250g red plums, stoned

75g dried apricots

1 shallot, sliced

125g demerara sugar

Seeds of 1 pomegranate

150ml apple cider vinegar

2 Granny Smith apples, peeled, cored and chopped

300ml pomegranate juice

Maldon sea salt, to taste

For the parsley root purée

650g parsley root (or parsnips, if you can't get hold of parsley root)

200ml full-fat milk

200ml double cream

100g unsalted butter

2 sprigs of thyme, leaves

Maldon sea salt, to taste

For the venison loin

1 venison loin from a 3–4kg saddle (I use Curtis Pitts)

100g unsalted butter

2 whole sprigs rosemary

Maldon sea salt and black pepper

To garnish

2 parsley roots

50g butter

2 sprigs thyme

40 pomegranate seeds

3 pieces celery cress

Equipment

Muslin cloth

Food processor

Piping bag or squeezy bottle

Chinois or fine sieve

Blender

Vacuum pack bags

Water bath

"I was the first chef to use Curtis Pitts Deer Services when I first started at the Angel. His family-run company rear their venison sustainably on Curtis's land and they are processed in his own on-site butchery. This recipe is beautiful way of showcasing Curtis's exceptional venison at its best. I use wild fallow deer and get it on the saddle, which has been dry aged for 28 days to give it that extra flavour when cooking."

Devonshire Lamb Loin | Brown Butter Artichokes | Sauce Picante

Serves 6

For the **braised lamb necks**, place the necks in the meat brine, ensuring they are fully immersed in the liquid. Cover and refrigerate for 12 hours. Once brined, wash them under cold running water and pat dry. Pour both stocks into a large saucepan. Place on a high heat, bring to the boil, then remove from the heat. In another large saucepan on high heat, add the lamb necks and sear them. Once seared, add the carrots, celery, herbs, garlic, coriander seeds, star anise and pink peppercorns. Now pour in the stock mixture and bring to the boil. Turn the heat down to low and simmer for 4–5 hours. The liquid should reduce by half during this time. The lamb necks will gently fall apart when ready and cooked. Gently allow the lamb necks to cool for 10–15 minutes. Reduce the remaining sauce further until the liquid coats the back of a spoon and is rich and glossy. Strain the sauce and pour over the lamb necks and mix in well. We gently roll necks into a ballotine by rolling out a piece of cling film, adding the braised lamb neck on top, then rolling it tightly to form a cylinder, making sure there is no air. Allow to set in the fridge. They can be made in advance and will keep well in the fridge for up to 5 days.

For the **sauce picante**, add the white wine and vinegar to a saucepan. Place the saucepan on a high heat and reduce the liquid by half. Once reduced, add the veal stock and lamb sauce. Then reduce by a further three-quarters until the sauce coats the back of a spoon. Remove from the heat and pass through a muslin cloth. Allow to cool and refrigerate until needed. Half-fill a small saucepan with water and place on a high heat. While it's coming to the boil, add the shallot, carrot and celery and blanch the vegetables in the water for 2 minutes. Refresh the vegetables under cold water to cool and put them in a container to use later. Put the gherkins and herbs into another container and set aside until needed.

Begin preparing the **Jerusalem artichoke purée** by half-filling a pan with water and the lemon juice. Peel the artichokes, then place them in the pan with the water and lemon juice until ready to slice. Then thinly slice them and place back into another pan. Once all the Jerusalem artichokes have been peeled and sliced, pour the milk and cream over them. Put the pan on a low heat and slowly cook them until soft. Strain the cooked artichokes in a colander and then place them into a blender. Now blend until you have smooth purée. Season with salt and allow to cool completely. Once cool, pour the purée into a squeezy bottle. Put the bottle in the fridge until needed. You can make the purée in advance and it will keep well in the fridge for up to 3 days.

Next, prepare the **stuffed artichokes**. Preheat the oven to 180°C (160°C fan/Gas Mark 4). Put the Jerusalem artichokes in a roasting tray, along with the rapeseed oil and a pinch of salt and pepper. Mix well and then roast in the oven for about 40 minutes. They may take a bit longer, depending upon the size of the artichokes. You are looking for them to be soft in the middle. Once cooked, remove from the oven and leave to cool slightly for 5-10 minutes. Using a small, serrated vegetable knife, cut the artichokes in half vertically and scoop out the insides with a teaspoon. Save both the shells and the filling of the artichokes. In a deep-fat fryer, or in a large pan of hot oil at about 180°C, fry the artichoke shells for 1-2 minutes until crispy, but not too dark, as they will taste bitter. Remove from the oil and sprinkle a small amount of salt over the shells. Keep to the side until required.

While the oil is still hot, quickly prepare the **artichoke crisps**. On a mandoline, finely slice the small artichoke horizontally. The slices should be almost translucent. Put the slices into a small bowl, add the flour, then mix until well covered. Fry these slices in the oil for 30 seconds-1 minute until they are golden and crispy. Remove from the oil and sprinkle with salt.

Now make the **Mornay cheese sauce**. Bring the milk to the boil in a small saucepan. Place another pan on the heat and melt the butter. Add the flour to the butter and gently mix. Continue whisking until a paste forms – this is called a roux. Continue cooking for a further 2-3 minutes. Add the milk to the roux, stirring as you go, until you get a smooth sauce. Cook the sauce for 10 minutes on a low heat, stirring continuously, until the sauce has thickened. Now add both the Parmesan and Cheddar and cook for a further 5 minutes. Season the sauce with salt and pepper.

In a small pan, add the artichoke filling and roughly an equal amount of Mornay sauce. Over a medium-low heat, combine both well and season with salt and pepper. Next, stir in the chopped chives. Once happy with the seasoning, transfer to a piping bag. Using an oven tray, line up your crispy artichoke shells and pipe in the filling. Use a palette knife to smooth the surface and they are now ready to be baked.

Get the **lamb** ready to cook. Vacuum seal the lamb loins individually in vacuum pack bags and set a water bath to 58°C. Cook the lamb loins in the water bath for 15 minutes. While the lamb is cooking, warm the picante sauce until it is at a simmer. After the 15 minutes, remove the lamb from the water bath and rest the meat in the bags for 5 minutes. Remove from the bags, season on all sides with salt and pepper and then sear in a very hot pan on all sides. Now let the lamb rest for 5-10 minutes. At this stage, add the blanched carrot, celery and shallot to the picante sauce and simmer until the vegetables are cooked, but not too soft – you want them to retain a little bite. Add the gherkins and herbs, then simmer for 1-2 minutes. In a hot frying pan, add the butter, rosemary and the sea salt. Foam the butter and add the rested lamb loins. Baste the lamb and keep moving it in the hot butter to make sure the meat is hot. Rest for another 2 minutes before carving and plating.

Take the **baby artichoke heart garnish** and cut them in half vertically, season with salt and cook in a frying pan on a high heat for about 2 minutes until a nice golden brown. Add a knob of butter and cook until the butter begins to brown. Remove from the heat and they are now ready serve.

Cook the **spinach garnish** in a hot pan with a knob of melted butter and a pinch of salt. It will take no longer than a couple of minutes to wilt. Remove from the pan and use kitchen paper to drain off the liquid. Use a tablespoon to ball the spinach into small parcels. They are now ready for plating.

Assembly and Plating Up

Cut 6 pieces of the braised lamb neck, and fry off until golden on each side, then place in the oven at 180°C (160°C fan/Gas Mark 4) for 5 minutes or until hot. Place your artichoke shells in the oven for 5 minutes, or until hot. Make sure your plates are warm before assembling the dishes. Place the spinach to the lefthand side of the plate, the filled artichoke to the righthand side, with artichoke crisps on top. Pipe a big dot of Jerusalem artichoke purée top right. Now place the carved lamb loin on top of the spinach and spoon the sauce picante over the loin. Serve with extra sauce if needed, or you just want to be indulgent.

For the braised lamb necks

1 portion of meat brine
5 lamb necks, boned
1 litre veal stock (see page 275)
500ml chicken stock (see page 274)
2 large carrots, sliced
1 celery stick, sliced
50g thyme
50g rosemary
4 garlic cloves, crushed
5g coriander seeds
2 star anise
Pinch of pink peppercorns

For the sauce picante

100ml white wine
100ml white wine vinegar
500ml veal stock (see page 275)
500ml lamb sauce (see page 277)
30g shallot, brunoised
30g carrot, diced
30g celery, diced
30g gherkins, brunoised or finely diced
10g chives, finely chopped
10g chervil, finely chopped
10g tarragon, finely chopped

For the Jerusalem artichoke purée

Juice of 1 lemon
500g Jerusalem artichokes
150ml full-fat milk
150ml double cream
Maldon sea salt

> *"This dish is based on Joyce Molyneux's sauce picante. Joyce used to serve it with hot grated beetroot, but I wanted to use an alternative vegetable, so decided on Jerusalem artichoke. At the Angel, I have slightly altered Joyce's original recipe but it remains a very clever sauce, which perfectly complements lamb loin and artichokes."*

For the stuffed artichokes

6 medium Jerusalem artichokes, cleaned
1 tbsp rapeseed oil
Oil, for frying
10g chives, finely chopped
Table salt and black pepper, to taste

For the artichoke crisps

1 small Jerusalem artichoke, cleaned
2 tbsp plain or gluten-free flour
Salt, to taste

For the Mornay cheese sauce

250ml full-fat milk
20g unsalted butter
25g plain flour
50g Parmesan, grated
50g Cheddar, grated
Salt and pepper, to taste

For the lamb

6 x 140g lamb loins (ask your butcher for the loins or a short saddle)
150g unsalted butter
6 sprigs of rosemary
20g Maldon sea salt
Table salt and black pepper, to taste

To garnish

3 cooked baby artichoke hearts (see page 64)
A couple of knobs of butter
200g bag of spinach leaves, picked from the stems and washed
Salt, to taste

Equipment

Muslin cloth
Blender
Squeezy bottle
Deep-fat fryer (optional)
Mandoline
Piping bag
Vacuum pack bags
Water batch

Serves 4

Roasted Line Caught Sea Bass | Caviar and Lettuce Cream

To make the **caviar and lettuce cream**, place a medium pan on a low heat, then add the butter. Gently melt and then add the onion. Once the onion has started to sweat down, add the garlic, celery and herbs. Allow the ingredients to sweat for a minute, then add the lettuce. Once all the ingredients have sweated down, pour in the chicken stock and bring to the boil. Add the double cream and let the mixture gently cook out for 5 minutes. Transfer to a blender and blend until smooth. Pass the liquid through a fine sieve. Cool over ice and place in the fridge until needed.

For the **grilled lettuce garnish**, add the butter and water to a pan and heat. Add the lettuce and cook for 30 seconds, then place on a metal tray and gently blowtorch the lettuce. Ideally you want the lettuce to be slightly coloured.

You are now ready to finish the dish with the **sea bass**. Preheat the oven to 180°C (160°C fan/Gas Mark 4). Remove the sea bass fillet from the fridge, portion it into four fillets, pat the skin dry with a clean J cloth and lightly season. Pour the oil into a non-stick pan and heat until the pan is hot but not smoking. Gently place the sea bass in the pan, skin-side down. Keep the pan on a medium heat until the edges of the fish skin gain a golden colouring. Transfer the sea bass to the oven and cook for a further 2 minutes. Take the sea bass out of the oven, add the butter to the pan, then baste it over the fish. Allow the fish to rest before serving.

Assembly and Plating Up

Place a piece of grilled lettuce on each plate, followed by the roasted sea bass. Add the caviar to the lettuce cream and bring to a simmer. Spoon on the side of the fish and lettuce.

> "I was inspired to create this dish by Joyce's recipe for sea bass in lettuce and herbs. It has a wonderful balance between the sweet flesh of the fish and the saltiness of the caviar, along with the lettuce cream, which brings everything together."

For the caviar and lettuce cream

100g unsalted butter
1 medium onion, thinly sliced
2 garlic cloves, crushed
1 celery stick, diced
1 sprig of rosemary, leaves only
2 sprigs of thyme, leaves only
4 iceberg lettuces, sliced into small pieces
700ml chicken stock (see page 274)
300ml double cream
10g caviar (I use Exmoor Caviar)

For the grilled lettuce garnish

50g unsalted butter
150ml tap water
1 iceberg lettuce, quartered

For the sea bass

3–4kg fillet of sea bass (we get ours from Flying Fish)
100g rapeseed oil
Knob of butter
Salt

Equipment

Blender
Fine sieve
Blowtorch

Apple Soufflé | Apple Syrup | Walnut and Maple Icecream

Serves 6 - 8

First, make the **walnut and maple ice cream**. I make this in the ThermoMixer. However, you can make this in a pan and gently cook out to 83°C. It's a brilliant recipe, as you can add any flavouring to this base of ice cream. Preheat the oven to 180°C (160°C fan/Gas Mark 4). Roast the walnuts for 6 minutes and allow to cool. Add the milk, cream, sugar, egg yolk and vanilla seeds to the ThermoMixer, then blitz on full speed. Pour in the maple syrup. Turn down to speed setting 3 and gently cook the ice cream, slowly turning up the temperature to reach 83°C. This process usually takes 5-10 minutes. When the custard is ready, add the walnuts and allow to infuse. Place the custard over a bowl of iced water to cool. Once cold, using a stick blender, gently blend the nuts into the ice cream and pass through a fine sieve. Put the ice cream into the freezer.

For the **apple syrup**, put the sugar in a pan and heat until it is a light golden caramel colour, then add the butter and deglaze the pan with the apple juice. Add the apples and gently simmer to infuse. Pass the syrup through a chinois and keep in the fridge until needed. This will last up to 3 days.

For the **apple purée base**, peel all the apples and place them into lemon water so they retain their colour. Chop the apples up into small pieces, making sure to discard the core and pips. Add all the apples to a large pan with the sugar and tap water. Cook the apples on a high heat, stirring continuously. Cover with cling film, allowing the apples to steam, and gently cook for 5-10 minutes. The apples should have no colour. Once the apples are cooked, blitz them in a food blender and pass the juice through a sieve. Weigh out 1kg apple purée and pour into a medium pan. Add 2 teaspoons of water to the cornflour to make a paste, then add to the apples. Cook the purée until it thickens and becomes glossy. Put into a container and allow to chill in the fridge, where it will keep for up to 2 days.

To make the **cinnamon sugar**, mix the cinnamon and sugar together well. Once thoroughly combined, pour into a container. Cover and store in the fridge. This will last for a couple of weeks.

Next, move on to the **oat crumble topping**. Preheat the oven to 180°C (160°C fan/Gas Mark 4). On a baking tray, add all the ingredients and mix very well with a spoon. Squeeze the oats together, making sure everything is well incorporated. Bake in the oven for up to 10 minutes. After 5 minutes, remove from the oven, quickly mix the ingredients with a spoon, then put back in to finish cooking. Remove from the oven, allow to cool, then transfer to a container with a lid and leave at room temperature. They will keep for 2 days.

Now, make the **soufflé**. Weigh out 300g of the apple purée base into a bowl. Next, weigh out the egg white in a stand mixer fitted with the whisk attachment. Have the caster sugar ready on the side as well. Brush the ramekins with the whipped butter, add a small amount of the cinnamon sugar, allowing it to coat all the sides and bottom, shaking out any excess. Keep the ramekins in the fridge until needed. Start whisking the egg white and, at the same time, gradually add the sugar, bit by bit. Do not stop whisking until the egg white looks like clouds. Once all the sugar has been added, you should have a glossy meringue. Fold one-third of the meringue into the apple base and whisk until combined. Then gently fold in the remaining meringue, making sure both are mixed together well.

Assembly and Plating Up

Preheat the oven to 200°C (180°C fan/Gas Mark 6). Fill the ramekins to the brim with the soufflé mixture and level off with a spatula or palette knife. Add three pieces of roasted walnut and some oat topping. Cook the soufflés in the middle of the oven for 3–4 minutes. The cooking time required depends on the size of your ramekins.

Serve the soufflés with a quenelle of the walnut and maple ice cream and some apple syrup.

For the walnut and maple ice cream

100g walnuts

330ml full-fat milk

80ml double cream

60g caster sugar

100g egg yolk

Seeds from 1 vanilla pod

40ml maple syrup

For the apple syrup

180g caster sugar

130g unsalted butter

200ml apple juice

2 Granny Smith apples, diced

For the apple purée base

1kg Bramley cooking apples

3 Granny Smith apples

3 Braeburn apples

1 lemon, for lemon water

75g caster sugar

100ml tap water

35g cornflour

For the cinnamon sugar

15g ground cinnamon

45g caster sugar

For the oat crumble topping

100g oats

20ml maple syrup

10ml olive oil

5g table salt

For the soufflé

300g apple base (see above)

180g egg whites

50g caster sugar

50g whipped unsalted butter

2g cinnamon sugar

For the garnish

12 roasted walnuts

Equipment

ThermoMixer

Stick blender

Fine sieve

Blender

Stand mixer with whisk attachment

6-8 ramekins, 7cm diameter

" Joyce served a Grand Marnier soufflé in the restaurant that was very popular, and customers still talk about it today. This inspired me to include one I used to serve at the beginning of my adventure with the Angel. It's a pure classic. "

'The Black Penny'

Serves 12

The first task is to make the **black sesame cake**. Preheat the oven to 160°C (140°C fan/ Gas Mark 3). Beat the butter and sugar together in a stand mixer fitted with the whisk attachment. Once fluffy, add the eggs and black sesame paste and continue to beat until combined. Remove the mixing bowl from the mixer and, using a silicone spatula, gently fold in the flour, ground almonds and baking powder. Take a large tray, line with a silicone mat or sheet of baking paper and evenly spread over the cake mixture. Bake in the oven for 9 minutes, or until cooked. Once cooked, place another silicone mat or sheet of baking paper over the top of the cake. Now place a heavy tray on top (or another heavy, flat-bottomed item) to cold-press the cake and then chill in the fridge for at least 1 hour. Once cold-pressed, remove the cake from the fridge. Now place the mousse ring in the centre of the tray and push down to cut out a square. Do not remove the mousse ring as we will build the dessert on this tray.

Next, prepare the **chocolate marquise**. Half-fill a medium pan with water and place it on a medium heat. In a metal mixing bowl, add the chocolate and butter. Cover with cling film and place on top of the pan of water to melt. Make sure the bowl does not meet the water. In a stand mixer, whisk the egg yolk and sugar together until pale and creamy. In another mixing bowl, whisk the cream to a soft peak stage, taking care not to overwork it, or it will not combine properly with the other ingredients. Mix the egg yolk, sugar and cocoa powder with the melted chocolate mixture until fully combined. Then fold the soft cream into the mix using a spatula. Fold until just combined, taking care not to beat the air out or overwork the cream. Transfer to a piping bag and pipe into the square mousse ring, on top of the cold-pressed cake. You are looking for about a 3.5cm depth of marquise in the ring mould. Smooth out with a palette knife and keep in the fridge until required.

To make the **banana and chocolate bavarois**, add the cream, banana purée, milk, black sesame paste and cornflour to a large saucepan. Place on a medium heat and bring to the boil, stirring continuously. Cook at boiling point until the mixture becomes quite thick, almost like a custard. Then add the white chocolate, the carbon black powder, and the sugar. Continue mixing until the chocolate has melted and incorporated into the bavarois. Remove from the heat and immediately pour into the square mousse ring. Allow a few minutes to cool, then keep in the fridge until needed.

Next, prepare the **banana and sesame sorbet**. Put some tepid water into a container and add the gelatine. Leave it for 5 minutes to bloom. Half-fill a bowl with ice cubes and cover with tap water. In a medium saucepan, pour the water, banana purée and sesame seed paste. Mix well, place on a high heat and bring to the boil. Once boiling, turn off the heat. In another bowl, mix the sugar and stabiliser together. Squeeze the water from the gelatine and add to the banana purée and water. Then add the sugar and stabiliser to the pan and mix well. Turn on the heat again and bring back to the boil. Once boiling, transfer the mixture to a container over the bowl of iced water. Pour the sorbet into a container and freeze until required. The sorbet will keep well in the freezer for up to a month.

Move on to the **sesame seed tuile**. Preheat the oven to 180°C (160°C fan/Gas Mark 4). Line an oven tray with a silicone mat or baking paper. In a medium pan, add the glucose, lime juice and butter. Place on a medium heat and bring to a simmer. Add the icing sugar and flour and cook out for 2–3 minutes. Then add both sesame pastes and mix well. Remove from the heat and spread evenly over the silicone mat or baking paper. Put the tray in the oven and cook for about 8 minutes. Remove from the oven and leave to cool completely. Once cooled, use the small ring cutter to cut out the tuiles. Keep them in an airtight container at room temperature until needed.

The final element to prepare is the **tempered chocolate sheet** (see page 280). I use a transfer sheet which is specially made for me, as it contains edible ink to replicate the iconic penny black stamp. I recommend making a tempered chocolate sheet at home with your own design to complete the dessert.

Assembly and Plating Up

Remove the layered mousse ring from the fridge. Pull the square ring off the dessert. If it is not pulling free easily, try using a small blowtorch around the ring mould to loosen it. Alternatively, if you do not have or want to use a blowtorch, use a hot knife around the edge. You can trim off any rough edges after getting the ring mould free. Using a hot knife, cut the penny black into twelve squares. Using a palette knife, place each one in the centre of a white plate, and top with a square of tempered chocolate sheet slightly bigger than each mousse. On a separate side plate, place a sesame seed tuile in the centre. Take the sorbet from the freezer and, using a hot spoon, scoop, rocher or quenelle the sorbet onto the tuile.

The dessert can be kept in the fridge for up to 2 days stored in a covered container.

> "This dessert holds wonderful memories for me. I first cooked it for the judges when competing for the South West of England during the 2021 series of BBC's *Great British Menu* and scored the maximum ten points from Richard Corrigan. The theme for that series was to celebrate a notable British invention."

For the black sesame cake

200g unsalted butter, softened
185g soft dark brown sugar
3 large eggs
100g black sesame paste
35g plain flour
100g ground almonds
1 tsp baking powder

For the chocolate marquise

145g good-quality dark chocolate (70% cocoa)
72g unsalted butter
60g egg yolk
72g caster sugar
3 tbsp cocoa powder
225ml double cream

For the banana and chocolate bavarois

185ml double cream
150g banana purée
75ml full-fat milk
23g black sesame paste
23g cornflour
45g white chocolate
1g carbon black powder
38g caster sugar

For the banana and sesame sorbet

½ gelatine leaf
110ml water
500g banana purée
1 tsp black sesame paste
105g caster sugar
25g sorbet stabiliser

For the sesame seed tuile

50g liquid glucose
2 tsp fresh lime juice
100g unsalted butter
150g icing sugar, sifted
50g plain flour
50g white sesame paste
50g black sesame paste

For the tempered chocolate sheet

300g white chocolate chips
3g cocoa butter

Equipment

Stand mixer with whisk attachment
Silicone mats
200mm square mousse ring
Hand-held electric whisk
Piping bag
5cm circle ring cutter
Acetate sheets
Temperature probe
Blowtorch (optional)

Serves 6

Chocolate and Bitter Orange | Pedro Ximénez | Roasted Pearl Barley

First, make the **bitter orange insert**. Mix the pectin and 6g sugar in a bowl. You need to mix these together before adding the liquid so it does not become lumpy. In a medium saucepan, add the bitter orange purée, liquid glucose and the 32g sugar, then bring to the boil. Once boiling, add the orange liqueur and the sugar and pectin mixture to the purée. Place back on the heat and bring to the boil, making sure you're always whisking the purée. Pour the purée into a measuring jug, then into your individual silicone pomponette moulds. Place the moulds into the freezer to set and freeze. Once frozen, pop the bitter orange inserts out of the moulds and cut in half. They can be made up in advance and will last in the freezer for up to 1 month after making.

For the **chocolate caramel mousse**, start by soaking the gelatine in cold water. When the gelatine has bloomed, squeeze out any excess water and keep in a container until needed. Fill a medium pan halfway with water and place on the heat. Place the milk chocolate in a mixing bowl and place on top of the pan to gently melt. With a stand mixer, whisk the egg yolk until you have a thick sabayon. While the egg yolk is whisking, add the sugar to a medium pan. Put this on the heat and start to make the caramel. You're looking for a dark caramel, but without it burning. Add 127ml of the cream to the caramel and allow to cook out. The caramel will boil, then settle down once the cream is mixed in. It should look like a glossy caramel sauce. Pass the caramel through a fine sieve to make sure no sugar pieces are left. Before adding the gelatine to the caramel, make sure it is still hot enough for the gelatine to dissolve in it. Mix the gelatine into the caramel using a spatula. While the eggs are still whisking, slowly add the caramel to the sabayon and continue whisking on full. The milk chocolate should now be melted. Add it slowly to the sabayon and mix until fully combined. In a separate bowl, add the remaining 450ml cream and whisk to soft peaks. You don't want to over whisk the cream, as it will not mix in properly and may spilt the mousse. You now want to gently fold the whisked cream into the chocolate. Do this by folding a third of the whisked cream into the chocolate at a time. Gently fold the mousse with the cream until they are fully incorporated. Pour the mousse into piping bags ready to pipe into your silicone moulds.

Pipe the chocolate mousse into the larger quenelle silicone moulds, making sure to fill only halfway. Place a piece of the bitter orange insert in the middle of each mousse. Pipe more of the chocolate mousse to cover the inserts. Pipe the remaining mousse to fill the smaller quenelle moulds. Smooth off the top of each mousse with a palette knife and place a piece of baking paper over the top and then put them into the freezer to firm up. They need to be completely frozen before spraying them.

For the **roasted pearl barley ice cream**, preheat the oven to 180°C (160°C fan/Gas Mark 4). Spread the pearl barley over a baking tray and roast for 8–10 minutes. Pour the milk and cream into a medium pan and bring to the boil. Then add the roasted pearl barley and infuse for 30 minutes. Strain the cream liquid off. Whisk the yolk and sugar together in a mixing bowl, then add the cream mixture. Place on the heat and cook the liquid to 83°C, stirring continuously. Pass through a fine sieve and into a bowl sitting over another bowl of iced water. Allow to cool and freeze in Pacojet containers. Churn the ice cream when ready to plate.

For the **bitter orange gel**, add the water, sugar and bitter orange purée to a saucepan. Bring to the boil and then add the agar-agar. Continue boiling for another 2 minutes, then pour into a container. Cover and allow to set. Once firmly set, transfer it to a blender and blend until smooth. Pass the gel through a chinois and then into a piping bag. Keep the bag in the fridge until required. You can make this in advance and it lasts up to 3 days.

Next, move on to the **cocoa oats**. Preheat the oven to 180°C (160°C fan/Gas Mark 4). On a baking tray, add all the ingredients and mix very well with your hands. Squeeze the oats together and make sure everything is well incorporated. Bake in the oven for 25–30 minutes, taking them out of the oven every 5 minutes to mix quickly using a spoon. Once they are done, remove from the oven, allow to cool, then transfer to a container with a lid and leave at room temperature. They will keep for 2 days.

To make the **sherry vinegar gel**, add the sherry vinegar, Pedro Ximénez and sugar to a medium saucepan. Whisk constantly and bring to the boil. Then continue to whisk while you add the agar-agar. Whisk for a further 2 minutes at boiling point. Remove from the heat and pour into a container. The mixture will set at room temperature, but you can place in the fridge to set more quickly. The larger the surface area of the container you use, the faster it will set. Once completely set, mix in a blender on high until smooth. Pass through a chinois and put in a piping bag or squeezy bottle. The gel can be kept in the fridge for up to a week.

With all the other elements prepared, now make the **chocolate cocoa spray**. Put the chocolate and cocoa butter into a mixing bowl. Fill a medium pan three-quarters full with water and put it on a medium heat. Now place the mixing bowl on top, making sure it does not touch the water. The chocolate should now gently melt. Keep an eye on it, making sure the water does not boil. Using a stick blender, blend the chocolate and cocoa butter until completely mixed. Once mixed, set the bowl aside until required.

Put the melted chocolate mixture into a chocolate sprayer, making sure the correct attachment is on the sprayer. Turn out all the mousses onto a silicone mat, making sure there is space between them all. Spray the mousses evenly, taking care there is an even covering. Once sprayed, place them back in the freezer to firm up and freeze again. Ideally this needs to be done in the morning or a few hours before serving.

Assembly and Plating Up

Place one large quenelle of chocolate mousse on a plate and another smaller quenelle of mousse to the side of it. Add three dots of the bitter orange gel to the plate and place the cocoa oats over the top of the gel. Place a rocher of roasted pearl barley ice cream on the side, then add two dots of the sherry vinegar gel.

For the bitter orange insert

6g pectin NH
6g plus 32g caster sugar
218g bitter orange purée
16g liquid glucose
37ml orange liqueur

For the chocolate caramel mousse

3 gelatine leaves
230g milk chocolate
90g egg yolk
65g caster sugar
577ml double cream

For the roasted pearl barley ice cream

60g pearl barley
250ml full-fat milk
125ml double cream
75g egg yolk
50g caster sugar
20g malt extract (I use Ovaltine)
75g milk chocolate
½ tsp vanilla bean paste

For the bitter orange gel

150ml tap water
50g caster sugar
300g bitter orange purée
6g agar-agar

For the cocoa oats

50g oats
10g maple syrup
1 tbsp cocoa powder
3g table salt
15ml extra virgin olive oil

For the sherry vinegar gel

100ml sherry vinegar
100ml Pedro Ximénez
200g caster sugar
7g agar-agar

For the chocolate and cocoa spray

250g milk chocolate (I use Callebaut)
125g cocoa butter (I use Callebaut)

Equipment

Stand mixer with whisk attachment
6 small moulds (15ml volume or smaller)
Fine sieve
Piping bags
6 24ml silicone quenelle moulds
6 10ml silicone quenelle moulds
Temperature probe
Pacojet
Blender
Chinois
Squeezy bottle (optional)
Stick blender
Chocolate sprayer
Silicone mat

"The acidity in the vinegar transforms this finished chocolate dessert into a deeper, more vibrant brown colour. It also brings out a tang within the flavour of bitter orange, which pairs well with the richness of the chocolate."

Chocolate | Coffee Curd | Lemon | Coffee Milk Sorbet

Serves 6

Start by making the **preserved lemon gel**. In a medium saucepan, add the sugar, lemons and tap water. Bring the mixture to the boil, then pour it into a blender and blitz on a high setting until you have a smooth gel. With a spatula, transfer the contents from the blender back into a saucepan on a medium heat. While constantly whisking, add the agar-agar. Then, still gently whisking, cook for 4 minutes. Pour the mixture into a dish, cover with cling film and place in the fridge to set. Once it has set, use a spatula to put it into a blender. Blitz on the high setting. After a couple of minutes blitzing, pass the mixture through a chinois or sieve. Once sieved, pour it into a squeezy bottle or piping bag. You can prepare the gel up to a day in advance of serving, but it must be kept in the fridge

For the **coffee curd**, boil the espresso, butter and sugar in a small saucepan. Put the chocolate in a mixing bowl. In another mixing bowl, add the egg yolk and whisk. Then pour the hot espresso mixture over the eggs to temper them. Pour the whole mixture back into the saucepan and cook until it thickens, making sure to stir continuously as it cooks. You will know it is cooked when the mixture coats the back of a spoon. Pour this mixture over the chocolate, then mix well until everything has combined. Add the chocolate curd to a piping bag and place in the fridge. This curd will last for up to 3 days. Before serving, it will need to come out of the fridge to be brought back up to room temperature.

To make the **coffee milk sorbet**, preheat the oven to 160°C (140°C fan/Gas Mark 3). Scatter the coffee beans over a baking tray and gently roast in the oven for 5–10 minutes. Put the milk, cream and trimoline into a pan and bring to the boil. Then add the condensed milk and coffee beans. Allow to cool, then pass through a fine sieve. Pour into Pacojet containers and freeze.

Next, move on to the **cocoa oats**. On a baking tray, add all the ingredients and mix very well with your hands. Squeeze the oats together making sure everything is well incorporated. Bake in the oven at 180°C (160°C fan/Gas Mark 4) for 25–30 minutes, taking them out of the oven every 5 minutes to mix quickly using a spoon. Remove from the oven, allow to cool, then transfer to a container with a lid and leave at room temperature. They will keep for 2 days.

To make the **chocolate ganache**, place the double cream into a pan and bring to the boil. Pour the cream over the chocolates in two parts to gently melt. Fold the cream into the chocolate. Spread the mixture into the pebble moulds and bang out the air. Place in the freezer to firm – this will take an hour at least. Release from the mould and place in the fridge until needed.

The last element to prepare is the **gold chocolate base**. Melt the chocolate and cocoa butter in a medium bowl over a bain-marie. Once totally melted, add the feuilletine pieces and mix. Allow to cool a little before rolling out in a thin layer. Once rolled out, place in the fridge to set. You will ring cut the pieces when plating.

Assembling and Plating Up

Using a ring cutter, cut out the gold chocolate base and place on the plate. Pipe coffee curd onto the gold chocolate bases. Make sure the curd is hard enough to hold the chocolate ganache, then place the ganache on top of the coffee curd. Spray the chocolate ganache with edible gold spray. Dot on the preserved lemon gel and more of the coffee curd. Sprinkle over the cocoa oats and four halves of roasted hazelnuts per serving. Finish off with a rocher of milk coffee sorbet, topped with a piece of gold leaf, and scatter over four pieces of lemon balm per serving.

For the preserved lemon gel

125g caster sugar

125g preserved lemons

400ml tap water

9g agar-agar

For the coffee curd

50ml espresso (I use the Angel's own blend)

75g unsalted butter

7g caster sugar

50g good-quality dark chocolate (70% cocoa)

40g egg yolk

For the coffee milk sorbet

30g coffee beans (I use the Angel's own beans)

500ml full-fat milk

50ml double cream

3g trimoline (inverted sugar)

400ml condensed milk

For the cocoa oats

50g oats

10g maple syrup

1 tbsp cocoa powder

3g table salt

15ml extra virgin olive oil

For the chocolate ganache

150ml double cream

170g dark chocolate (70% cocoa)

150g Cluizel Z-Karamel 43% chocolate

For the gold chocolate base

120g gold chocolate

80g cocoa butter

115g feuilletine pieces

To garnish

Edible gold spray

12 halved roasted hazelnuts

Edible gold leaf

24 pieces of lemon balm

Equipment

Blender

Chinois or fine sieve

Squeezy bottle (optional)

Piping bags

Pacojet

Pebble moulds

5cm ring cutter

❝This dessert is very special to me as it brings back wonderful memories of someone who I will always dearly miss. It was the last dessert Craig and I put together on the menu. A dessert which we will always cherish. A true statement to the Angel.❞

Serves 4

Toffee Apple and Cinnamon Chocolates

For the **dark chocolate shells**, remove the metal base sheet from the magnetic polycarbonate chocolate moulds. Using a glass cloth, polish the moulds. Decorate the moulds using edible gold leaf and coloured cocoa butter. Cut a transfer sheet to size and place it on the metal sheet before attaching it to the mould. To line the moulds, temper the dark chocolate (see page 280). Fill the moulds completely with the chocolate, then tap the moulds firmly on the work surface to remove any air bubbles. Turn the moulds over, allowing the excess chocolate to run out into a large bowl. Save the excess chocolate to cap the shells the next day. While still inverted, tap the moulds gently to produce a thin shell, then scrape the top and sides of the moulds to remove excess chocolate. Place face down on a silicone sheet for 2 minutes to prevent any chocolate pooling in the base of the shells. Turn the chocolate-lined moulds right way up and allow to crystallise in a cool, dry place overnight (not the fridge, which has too much moisture).

To make the **caramel**, add the sugar and water to a heavy-based frying pan. Dissolve on a medium heat, then turn up the heat and allow to bubble for 4–5 minutes until you have a caramel. Remove from the heat and stir in the cream and butter. Leave the sauce to cool to 32°C, then transfer to a piping bag. Pipe a thin layer into the base of each chocolate shell.

Now for the **toffee apple and cinnamon ganache**. Place the apple juice and cinnamon in a saucepan and simmer until reduced by half. Remove from the heat and stir in the liquid glucose. Pass through a fine sieve and allow to cool to 50°C. Finely chop the chocolate, then pour the juice over the chocolate and allow to stand for 1 minute to begin melting. Add the butter, then transfer to a blender and blend for 3 minutes until fully emulsified. Allow to cool to 32°C before transferring to a piping bag and filling the moulds. Leave 2mm at the top of each mould for capping off. Allow to set in a cool place for a couple of hours before capping the top of the moulds with the reserved tempered dark chocolate. Crystallise overnight before turning the chocolates out from their moulds.

Finally, make the **angel wing discs**. Put the tempered chocolate into a piping bag and pipe roughly 20mm discs onto a silicone sheet. Then, with a wax stamp (which has been pre-cooled in the freezer), press it onto each disc to create a decorative imprint, cooling the stamp on ice between each disc. I use an angel wing stamp. Allow the chocolate discs to set and crystallise for at least 1 hour. Place a disc onto a hot plate for 2 seconds to melt the back, before topping each petit four chocolate.

I serve these petit fours together with the Angel's own fine coffee blend.

For the dark chocolate shells

24-carat edible gold leaf

Coloured cocoa butter (we tend to use greens, browns and golds, which can be bought online)

500g dark chocolate (Callebaut or any good-quality chocolate)

For the caramel

250g caster sugar

4 tbsp tap water

150ml double cream

50g unsalted butter

For the toffee apple and cinnamon ganache

700ml apple juice

1 tsp ground cinnamon

20ml liquid glucose

300g gold or blonde chocolate

50g unsalted butter

For the angel wing discs

200g gold or blonde chocolate, tempered (see page 280)

Equipment

8 30mm round magnetic polycarbonate chocolate moulds

Glass cloths

Scissors

Transfer sheet (we have our own Angel wing feather ones, but you can buy different designs online)

2 silicone sheets

Piping bags

Temperature probe

Blender

Wax stamp

“Umber & Ecru, our chocolatier, are also based in Dartmouth, on the beautiful river Dart. Their kitchen studio overlooks Dartmouth town and out to sea. It is a truly inspirational setting. The changing seasons and scenery influence the style and design of their creations. They make and decorate all our chocolates by hand, so that each one is unique and exclusive. U & E source only the finest and freshest organic ingredients and, where possible, obtain them from Devon-based suppliers. They look amazing and provide our diners with a wonderful end-of-meal treat. It has been a great pleasure to work with Heather of U & E to create and evolve our range of chocolates.”

AND A LITTLE EXTRA...

The Angel Brines

Put all the ingredients in a large saucepan, adding the water last. Bring to the boil, then remove from the heat and allow to cool completely. I leave the herbs and spices to infuse for 24 hours before using the brines. Once the mixture has had time to infuse, pass the liquid through a chinois.

The length of time you brine your fish or meat for is very much dependent on size. Fish takes much less time to brine. I brine each portion to order, whether it's for a tasting or à la carte menu. For example, for the à la carte menu, I weigh 140g fish and brine it for 25 minutes. For meat, regardless of weight and size of the portions, I brine it overnight.

> *These brines are used daily in the restaurant to season fish and cuts of meat, prior to cooking. Brining proteins such as fish and meat allows for a more balanced flavour overall when cooked.*

For fish brine

500ml tap water

30g caster sugar

50g table salt

2 sprigs of thyme

8g coriander seeds

2 star anise

8g fennel seeds

1 bay leaf

For meat brine (use secondary cuts such as lamb neck, pork belly, pork cheeks)

1 litre tap water

100g caster sugar

100g table salt

2 sprigs of thyme

2 sprigs of rosemary

25g coriander seeds

10g star anise

15g black peppercorns

10g fennel seeds

15g mustard seeds

1 bay leaf

Equipment

Chinois

Fish Stock

Place a large saucepan on a medium heat. Now add the carrot, leek, celery, coriander seeds and fennel seeds. Give the ingredients time to sweat but not colour. Then add the fish bones and head, followed by the white wine. Still on a medium heat, reduce the liquid by two-thirds. Once reduced, add water until the bones are covered. Bring the liquid to the boil and then reduce the heat. Simmer for about 45 minutes, occasionally skimming the surface. After 45 minutes and a final skim, stir in the parsley and lemon juice. Take the saucepan off the heat and allow to cool for 45 minutes.

Once cool, pass the liquid through a chinois into a bowl, cover with cling film and set aside. This can be made in advanced and I normally vacuum pack this fish stock for use when required. It can be frozen and kept in a sealed container for up to a month.

> "By making your own stock, you have total control of the ingredients used to create it. Also, by carefully choosing the right type of fish to make your stock with, you know its flavour will go well with the rest of the recipe. Ideally you want to use a flat fish – turbot, brill, plaice, or sole work perfectly to make fish stock."

1 carrot, roughly chopped
1 leek, roughly chopped
1 celery stick, diced
8 coriander seeds
8 fennel seeds
3–4kg fish bones and head, gills removed
300ml dry white wine
3 sprigs of flat-leaf parsley
Juice of ½ lemon

Equipment
Chinois

Chicken Stock

Put the chicken carcasses into the large stock pot. Fill the pot with cold water until the carcasses are just covered. Place the pot on a high heat and bring to the boil. With a ladle, remove the scum from the surface of the stock. Once removed, reduce to a simmer, and cook for 30 minutes. Add the ice cubes to the stock and cook it out again to remove any fat.

Once it starts to boil again, reduce the heat to low and remove the surface fat with the ladle. Add the carrots, leeks, white onions, celery, garlic and thyme. Simmer for 3 hours and keep skimming off the impurities as they rise to the surface. Take the pot off the heat and allow to cool for 30 minutes.

Once cooled, first pass the liquid through a colander, followed by a double layer of muslin cloth. Allow the stock time to cool and then put it into a container. Close the lid or cover with cling film and place in the fridge. The stock will keep well in the fridge for up to 5 days.

“ Making your own chicken stock is the perfect starting point to gain a real understanding of how stocks and sauces are made. Once you have mastered this recipe, I am sure you will go on to make a range of your own stocks and sauces. ”

4kg chicken carcasses

500g ice cubes

4 medium carrots, diced

2 leeks, sliced

2 large white onions, chopped

2 celery sticks, sliced

1 head of garlic, diced

2 sprigs of thyme

Equipment
Large stockpot
Muslin cloth

Veal Stock

Preheat the oven to 110°C (90°C fan/Gas Mark ¼). Put all the bones on a roasting tray and place in the oven for 12 hours. Remove from the oven and put the bones into a colander to drain off the excess fat. Once drained, put them into a stock pot and cover with cold water. Bring the stock to the boil, then add the ice cubes. Use the ladle to skim off any scum or fat from the surface.

Preheat the oven to 200°C (180°C fan/Gas Mark 6). Put the carrots, leeks, onions and celery onto an oven tray. Coat them generously with rapeseed oil, then roast in the oven until they are a dark golden brown. Once coloured, remove from the oven and add the vegetables to the stock, along with the thyme and rosemary. Simmer the stock for 8 hours. In a separate pan, add the tomato paste and cook on a medium heat until it has darkened. Then pour in the wine to deglaze the tomato, and cook off the alcohol. After a couple of minutes, pour the mixture into the veal stock and add the garlic. Gently simmer for a further 16 hours. Top up the stock with water if it has reduced too much. Once the stock has simmered for a total of 24 hours, remove from the heat and allow to rest for 1 hour. Next, pass it through a colander, followed by a double layer of muslin cloth. Put the clear, filtered stock into a saucepan, place on a low heat and reduce the liquid by a third. You can make this stock up to 7 days in advance and keep it refrigerated until needed. Alternatively, it can be frozen for up to 3 months.

> "We regularly make this veal stock at the Angel. You could make a veal stock in just one day by cooking the bones at a high temperature. However, it is worth taking the extra time which this recipe requires to get the perfect result. I learned to make veal stock this way when working with Hywel Jones at Luckman Park. He always insisted that a veal stock is the base of every good sauce, so it is very important to get it right. I fully agree with Hywel that to make the perfect sauce for any dish, you must have the perfect stock."

2kg beef bones

4kg veal bones

400g ice cubes

2 carrots, roughly chopped

2 leeks, roughly chopped

2 large white onions, sliced

1 celery stick, roughly chopped

Rapeseed oil, for drizzling

3 sprigs of thyme

4 sprigs of rosemary

800g tomato paste

750ml red wine

1 head of garlic, chopped

Equipment

Muslin cloth

Lamb Stock

Preheat the oven to 180°C (160°C fan/Gas Mark 4). Spread out the bones on a large roasting tray and drizzle with a little rapeseed oil. Roast for 45 minutes–1 hour, turning them over halfway, until evenly browned. Then remove from the oven and, using a colander, drain off all the fat.

Put a large pan on a medium heat, add in 2 teaspoons of rapeseed oil and the leek, onion, carrots, celery and garlic. Turn up the heat and cook until golden brown, stirring occasionally. Now add the tomato purée and cook for a further 5 minutes on a high heat, again stirring occasionally. Then add the wine and cook until the liquid has reduced by half.

Once reduced, add the lamb bones, then pour over enough water to cover them. Add the bay leaves, peppercorns, rosemary and thyme. Simmer the stock for 3–4 hours or until you are happy with the depth of flavour of your lamb stock. Remove from the heat and allow to cool for at least 20 minutes.

Pass the stock through a fine sieve and allow to cool to room temperature. Then cover and refrigerate for up to 2 days. Fat from the stock will rise and congeal on the surface. Remove and discard with a ladle so that you are left with a clear liquid stock. Put the clear stock into a container, cover and keep in the fridge until needed. Fresh stock should be used within 4 days, or it can be stored in the freezer for up to 3 months.

2 whole lamb saddle bones or 2kg lamb bones, chopped into small pieces
Rapeseed oil, for drizzling
1 leek, roughly diced
1 large onion, roughly diced
2 carrots, diced
3 celery sticks, diced
½ head of garlic, cut into 2 pieces with the skin on (keep the remaining garlic for the lamb sauce, see page 277)
300g tomato purée
100ml white wine
2 bay leaves
1 tsp black peppercorns
2 sprigs of rosemary
2 sprigs of thyme

Equipment
Fine sieve

" Making stock is one of the core skills to master, as it is the base of all good sauces. This lamb stock is simple, delicious and provides a solid foundation to the lamb sauce. "

Lamb Sauce

Preheat the oven to 180°C (160°C fan/Gas Mark 4). Put the lamb trim and bones in an oven tray and roast for 30–45 minutes.

While the bones are roasting, place a large saucepan on a medium heat. Add the oil, onions, carrots and celery, then allow them to sweat for 5 minutes. Now add the rosemary, thyme and garlic. Stir and continue the sweating process for another 2 minutes. You want the vegetables to become soft and nicely caramelised. Next, add the tomatoes and continue to cook on a medium heat, stirring occasionally, until you have a jammy consistency. Finally, add the alcohol and reduce the liquid by half. By the time the liquid has reduced, the bones will be roasted. Add them to the saucepan, followed by the stocks. Turn up the heat and bring to the boil. Once boiling, reduce the heat to low and simmer for 3 hours. Check every 30 minutes and skim the top of impurities.

After 3 hours of simmering, no more impurities should be rising to the surface. Now pass the liquid through a chinois or fine sieve and then a muslin or cheesecloth. Use a large length of muslin, hold two corners in each hand and gently pull from side to side by lifting your hands alternately. Allow the liquid to naturally pass though. Do not squeeze or press through the liquid, as any impurities that remain will also pass through. Cover with cling film and set aside ready to reduce when needed. This can be kept in the fridge for at least 3 days.

"A simple lamb sauce that will elevate all of your favourite lamb recipes to the next level."

3kg lamb trim (any cut of lamb will work fine)
2kg lamb bones, cut into very small pieces
Oil, for frying
2 white onions, diced
2 large carrots, diced
2 celery sticks, diced
3 sprigs of rosemary
3 sprigs of thyme
5 garlic cloves, crushed
500g chopped tomatoes
400ml Madeira wine
400ml dry white wine
1.5 litres lamb stock (see page 276)
1 litre veal stock (see page 275)
1 litre chicken stock (see page 274)

Equipment

Chinois or fine sieve
Muslin cloth

Herb Oils

Fill a large pan three-quarters full with water, set on a high heat and bring to the boil. While the water is boiling, half-fill a mixing bowl with ice cubes and cover with water. You will need this later to refresh the herb.

Add your chosen herb to the boiling water, then cook for about 15 seconds. Once the stems are bright green, quickly transfer the herb into the bowl of iced water and allow to cool completely. Once cool, remove from the iced water and place the herb on a J cloth (or kitchen towel) and squeeze out as much excess water as you can. Be sure to get all the water out, otherwise it will dilute your oil. You want to end up with a nice, thick oil.

Line a fine sieve with a piece of muslin. Pour the oil into a blender and then add the drained herb. Blend on a high speed for at least 1 minute until you have a smooth oil. If it looks a little too thick, add a drop or two more oil, but not water. Pour the blended oil into the sieve set over a bowl, and let it sit for a few hours. Stir occasionally while the oil is draining through. Do not press the oil through, as any impurities could be pushed through and ruin the clear, pure oil you are looking for. Once thoroughly drained, transfer the oil to a squeezy bottle and store in the fridge. It will keep well for up to a week.

> "This recipe can be used to make a number of different oils using the same method. I use it to make coriander, dill, nasturtium, parsley and tarragon oils, which all regularly feature on the dishes we serve at the Angel.
>
> Use the same amount of oil and weight for each herb."

2 x 100g bags of any herb
100ml rapeseed oil

Equipment
Fine sieve
Muslin cloth
Blender
Squeezy bottle

Red Wine Jus

Preheat the oven to 180°C (160°C fan/Gas Mark 4). Dice the beef trim into small pieces, place onto an oven tray and drizzle with the rapeseed oil. Roast in the oven until dark golden brown. This will usually take 25–35 minutes.

Meanwhile, start to make the base of the sauce. Heat a saucepan on a high heat. Add the shallots and garlic. Begin to sweat and caramelise them both until golden brown. Now add the chopped tomatoes, along with the thyme and rosemary, then cook out until you have a sticky jam consistency. Then pour in the red wine and ruby port and reduce by a third. Remove the meat from the oven and drain off the excess fat using a chinois or colander. Now put the beef trim into the sauce. Deglaze the oven tray used to cook the beef trim with a little of the chicken stock to get all that sediment of concentrated flavour into the sauce. Pour the deglazed liquid from the oven tray, along with the remaining chicken stock and veal stock, into the saucepan containing the shallots and the beef trim. Bring to the boil and skim the excess fat that comes to the surface with a ladle. Once boiling, reduce the heat to low and let the stock gently simmer for 2–3 hours. Remove from the heat and let the pan sit for 30 minutes before passing the contents through a colander, followed by a double layer of muslin cloth. Put the sieved liquid into a saucepan and place on a medium heat until it reaches boiling point. Skim off any excess fat, reduce the heat to low and reduce the liquid until it has your desired consistency. When you have the consistency you want, pour it into a container, close the lid or cover with cling film and put it in the fridge. The sauce will last in the fridge for up to 5 days.

> "This is a classic French sauce made with red wine, port and shallots."

1kg beef trim

Rapeseed oil, for drizzling

6 banana shallots, finely sliced

1 head of garlic, halved

1kg large tomatoes on the vine, cut into small pieces

¼ bunch of thyme

¼ bunch of rosemary

750ml red wine

200ml ruby port

1.5 litres chicken stock (see page 274)

2 litres veal stock (see page 275)

Equipment

Chinois or colander

Muslin cloth

Tempering Chocolate

There are several ways to temper chocolate. Whichever method you choose, it is important to note that all chocolates will not contract and release from the polycarbonate moulds unless they have been perfectly tempered. Tempering is also what gives chocolate that perfect shine.

One simple tempering method is called seeding. To temper chocolate using this method, first finely chop the chocolate and then gently melt two-thirds of it over a bain-marie, stirring until it is fully melted. Make sure it does not overheat. Check the temperature of the chocolate with a temperature probe. Once it has reached 55°C, remove from the heat and add the remaining third of the chopped chocolate. Stir continuously until all the chocolate has melted. Once the temperature has reduced to 32°C, it is at the perfect working temperature. Pour the melted chocolate into moulds of your choice and put aside to set.

You will always need to temper more chocolate than you believe you will actually need, but leftover tempered chocolate can be reused again.

Index

A

almonds
  'the black penny' 256–8
  'chocolate bar' poached cherries | salted almond 94–6
  lamb loin | apricots | hispi cabbage | smoked almond 68–71
  tomato and peach gazpacho | natural almonds 110
apples
  apple soufflé | apple syrup | walnut and maple ice cream 252–4
  black garlic risotto | sherry vinegar | crispy quail egg 232–3
  carrot cream | miso | black garlic 42–3
  cured brill | Exmoor caviar | Granny Smith dressing 46–7
  Devonshire clotted cream parfait | golden raisin | sesame and apple 86–7
  duck ravioli | bitter orange | cranberry | duck consommé 236–9
  lamb loin | apricots | hispi cabbage | smoked almond 68–71
  milk-cured duck liver | salted peach | Sauternes 116–18
  red cabbage gazpacho | olive oil 172
  toffee apple and cinnamon chocolates 268
  venison loin | parsley root | pomegranate 242
apricots
  apricot sorbet | toasted honey | chamomile | bee pollen 74–5
  Dartmouth pie 194
  lamb loin | apricots | hispi cabbage | smoked almond 68–71
  milk-cured duck liver | salted peach | Sauternes 116–18
  venison loin | parsley root | pomegranate 242
artichokes
  artichoke | lovage tartlet 168–9
  red mullet | baby artichokes | langoustine bisque 64–7
  tomato millefeuille | ricotta | artichokes | smoked tomato jam 128–9
asparagus
  roasted turbot | baby gem | broad bean | makrut lime butter sauce 136–9
  white asparagus tortellini | potato | truffle tea 50–3

B

bananas: 'the black penny' 256–8
beef: ruby red beef fillet | caramelised onion | horseradish buttermilk | red wine jus 132–4
beer
  cod brandade | malt vinegar jam 104–7
  roasted brill | turnip | smoked sea lettuce sauce 60–3
beetroot tarts | poppy seed goat's cheese | puffed wild rice and celery cress 226–9
black garlic
  black garlic risotto | sherry vinegar | crispy quail egg 232–3
  carrot cream | miso | black garlic 42–3
'the black penny' 256–8
blackberry millefeuille | crème fraîche sorbet 206–7
blackcurrants: cassis | fermented red currants | lemon thyme 196–7
bread: milk bread rolls 38–9
brill
  cured brill | Exmoor caviar | Granny Smith dressing 46–7
  roasted brill | turnip | smoked sea lettuce sauce 60–3
brines 272
broad beans: roasted turbot | baby gem | broad bean | makrut lime butter sauce 136–9
buttermilk
  ruby red beef fillet | caramelised onion | horseradish buttermilk | red wine jus 132–4
  sea bream | gooseberry dashi | buttermilk | borage 120–1

C

cabbage
  lamb loin | apricots | hispi cabbage | smoked almond 68–71
  red cabbage gazpacho | olive oil 172
calamansi | lime curd | fennel rice crisp 142–3
capers
  red mullet | baby artichokes | langoustine bisque 64–7
  tomato millefeuille | ricotta | artichokes | smoked tomato jam 128–9
carrots
  artichoke | lovage tartlet 168–9
  carrot cream | miso | black garlic 42–3
  chicken stock 274
  crab risotto | lemon | sea vegetables 124–6
  Devonshire lamb loin | brown butter artichokes | sauce picante 246–9
  duck ravioli | bitter orange | cranberry | duck consommé 236–9
  fish stock 273
  Jerusalem artichoke ravioli | Serrano ham | roasted chicken consommé 174–7
  lamb loin | apricots | hispi cabbage | smoked almond 68–71
  lamb sauce 277
  lamb stock 276
  mushroom tartlet | cep custard | Wiltshire truffle | garlic chive cress 178–80
  red mullet | baby artichokes | langoustine bisque 64–7
  roasted pigeon | glazed salsify | cocoa nib | hazelnut 182–5
  tomato millefeuille | ricotta | artichokes | smoked tomato jam 128–9
  veal stock 275
  white asparagus tortellini | potato | truffle tea 50–3
cassis | fermented red currants | lemon thyme 196–7
caviar
  crab tartlet | grapefruit | smoke caviar 108
  cured brill | Exmoor caviar | Granny Smith dressing 46–7
  roasted line caught sea bass | caviar and lettuce cream 250
celeriac: oat crusted king oyster mushrooms | salt baked celeriac | mushroom foam 188–91
celery
  artichoke | lovage tartlet 168–9
  chicken stock 274
  crab risotto | lemon | sea vegetables 124–6
  Dartmouth pie 194
  Devonshire lamb loin | brown butter artichokes | sauce picante 246–9
  fish stock 273
  lamb loin | apricots | hispi cabbage | smoked almond 68–71
  lamb sauce 277
  lamb stock 276
  mushroom tartlet | cep custard | Wiltshire truffle | garlic chive cress 178–80
  red mullet | baby artichokes | langoustine bisque 64–7
  roasted pigeon | glazed salsify | cocoa nib | hazelnut 182–5
  roasted turbot | baby gem | broad bean | makrut lime butter sauce 136–9
  veal stock 275
  white asparagus tortellini | potato | truffle tea 50–3
cheese
  beetroot tarts | poppy seed goat's cheese | puffed wild rice and celery cress 226–9
  black garlic risotto | sherry vinegar |

crispy quail egg 232–3
cured salmon | watermelon salsa | oyster 112–14
Devonshire lamb loin | brown butter artichokes | sauce picante 246–9
Jerusalem artichoke ravioli | Serrano ham | roasted chicken consommé 174–7
truffle cheese gougère 220–1
white asparagus tortellini | potato | truffle tea 50–3
cherries: 'chocolate bar' poached cherries | salted almond 94–6
chicken
   chicken stock 274
   Jerusalem artichoke ravioli | Serrano ham | roasted chicken consommé 174–7
chocolate
   apricot sorbet | toasted honey | chamomile | bee pollen 74–5
   'the black penny' 256–8
   calamansi | lime curd | fennel rice crisp 142–3
   cassis | fermented red currants | lemon thyme 196–7
   chocolate and bitter orange | Pedro Ximénez | roasted pearl barley 260–2
   'chocolate bar' poached cherries | salted almond 94–6
   chocolate | coffee curd | lemon | coffee milk sorbet 264–5
   coconut | lychee | yuzu 'all white' 80–3
   cucumber | white chocolate curd | lime 146
   espresso fudge chocolate dome 160
   gin and tonic 'Angel Style' 78–9
   malt mousse | blackout coffee sponge | hazelnut ice cream 90–3
   'peach melba' | smoked white chocolate ice cream 152–4
   roasted coffee parfait | mascarpone | white chocolate granita 202–3
   roasted pigeon | glazed salsify | cocoa nib | hazelnut 182–5
   tempering 279
   toffee apple and cinnamon chocolates 268
coconut
   coconut | lychee | yuzu 'all white' 80–3
   yuzu cream | toasted coconut meringue | mandarin | vanilla sorbet 148–51
cod brandade | malt vinegar jam 104–7
coffee
   chocolate | coffee curd | lemon | coffee milk sorbet 264–5
   espresso fudge chocolate dome 160
   malt mousse | blackout coffee sponge | hazelnut ice cream 90–3
   roasted coffee parfait | mascarpone | white chocolate granita 202–3
   roasted pigeon | glazed salsify | cocoa nib | hazelnut 182–5

condensed milk: espresso fudge chocolate dome 160
crab
   crab risotto | lemon | sea vegetables 124–6
   crab tartlet | grapefruit | smoke caviar 108
cranberries: duck ravioli | bitter orange | cranberry | duck consommé 236–9
cream
   apple soufflé | apple syrup | walnut and maple ice cream 252–4
   apricot sorbet | toasted honey | chamomile | bee pollen 74–5
   artichoke | lovage tartlet 168–9
   black garlic risotto | sherry vinegar | crispy quail egg 232–3
   'the black penny' 256–8
   blackberry millefeuille | crème fraîche sorbet 206–7
   chocolate and bitter orange | Pedro Ximénez | roasted pearl barley 260–2
   'chocolate bar' poached cherries | salted almond 94–6
   coconut | lychee | yuzu 'all white' 80–3
   cod brandade | malt vinegar jam 104–7
   Devonshire clotted cream parfait | golden raisin | sesame and apple 86–7
   Devonshire lamb loin | brown butter artichokes | sauce picante 246–9
   duck ravioli | bitter orange | cranberry | duck consommé 236–9
   free dived scallops | cucumber butter | pickled mustard seed 56–9
   leek and potato velouté | chive gnocchi 224
   malt mousse | blackout coffee sponge | hazelnut ice cream 90–3
   milk-cured duck liver | salted peach | Sauternes 116–18
   mushroom tartlet | cep custard | Wiltshire truffle | garlic chive cress 178–80
   nut butter brulée | nashi pear | pine nut ice cream 210–11
   orange blossom sorbet | crème fraîche | grapefruit | cocoa granola 200
   'peach melba' | smoked white chocolate ice cream 152–4
   raspberry cannelloni | macadamia nut | tarragon ice cream 156–7
   roasted brill | turnip | smoked sea lettuce sauce 60–3
   roasted coffee parfait | mascarpone | white chocolate granita 202–3
   roasted line caught sea bass | caviar and lettuce cream 250
   roasted pigeon | glazed salsify | cocoa nib | hazelnut 182–5
   toffee apple and cinnamon chocolates 268
   venison loin | parsley root | pomegranate 242

crème fraîche
   black garlic risotto | sherry vinegar | crispy quail egg 232–3
   blackberry millefeuille | crème fraîche sorbet 206–7
   duck ravioli | bitter orange | cranberry | duck consommé 236–9
   orange blossom sorbet | crème fraîche | grapefruit | cocoa granola 200
cucumber
   cucumber | white chocolate curd | lime 146
   free dived scallops | cucumber butter | pickled mustard seed 56–9
   red cabbage gazpacho | olive oil 172
   tomato and peach gazpacho | natural almonds 110

D

Dartmouth pie 194
Devonshire clotted cream parfait | golden raisin | sesame and apple 86–7
duck
   duck ravioli | bitter orange | cranberry | duck consommé 236–9
   milk-cured duck liver | salted peach | Sauternes 116–18

E

eggs: black garlic risotto | sherry vinegar | crispy quail egg 232–3
elderflower tonic: gin and tonic 'Angel Style' 78–9
espresso fudge chocolate dome 160

F

fennel
   calamansi | lime curd | fennel rice crisp 142–3
   crab risotto | lemon | sea vegetables 124–6
   red mullet | baby artichokes | langoustine bisque 64–7
   roasted turbot | baby gem | broad bean | makrut lime butter sauce 136–9
fish
   cod brandade | malt vinegar jam 104–7
   cured brill | Exmoor caviar | Granny Smith dressing 46–7
   cured salmon | watermelon salsa | oyster 112–14
   fish stock 273
   red mullet | baby artichokes | langoustine bisque 64–7
   roasted brill | turnip | smoked sea lettuce sauce 60–3
   roasted line caught sea bass | caviar and

lettuce cream 250
roasted turbot | baby gem | broad bean | makrut lime butter sauce 136-9
sea bream | gooseberry dashi | buttermilk | borage 120-1
fish brine 272

G

garlic
    black garlic risotto | sherry vinegar | crispy quail egg 232-3
    carrot cream | miso | black garlic 42-3
gherkins: Devonshire lamb loin | brown butter artichokes | sauce picante 246-9
gin and tonic 'Angel Style' 78-9
gnocchi: leek and potato velouté | chive gnocchi 224
gooseberries: sea bream | gooseberry dashi | buttermilk | borage 120-1
granita
    cucumber | white chocolate curd | lime 146
    gin and tonic 'Angel Style' 78-9
    roasted coffee parfait | mascarpone | white chocolate granita 202-3
grapefruit
    crab tartlet | grapefruit | smoke caviar 108
    orange blossom sorbet | crème fraîche | grapefruit | cocoa granola 200

H

ham: Jerusalem artichoke ravioli | Serrano ham | roasted chicken consommé 174-7
hazelnuts
    chocolate | coffee curd | lemon | coffee milk sorbet 264-5
    Jerusalem artichoke ravioli | Serrano ham | roasted chicken consommé 174-7
    malt mousse | blackout coffee sponge | hazelnut ice cream 90-3
    nut butter brulée | nashi pear | pine nut ice cream 210-11
    roasted pigeon | glazed salsify | cocoa nib | hazelnut 182-5
herb oils 278
honey
    apricot sorbet | toasted honey | chamomile | bee pollen 74-5
    red mullet | baby artichokes | langoustine bisque 64-7
horseradish: ruby red beef fillet | caramelised onion | horseradish buttermilk | red wine jus 132-4

I

ice creams
    apple soufflé | apple syrup | walnut and maple ice cream 252-4
    chocolate and bitter orange | Pedro Ximénez | roasted pearl barley 260-2
    malt mousse | blackout coffee sponge | hazelnut ice cream 90-3
    nut butter brulée | nashi pear | pine nut ice cream 210-11
    'peach melba' | smoked white chocolate ice cream 152-4
    raspberry cannelloni | macadamia nut | tarragon ice cream 156-7

J

Jerusalem artichokes
    Devonshire lamb loin | brown butter artichokes | sauce picante 246-9
    Jerusalem artichoke ravioli | Serrano ham | roasted chicken consommé 174-7

L

lamb
    Devonshire lamb loin | brown butter artichokes | sauce picante 246-9
    lamb loin | apricots | hispi cabbage | smoked almond 68-71
    lamb sauce 277
    lamb stock 276
langoustines
    crab risotto | lemon | sea vegetables 124-6
    red mullet | baby artichokes | langoustine bisque 64-7
leeks
    black garlic risotto | sherry vinegar | crispy quail egg 232-3
    chicken stock 274
    duck ravioli | bitter orange | cranberry | duck consommé 236-9
    fish stock 273
    Jerusalem artichoke ravioli | Serrano ham | roasted chicken consommé 174-7
    lamb stock 276
    leek and potato velouté | chive gnocchi 224
    mushroom tartlet | cep custard | Wiltshire truffle | garlic chive cress 178-80
    veal stock 275
    white asparagus tortellini | potato | truffle tea 50-3
lemons
    artichoke | lovage tartlet 168-9
    cured brill | Exmoor caviar | Granny Smith dressing 46-7
    cured salmon | watermelon salsa | oyster 112-14
    gin and tonic 'Angel Style' 78-9
    malt mousse | blackout coffee sponge | hazelnut ice cream 90-3
    red mullet | baby artichokes | langoustine bisque 64-7
    roasted coffee parfait | mascarpone | white chocolate granita 202-3
    roasted pigeon | glazed salsify | cocoa nib | hazelnut 182-5
    sea bream | gooseberry dashi | buttermilk | borage 120-1
    tomato millefeuille | ricotta | artichokes | smoked tomato jam 128-9
    white asparagus tortellini | potato | truffle tea 50-3
lemons, preserved
    chocolate | coffee curd | lemon | coffee milk sorbet 264-5
    crab risotto | lemon | sea vegetables 124-6
    roasted brill | turnip | smoked sea lettuce sauce 60-3
lettuce
    roasted line caught sea bass | caviar and lettuce cream 250
    roasted turbot | baby gem | broad bean | makrut lime butter sauce 136-9
limes
    'the black penny' 256-8
    blackberry millefeuille | crème fraîche sorbet 206-7
    calamansi | lime curd | fennel rice crisp 142-3
    coconut | lychee | yuzu 'all white' 80-3
    crab tartlet | grapefruit | smoke caviar 108
    cured brill | Exmoor caviar | Granny Smith dressing 46-7
    gin and tonic 'Angel Style' 78-9
    roasted turbot | baby gem | broad bean | makrut lime butter sauce 136-9
liver: milk-cured duck liver | salted peach | Sauternes 116-18
lovage: artichoke | lovage tartlet 168-9
lychees: coconut | lychee | yuzu 'all white' 80-3

M

macadamia nuts: raspberry cannelloni | macadamia nut | tarragon ice cream 156-7
malt mousse | blackout coffee sponge | hazelnut ice cream 90-3
mandarins
    milk-cured duck liver | salted peach | Sauternes 116-18
    yuzu cream | toasted coconut meringue |

mandarin | vanilla sorbet 148-51
mascarpone: roasted coffee parfait | mascarpone | white chocolate granita 202-3
meat brine 272
milk bread rolls 38-9
miso: carrot cream | miso | black garlic 42-3
mushrooms
   duck ravioli | bitter orange | cranberry | duck consommé 236-9
   Jerusalem artichoke ravioli | Serrano ham | roasted chicken consommé 174-7
   mushroom tartlet | cep custard | Wiltshire truffle | garlic chive cress 178-80
   oat crusted king oyster mushrooms | salt baked celeriac | mushroom foam 188-91
   ruby red beef fillet | caramelised onion | horseradish buttermilk | red wine jus 132-4
   white asparagus tortellini | potato | truffle tea 50-3
mutton: Dartmouth pie 194

N

nashi pears: nut butter brulée | nashi pear | pine nut ice cream 210-11
nut butter brulée | nashi pear | pine nut ice cream 210-11

O

oats
   apple soufflé | apple syrup | walnut and maple ice cream 252-4
   chocolate and bitter orange | Pedro Ximénez | roasted pearl barley 260-2
   chocolate | coffee curd | lemon | coffee milk sorbet 264-5
   lamb loin | apricots | hispi cabbage | smoked almond 68-71
   oat crusted king oyster mushrooms | salt baked celeriac | mushroom foam 188-91
   orange blossom sorbet | crème fraîche | grapefruit | cocoa granola 200
   roasted pigeon | glazed salsify | cocoa nib | hazelnut 182-5
onions
   chicken stock 274
   lamb sauce 277
   lamb stock 276
   red mullet | baby artichokes | langoustine bisque 64-7
   roasted line caught sea bass | caviar and lettuce cream 250
   roasted pigeon | glazed salsify | cocoa nib

| hazelnut 182-5
ruby red beef fillet | caramelised onion | horseradish buttermilk | red wine jus 132-4
veal stock 275
orange blossom sorbet | crème fraîche | grapefruit | cocoa granola 200
oranges
   chocolate and bitter orange | Pedro Ximénez | roasted pearl barley 260-2
   cured brill | Exmoor caviar | Granny Smith dressing 46-7
   Dartmouth pie 194
   duck ravioli | bitter orange | cranberry | duck consommé 236-9
   gin and tonic 'Angel Style' 78-9
   orange blossom sorbet | crème fraîche | grapefruit | cocoa granola 200
   sea bream | gooseberry dashi | buttermilk | borage 120-1
ox cheek: roasted pigeon | glazed salsify | cocoa nib | hazelnut 182-5
oysters: cured salmon | watermelon salsa | oyster 112-14

P

parfait
   Devonshire clotted cream parfait | golden raisin | sesame and apple 86-7
   roasted coffee parfait | mascarpone | white chocolate granita 202-3
parsley root: venison loin | parsley root | pomegranate 242
parsnips: venison loin | parsley root | pomegranate 242
pasta
   duck ravioli | bitter orange | cranberry | duck consommé 236-9
   Jerusalem artichoke ravioli | Serrano ham | roasted chicken consommé 174-7
   white asparagus tortellini | potato | truffle tea 50-3
peaches
   milk-cured duck liver | salted peach | Sauternes 116-18
   'peach melba' | smoked white chocolate ice cream 152-4
   tomato and peach gazpacho | natural almonds 110
pearl barley: chocolate and bitter orange | Pedro Ximénez | roasted pearl barley 260-2
pears: nut butter brulée | nashi pear | pine nut ice cream 210-11
pigeon: roasted pigeon | glazed salsify | cocoa nib | hazelnut 182-5
pine nuts
   calamansi | lime curd | fennel rice crisp 142-3

nut butter brulée | nashi pear | pine nut ice cream 210-11
plums: venison loin | parsley root | pomegranate 242
pollen
   apricot sorbet | toasted honey | chamomile | bee pollen 74-5
   cured salmon | watermelon salsa | oyster 112-14
   red mullet | baby artichokes | langoustine bisque 64-7
pomegranate: venison loin | parsley root | pomegranate 242
potatoes
   black garlic risotto | sherry vinegar | crispy quail egg 232-3
   carrot cream | miso | black garlic 42-3
   cod brandade | malt vinegar jam 104-7
   duck ravioli | bitter orange | cranberry | duck consommé 236-9
   lamb loin | apricots | hispi cabbage | smoked almond 68-71
   leek and potato velouté | chive gnocchi 224
   ruby red beef fillet | caramelised onion | horseradish buttermilk | red wine jus 132-4
   white asparagus tortellini | potato | truffle tea 50-3
prunes: Dartmouth pie 194

Q

quail eggs: black garlic risotto | sherry vinegar | crispy quail egg 232-3
quinoa: red mullet | baby artichokes | langoustine bisque 64-7

R

radishes: sea bream | gooseberry dashi | buttermilk | borage 120-1
raisins
   Dartmouth pie 194
   Devonshire clotted cream parfait | golden raisin | sesame and apple 86-7
raspberries
   'peach melba' | smoked white chocolate ice cream 152-4
   raspberry cannelloni | macadamia nut | tarragon ice cream 156-7
red cabbage gazpacho | olive oil 172
red mullet | baby artichokes | langoustine bisque 64-7
red wine jus 279
redcurrants: cassis | fermented red currants | lemon thyme 196-7
rice
   beetroot tarts | poppy seed goat's cheese | puffed wild rice and celery cress 226-9

black garlic risotto | sherry vinegar | crispy quail egg 232–3
crab risotto | lemon | sea vegetables 124–6
Rice Krispies: calamansi | lime curd | fennel rice crisp 142–3
ricotta: tomato millefeuille | ricotta | artichokes | smoked tomato jam 128–9

S

salmon: cured salmon | watermelon salsa | oyster 112–14
salsify: roasted pigeon | glazed salsify | cocoa nib | hazelnut 182–5
Sauternes
    lamb loin | apricots | hispi cabbage | smoked almond 68–71
    milk-cured duck liver | salted peach | Sauternes 116–18
scallops
    free dived scallops | cucumber butter | pickled mustard seed 56–9
    roasted brill | turnip | smoked sea lettuce sauce 60–3
sea bass: roasted line caught sea bass | caviar and lettuce cream 250
sea beet: free dived scallops | cucumber butter | pickled mustard seed 56–9
sea bream | gooseberry dashi | buttermilk | borage 120–1
sea fennel
    cured brill | Exmoor caviar | Granny Smith dressing 46–7
    cured salmon | watermelon salsa | oyster 112–14
    free dived scallops | cucumber butter | pickled mustard seed 56–9
    sea bream | gooseberry dashi | buttermilk | borage 120–1
sea lettuce: roasted brill | turnip | smoked sea lettuce sauce 60–3
sea purslane
    crab risotto | lemon | sea vegetables 124–6
    cured brill | Exmoor caviar | Granny Smith dressing 46–7
    cured salmon | watermelon salsa | oyster 112–14
    free dived scallops | cucumber butter | pickled mustard seed 56–9
    roasted brill | turnip | smoked sea lettuce sauce 60–3
    sea bream | gooseberry dashi | buttermilk | borage 120–1
seafood
    crab risotto | lemon | sea vegetables 124–6
    crab tartlet | grapefruit | smoke caviar 108
    free dived scallops | cucumber butter | pickled mustard seed 56–9

red mullet | baby artichokes | langoustine bisque 64–7
shallots
    Dartmouth pie 194
    free dived scallops | cucumber butter | pickled mustard seed 56–9
    red wine jus 279
    white asparagus tortellini | potato | truffle tea 50–3
sorbets
    apricot sorbet | toasted honey | chamomile | bee pollen 74–5
    blackberry millefeuille | crème fraîche sorbet 206–7
    calamansi | lime curd | fennel rice crisp 142–3
    chocolate | coffee curd | lemon | coffee milk sorbet 264–5
    coconut | lychee | yuzu 'all white' 80–3
    Devonshire clotted cream parfait | golden raisin | sesame and apple 86–7
    orange blossom sorbet | crème fraîche | grapefruit | cocoa granola 200
spinach: ruby red beef fillet | caramelised onion | horseradish buttermilk | red wine jus 132–4
split peas
    cod brandade | malt vinegar jam 104–7
    roasted brill | turnip | smoked sea lettuce sauce 60–3
stocks
    chicken stock 274
    fish stock 273
    lamb stock 276
    veal stock 275

T

toffee apple and cinnamon chocolates 268
tomatoes
    crab risotto | lemon | sea vegetables 124–6
    lamb sauce 277
    red mullet | baby artichokes | langoustine bisque 64–7
    red wine jus 279
    roasted turbot | baby gem | broad bean | makrut lime butter sauce 136–9
    tomato and peach gazpacho | natural almonds 110
    tomato millefeuille | ricotta | artichokes | smoked tomato jam 128–9
truffles
    mushroom tartlet | cep custard | Wiltshire truffle | garlic chive cress 178–80
    oat crusted king oyster mushrooms | salt baked celeriac | mushroom foam 188–91
    ruby red beef fillet | caramelised onion | horseradish buttermilk | red wine jus 132–4

truffle cheese gougère 220–1
    white asparagus tortellini | potato | truffle tea 50–3
turbot: roasted turbot | baby gem | broad bean | makrut lime butter sauce 136–9
turnips: roasted brill | turnip | smoked sea lettuce sauce 60–3

V

veal stock 275
venison loin | parsley root | pomegranate 242

W

walnuts: apple soufflé | apple syrup | walnut and maple ice cream 252–4
watermelon: cured salmon | watermelon salsa | oyster 112–14
white asparagus tortellini | potato | truffle tea 50–3

Y

yoghurt
    calamansi | lime curd | fennel rice crisp 142–3
    cucumber | white chocolate curd | lime 146
yuzu
    coconut | lychee | yuzu 'all white' 80–3
    yuzu cream | toasted coconut meringue | mandarin | vanilla sorbet 148–51

Acknowledgements

I would like to thank the following people who contributed to the history of the restaurant: Tom and Sally Jaine, Tony Mulliken, Stephen Marwick, Nick Coiley, Jane Baxter, Alan Murchison, Tim and Helen Withers, Clive Jacobs, Peter Gorton, David Jones, Sophie Grigson, Pierre Koffmann and Richard Corrigan.

A big thank you to the exceptional chefs I have worked with, who inspired and encouraged me, and who remain mentors for me today: Chris and James Tanner, Richard Davies, Hywel Jones and Simon Hulstone.

I would also like to thank the people and businesses who have supplied me with their fantastic ingredients.

Kate Stephenson & Johnny Godden (Flying Fish)

Peter Harris & Dave Edwards (Wellocks)

Alex (Roots)

Heather James (Umber & Ecru)

Jamie Kirkaldy (Greenstraight Scallops)

Zak Frost (Wiltshire Truffles)

Jack & Charlie Cook (Walter Rose & Sons)

Villeroy & Boch

Donna Dalby (Alliance)

Thanks to my friends and colleagues:
Brandon Head (chef at the Angel),
Thomas Brind (previously at the Angel), James Pike (General Manager of The Holland Group) and Josh Campbell (for the superb photography).

Last, but not least, I would like to say a big thank you to Paul McCarthy who worked closely with me throughout the project to get the book written.

Ebury Press, an imprint of Ebury Publishing
20 Vauxhall Bridge Road
London SW1V 2SA

Ebury Press is part of the Penguin Random House group of companies whose addresses can be found at global.penguinrandomhouse.com

Text © Ebury Press 2024
Design © Ebury Press 2024
Photography © Ebury Press 2024

Photography: Josh Campbell
Design: Lucie Stericker/Studio 7:15
Production: Percie Bridgwater
Publishing Assistant: Izzy Frost
Publishing Director: Elizabeth Bond

Elly Wentworth has asserted her right to be identified as the author of this Work in accordance with the Copyright, Designs and Patents Act 1988.

First published by Ebury Press in 2024

www.penguin.co.uk
www.theangeldartmouth.co.uk

A CIP catalogue record for this book is available from the British Library.

ISBN 978-1-52991-790-1
Printed and bound in China by C&C Offset Printing Co., Ltd

The authorised representative in the EEA is Penguin Random House Ireland, Morrison Chambers, 32 Nassau Street, Dublin D02 YH68.

Photography © Josh Campbell

Additional illustrations and photography:

Pg 9, illustration of the Angel © Angela Dawes, Keyscape Design

Pg 11, 12, 13, 14, 17, 18, photographs, menus and letter, courtesy of Tom Jaine

Pg 15, awards and photograph, courtesy of the Angel, Dartmouth, The Holland Group

Pg 16, newspaper cutting from The Totnes Times, courtesy of Tindle Newspapers

Pg 19, Joyce Molyneux, credit Frank Baron/The Guardian

Pg 20, Peter Gorton, courtesy of Kaz Gorton, Alan Murchison, courtesy of Alan Murchison

Pg 26, 27, 28, 29, courtesy of Elly Wentworth

Penguin Random House is committed to a sustainable future for our business, our readers and our planet. This book is made from Forest Stewardship Council® certified paper.